DATE DUE

MR 18 '98			

DEMCO 38-296

THE CLEAR MIRROR

A traditional account of Tibet's Golden Age

Sakyapa Sonam Gyaltsen's
Clear Mirror on Royal Genealogy

Translated by
McComas Taylor
and
Lama Choedak Yuthok

Foreword by
H.H. the Fourteenth Dalai Lama

Illustrated by
Delek Chokjin Shastri

Snow Lion Publications
Ithaca, New York

Snow Lion Publications
P.O. Box 6483
Ithaca, New York 14850 USA
607-273-8519

Printed in the USA.

ISBN 1-55939-048-4

Library of Congress Cataloging-in-Publication Data

Bsod-nams-rgyal-mtshan, Sa-skya-pa Bla-ma Dam-pa, 1312-1375.
    [Rgyal rabs gsal ba'i me long. English]
    The clear mirror ; a traditional account of Tibet's golden age / Sakyapa
Sonam Gyaltsen's Clear mirror on royal genealogy ; translated by
McComas Taylor and Lama Choedak Yuthok ; foreword by H.H. the fourteenth Dalai Lama : illustrated by Delek Chokjin Shastri.
      p. cm.
    Includes bibliographical references and index.
    ISBN 1-55939-048-4
    1. Tibet (China)--History. 2. Buddhism--China--Tibet--History. I. Tay-
lor, McComas, 1956-   . II. Choedak Yuthok, Lama, 1954-   . III. Title.
DS785.B813 1996
951'.5—dc20
                                                       95-45728
                                                       CIP

Contents

List of Illustrations

THE DALAI LAMA

Foreword

Tibet has long been geographically, culturally, racially and linguistically an independent country. According to some the first people lived in Tibet more than twelve thousand years ago. In the course of time Tibetans developed a way of life suited to the unique environment they found themselves in. Meanwhile, Tibetan culture evolved under the sway of many influences. Predominant among these was the introduction of Buddhism, principally from India. Buddhist influence was pervasive. In addition to the achievements of accomplished religious adepts, it lead to the acquisition and development of a vast and profound literature and a far-reaching education system. Ultimately it even affected the system of government, the administration of the country and its foreign relations.

This book, *Gyalrab Salwa'i Melong*, by Sakyapa Sonam Gyaltsen (1312-1375), translated here as *The Clear Mirror*, provides a traditional historical account of these developments. An excellent example of its genre, it shows how Tibetans have viewed their history, how religion has always been important, but also how the distinct Tibetan identity has never been in doubt. I congratulate the translators, McComas Taylor and Lama Choedak Yuthok, for their efforts in making it accessible to an English readership, thereby throwing further light on the rich Tibetan heritage.

December 30, 1994

May the Tibetans enjoy
happiness in Tibet,
and may the Chinese enjoy
happiness in China.

Sino-Tibetan Treaty of 821-822

Preface

What makes Tibetans different? What sets them apart from their Chinese, Nepali, Indian, Turkic and Mongolian neighbours? What binds them together as a single, identifiable people? Ethnicity, language and religion are all important elements in Tibetanness. A fourth component is the acknowledgment of a common past, the subscription to a common mythology, the sharing of a single history.

The themes of Sakyapa Sonam Gyaltsen's *Clear Mirror on Royal Genealogy* are all central to the Tibetan national consciousness: the origins of the race, the advent of the early kings, the arrival of Buddhism, and the subsequent construction of the great shrines. These events form and inform the national psyche to this day.

Anyone who knows Tibet will have experienced the contrast between the savage beauty of the physical setting and the inner spiritual warmth of its inhabitants. It is not difficult to imagine that this land is indeed the primordial ogress lying on her back, barely restrained by the twelve strategically located Buddhist shrines. Nor is it difficult to see in the Tibetan people the rugged descendants of the monkey and the rock-demon, subdued by Avalokiteshvara, the lotus-born bodhisattva. *The Clear Mirror* vividly portrays a land bathed in the light of the Buddha's teachings, and thereby pacified, civilised, sanctified and uplifted. Travellers who have breathed the thin, clear air or experienced the intensity of the Tibetan sky can attest to the reality of this image.

Despite the horrors of the past four decades, much of the Tibetan heritage endures, and we must ensure its continued survival. The need for international recognition of the unique and distinctive nature of Tibet and Tibetanness grows more urgent by the day. This country, its people and its culture are now facing greater threats than at any preceding time in history. We hope that readers who enjoy the tales, legends, verses and discourses that comprise this folk-history will gain some insight into the Tibetan national consciousness. Perhaps for a moment, they may even glimpse the world through Tibetan eyes.

McComas Taylor   Lama Choedak Yuthok

Introduction

History and 'folk-history'

The Tibetan nation sprang from relative obscurity in the seventh century to become a regional superpower. The great kings Songtsen Gampo, Trisong Detsen and Relpachen welded local clan chieftains into an invincible war-machine and overran most of Central Asia. As early as 635, the Tibetans were able to demand a princess from their mighty Chinese neighbours. In 648 they attacked India, and in 670, their empire extended to Kokonor in the north. They captured Chinese outposts along the Silk Road in Turkestan, and held vast tracts stretching as far as modern Pakistan in the west. To the south of the Himalayas, Tibet advanced into Nepal, Sikkim, Bhutan and Burma. The Chinese emperor agreed to pay a yearly ransom of 50,000 bolts of silk to hold the Tibetan armies at bay. When he defaulted, Tibet retaliated by occupying the capital of Chang'an and installing a puppet emperor.

Buddhism was first introduced from India during this age of greatness. An alphabet, based on the Kashmiri script, was devised to facilitate the translation of Buddhist writings from Sanskrit into Tibetan. The kings established monasteries and shrines that have endured until the present. While the new religion was adopted by some sections of the ruling elite, it met with hostility from others and from the populace at large, who chose to adhere to their own indigenous, shamanist traditions known as Bon.

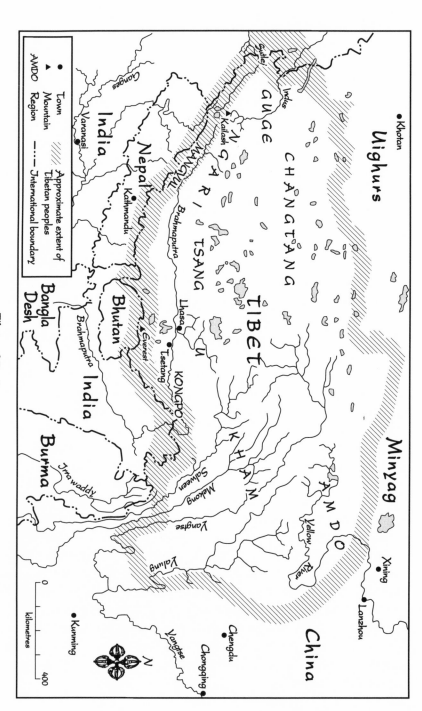

Tibet and Environs

The adoption of Buddhism and the threat it posed to the vested interests of the pro-Bon aristocrats led ultimately to deep divisions within the ruling stratum. Relpachen's brother King Langdarma attempted to extirpate Buddhism altogether, and very nearly succeeded. By the time of Langdarma's assassination in 842, internecine strife had so weakened the leadership that the once great empire collapsed. Tibet reverted to a loose alliance of minor local potentiaries, and its Golden Age drew to a close.

The Chinese dynastic histories contain manifold references to the troublesome Tibetan barbarians who harried the borderlands of their empire. The deeds of the Tibetan kings and their ministers were inscribed upon stone monuments that still dot the land. A priceless cache of contemporary documents was found in a cave in what had been a Tibetan military garrison at Dunhuang. From these and other fragmentary accounts, modern historians have reconstructed the bare bones of the 'real' history of early Tibet.

But what of the nation's folk-history? The Tibetans, like every people, have their own traditional accounts of the beginning of the world, the origins of their race, the rise of agriculture and technology, their great kings and the birth of their civilisation. Such mythological folk-history exists to inform, instruct and entertain its natal society. Yet folk-history is a living, evolving entity. It shapes the society in which it evolves and is also shaped by that society. As the influence of Buddhism expanded in Tibetan society, so the themes of folk-history came to be reinterpreted through the lens of the Buddhist world-view. *The Clear Mirror* falls into what Haarh has called the 'orthodox Buddhist tradition' of Tibetan history.[1] The text was expressly written to glorify the Dharma and the Dharma-kings, a fact to which the author himself attests. These same kings who, according to 'real' history, may have had little more than a pragmatic, passing interest in the new religion are elevated in our text to the status of major religious figures. So dense is the overlay of Buddhist ideology that the indigenous Tibetan account of the creation of the universe, for example, has been replaced by the Buddhist, Indian version. Similarly, the author seeks legitimacy for the first Tibetan king, Nyatri Tsenpo, by tracing his descent from the great kings of India.

Not only is folk-history ever-fluid, but it can accommodate mul-
tiple versions of a single event. Names, dates, places, characters
and motives vary from one source to another. These tales have been
told and retold by countless voices, each with its own idiosyncra-
sies. The accounts contained in *The Clear Mirror* are typical of their
genre, but are no more or less authoritative than versions found in
other vernacular histories.[2]

The fact that folk-history may share little or no common ground
with 'real' history is not important, as long as the two are not confounded. We can confirm from Chinese sources that Minister Gar
visited the imperial court to obtain a bride for King Songtsen
Gampo. Folk-history has constructed around this simple factual
kernel an elaborate literary corpus of intrigue and ingenuity. We
know the thoughts and hear the words, not only of the major players, but of many incidental figures. In a rich tapestry of verse and
prose, intellect conquers strength, good triumphs over evil, the
humble Tibetans outwit the Chinese, and the best man wins. So-
cially desirable mores are upheld and instilled in the audience, the
race is glorified and society is strengthened by the telling of this
tale. The past is alive and tangible. For Tibetans, folk-history is their
real history.

The Khon family, the Sakya hierarchs and Sonam Gyaltsen

Sakyapa Sonam Gyaltsen was a scion of one of Tibet's greatest families, the Khon, which even in the author's day could trace its roots
back six hundred years. The first prominent member of the clan
was Khon Palpoche, a minister at the court of King Trisong Detsen
in the eighth century. This figure is not mentioned in *The Clear Mirror*, but his son, Khon Luiwangpo Sungwa, is mentioned among
the 'Seven Chosen Ones', who were the first Tibetans to be ordained
as Buddhist monks. Khon Luiwangpo Sungwa later became one of
the great scholars who translated the Buddhist scriptures from Sanskrit into Tibetan.

Khon Konchog Gyalpo (1034-1102) founded a monastery in his
hometown of Sakya in 1073, and he and his son Kunga Nyingpo
(1092-1158) went on to establish the Sakya tradition, one of the four
great traditions within Tibetan Buddhism.

The rising power of the Mongols began to pose a threat to Tibet from about 1207. To stave off Mongol aggression, the Tibetans offered to accept Mongol overlordship in exchange for peace. Despite an invasion that penetrated nearly to Lhasa in 1239, this agreement proved sustainable, and was formalised in 1247 when the Mongolian emperor appointed the eminent member of the Khon family, Sakya Pandita (1182-1251), as his vice-regent in Tibet. The Sakya hierarchs were already the pre-eminent Tibetan spiritual leaders of their day. Under Mongol tutelage, they now acquired secular authority over Tibet. In 1253, Sakya Pandita's nephew and great-uncle of the author, Pagpa (1235-1274),[3] travelled to the court of the Mongolian emperor, Kubilai Khan. So great was Pagpa's influence over the emperor that Kubilai made him his personal chaplain and adopted Buddhism.

Sonam Gyaltsen's father was the High Lama of Sakya, Dagnyi Chenpo Zangpo Pal (1262-1325). He was conceived at Zhalu, the home monastery of another of Tibet's great historians, Buton Rinpoche (1290-1364), and was born at Rinchen Gang in Sakya on the eighth day of the fourth month of 1312. Sonam Gyaltsen was predestined for greatness: his birth was attended by portentous events, including an earthquake, a rainbow in the form of a tent above the palace in which he was born, and a sudden rise in level of the Trom River, which flows through Sakya township. This child, known as Nyima Dewai Lodro, was to be the second youngest of his father's many children. He was a prodigious child, and at the age of eight he astonished a learned gathering by delivering discourses on many fields of knowledge.

Acting on a prediction that Sakya would collapse through a lack of heirs, Sonam Gyaltsen's father, Dagnyi Chenpo Zangpo Pal, attempted to increase the family by dividing the House of Sakya into four *labrang*, or lineages, each headed by one of his sons. As head of Rinchen Labrang, Sonam Gyaltsen came under great pressure from his family to ensure the continuation of the lineage, and it was only with some difficulty that he secured permission to be ordained. At the age of eleven, he took Upasaka vows from his half-brother Tishri Kunga Lodro (1296-1327).[4] When he was seventeen, in 1329, he received novitiate vows and his religious name,

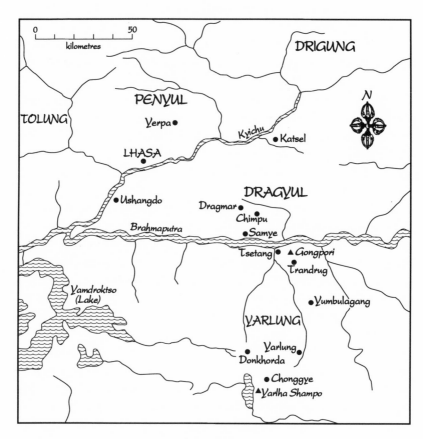

Central Tibet

Sonam Gyaltsen. At twenty, he became fully ordained and continued his studies under many great teachers, including his elder half-brothers Tishri Kunga Lodro and Jamyang Donyo Gyaltsen (1310-1344). He received Kalachakra initiation from Buton Rinpoche. His main root guru, Dragpugpa Sonam Pal (1277-1350), foretold that Sonam Gyaltsen would be invited to become Tishri at the court of the Mongolian emperors in China, but advised his student to decline the offer.

After he was fully ordained, in accordance with the strictest monastic discipline, Sonam Gyaltsen refrained from eating after midday and became a pure vegetarian. It is said that even in the middle of winter, he never wore shirts with sleeves. These rules are often overlooked by all but the most highly disciplined devotees, as compliance demands great personal sacrifice.

At the age of thirty-five, in 1345, he was installed on the Sakya throne, and as head of Sakya he held the highest political and religious position in Tibet for four years. Seeing the internal rivalry among his half-brothers, he renounced the throne and retired to live in various hermitages. Continued internecine strife severely eroded the position of the royal house, and at the same time, the prestige of its Mongol sponsors declined as the dynasty began to falter.

In 1354 temporal authority over Tibet finally passed from the Sakya lineage to Jangchub Gyaltsen, a former regional governor of the Pagmo Drupa clan whose home was in the Yarlung Valley. His rule ushered in a period of rapid social reform and sparked a renewed interest in the Tibetan national identity. Jangchub Gyaltsen's incumbency was cast as a return to the Golden Age of the great kings Songtsen Gampo and Trisong Detsen, who had reigned seven centuries earlier.

Having retired from political life, Sonam Gyaltsen gained a reputation as a great yogin who spurned the mundane world and all its trappings. Among the many faithful devotees whom he attracted was the young Je Tsongkapa, who later founded the Gelug tradition and is one of the greatest figures in the history of Tibetan Buddhism.

Famed for his erudition and sanctity, Sonam Gyaltsen was universally acclaimed as the *Lama dampa*, or 'Holy Guru', a title with which he is still honoured today. Tradition holds that Lama Dampa consecrated a reliquary stupa containing the skull of Shantarakshita, the first abbot of Samye. Many miracles followed the ceremony, and Lama Dampa became abbot of the monastery thereafter. From his day, this great establishment came under Sakya control. Lama Dampa redirected all the offerings that he received to the restoration of various religious establishments, including the throne of the Jowo Shakyamuni in Lhasa. It is said that on one occasion, he gave a gold coin to every monk at Samye.

The author noted in the colophon that *The Clear Mirror* was compiled in an Earth-male-dragon Year. The only such year during the author's lifetime was 1328, when he was only 16 years of age. It has been argued that he began the compilation in that year.[5] It seems more likely, however, that *'brug* (dragon) is a scribal error for *spre'u* (monkey), and that Sonam Gyaltsen wrote the work in the Earth-male-monkey Year 1368.[6]

Lama Dampa died at Samye on the twenty-fifth day of the sixth month in 1375 at the age of sixty-four. His reliquary stupa was constructed at Netang but was destroyed sometime during the Cultural Revolution.[7]

The history of the text

Sonam Gyaltsen was one of the leading figures of his day, and his reputation undoubtedly helped to assure the evergreen popularity enjoyed by *The Clear Mirror* over the succeeding six centuries. It ranks among the great works of early Tibetan historiographical writing, but outshines all others in both the depth and breadth of its coverage. *The Clear Mirror* encompasses the full course of history, from the creation of the physical universe in the vast primordial void, to the genealogies of the local potentiaries who dominated the political scene when the book was written. Sonam Gyaltsen states that he compiled *The Clear Mirror* to 'give pleasure to the faithful and to those who desire a history of the propagation of the Buddha's teachings' and to 'provide amusement for their ears'.

The text is a rich blend of history, legend, poetry, adventure and romance. It may properly be regarded as a literary work, albeit a morally and spiritually uplifting one. Its eclectic style and its treatment of both secular and sacred subjects sets it apart from other well-known ecclesiastical works like Buton's *History of the Dharma* and the *Blue Annals* of Go Lotsawa (1392-1481). As secular literature, *The Clear Mirror* has never been regarded as entirely respectable, even though it may appear to the Western reader to be thoroughly steeped in religious sentiment.

The Clear Mirror is as much a compilation of earlier historical documents as it is a piece of original writing, a fact which the author himself readily acknowledges.[8] In the concluding lines of each chapter, he usually directs the reader to the original works upon which he has drawn. In some cases, the quotations and summaries of earlier documents are particularly significant, as the originals are no longer extant. In addition to the many references throughout the text, the closing paragraphs of the final chapter list the most important sources to which the author has referred.

This text has been known by several names. The original Tibetan title, and the one that is most widely recognised, is *Clear Mirror on Royal Genealogy*, although in the final paragraph the author himself calls the work *Clear Mirror on the History of the Dharma*. The first wood-block edition was printed at the Tsuglagkhang in 1478 and is therefore known as the Lhasa redaction. In the colophon of that version, one finds the title *Clear Mirror on Royal Genealogy and the History of the Dharma*.[9] A second redaction was printed at the famous Derge printing-monastery during the eighteenth century.

The *Clear Mirror* was twice translated into Mongolian in the seventeenth century. A German translation of one of these versions in 1824 marked the beginning of modern scholarly interest in the work. Since that time, more than a dozen translations of various sections of the Tibetan original have appeared in English, German, Italian, Chinese and Russian.[10]

The present work is a translation of a modern edition of the Derge redaction, published by the Chinese Nationalities Publishing House in 1981, and reprinted several times since then.[11] The modern editors corrected some (but not all) orthographical errors found in the

Derge text. The original lengthy eighteenth chapter, which contains the biographies of all the kings after Songtsen Gampo, was divided into sixteen new chapters, a convenience which we have retained. Following tradition, each of the original chapters closes with a summary of its contents. The editors adopted the modern convention of giving each chapter a title based on the traditional summary. We have further abbreviated and simplified some of these.

The publication of *The Clear Mirror* by an organ of the Chinese government is surprising, given the strongly nationalistic flavour of the work. *The Clear Mirror* could be considered subversive, as it might inflame 'separatist' sentiments. It paints a picture of a strong, independent nation with its own distinct race, language, culture, history and polity. In fact, Tibet's cultural ties with India are pre-eminent. The material in *The Clear Mirror* undermines China's own claim that Tibet has been under its thrall since Songtsen Gampo married the Chinese princess in the seventh century.

Translation and conventions

Our philosophy in translating *The Clear Mirror* is simply to further the author's own stated goals of pleasing and informing his readership. This is not a translation in the discipline of philology, textual criticism or history, nor is it by any means an academic rendering. Our translation is literary, not literal. We feel sure that the scholarly community will find many shortcomings with our approach, but to paraphrase the author, 'Although this endeavour lay beyond our own inferior capabilities, we undertook it nevertheless!' It is our great regret that we have been unable to pursue the manifold avenues of inquiry that opened before us during the course of our labours. We hope that by placing this document in the public domain, it will attract the attention from ethnologists, historians, folklorists and anthropologists that it so richly deserves.

We believe that the author intended his work for a general readership; this is also our intention. While maintaining fidelity to the original, we have stressed fluency and accessibility in the translation. This lends us as translators a certain licence with language but also devolves upon us the responsibility to ensure that the text remains uncontrived and fluent. Where the original is ambiguous, inconsistent, incorrect or incomplete, we have used common sense to resolve or correct shortcomings, rather than burden the reader with the full range of possibilities.

We have retained the original textual annotations which were added by one or more unidentified Tibetan editors, possibly even by the author himself. They provide interpretation or expansion of certain details, and in some cases, alternative accounts of events from other sources. These remarks have been set in square brackets. We have added our own footnotes where we felt that the reader might benefit from additional explanation. Where the original text presented material in verse form, we have indented the text and retained the author's linebreaks.

Tibetan names and terms have been transliterated into English to enable readers who do not know Tibetan to approximate the original pronunciation in the standard dialect of the central provinces. The Tibetan spellings of all names and places are given in the index. Sanskrit words have been transliterated without diacritics in the text, but are given in complete form in parentheses in the index. We have used the Pinyin system for romanising Chinese names.

As translators we can only restate Lama Dampa Sonam Gyaltsen's closing prayer that *The Clear Mirror* may ultimately 'bring forth blooms in the lotus garden of benefits and happiness, and redouble the enjoyment of the faithful bees'.

Tibetan calendrical system

Each year in the traditional Tibetan calendrical cycle has a trinomial title consisting of an element, a gender and an animal. Five elements, namely earth, iron, water, wood and fire, are joined with twelve animals, dog, pig, mouse, ox, tiger, hare, dragon, snake, horse, sheep, monkey and bird. Each element appears twice, first as male, and then as female.[12] The cycle begins as follows:

Earth-male-dog
Earth-female-pig
Iron-male-mouse
Iron-female-ox

There are sixty years in each cycle. The Western equivalents of the Tibetan sixty-year cycle are indicated in the text in brackets. These were derived from the calendrical appendix to the Tibetan-Chinese Dictionary.[13] There is great variation among the various Tibetan sources on the dates of early historical events. With the exception of those that can be corroborated by the Chinese dynastic histories, few other dates can be verified. A comprehensive study of dates for the period covered by *The Clear Mirror* was undertaken by Aoki.[14]

PART I
THE BEGINNINGS

Prologue

REVERENT HOMAGE
TO LORD AVALOKITESHVARA,
SUBLIME MASTER OF COMPASSION!

I pay reverent homage with body, voice and mind
To the fulfilment of the hopes of all beings,
To the glory that satisfies all needs and desires,
To the foremost among humans and treasury of all qualities,
To the teacher of gods and humans, the King of Shakya![15]

I pay homage to Lord Avalokiteshvara
Who, by the excellent development of compassion
Of immeasurable omniscience and love,
Manifests in appropriate forms to subdue every candidate,
And who establishes all beings in Tibet upon the path of
maturity and liberation.

I pay homage to the miraculously accomplished masters of men
Who possess boundless merit,
The precious descendants of Mahasammata,[16]
The pure, royal lineage of India
Of Ikshvaku and his like.[17]

I pay homage to the miraculous kings and ministers
Who lit the great lamp of the Holy Dharma
In the murky darkness of this wild land of Tibet,
And led the people and all other sentient beings to happiness.

I pay homage to the profoundly learned translators and pandits,
Who are the source of all benefits and happiness,
Who are beautified by the ornaments of the three classes
of learning,
Who established the translations of the precepts and treatises,
And who caused the teachings of the Buddha to flourish in
every direction.

Although it is beyond my own inferior capabilities
To compile this collection of brief biographies
Of Avalokiteshvara and the successive generations of
Dharma-kings
Whose infinite qualities defy imagination,
I wrote it nevertheless to engender boundless piety
and reverence
Among those faithful persons who wish to know the history
of the teachings
And to provide amusement for their ears!

The precious teachings of the Buddha are the foundation on which
goodness, benefits and happiness are achieved in this world. The
agency by which these teachings spread and developed was the
magnanimity of the bodhisattva Dharma-kings of India and Tibet.
This work therefore propagates their respective histories. In particular, the sublime bodhisattva Lord Avalokiteshvara established
all sentient beings in this barbaric Land of Snows on the path of
liberation and enlightenment by manifesting in appropriate forms
for the subjugation of every being, as prophesied by the most
perfectly accomplished sage, the Buddha. Thus, the Dharma-protecting king Songtsen Gampo, who was the mind-emanation of

Avalokiteshvara, this especially noble being, and the successive generations of Dharma-kings spread and developed the Buddha's teachings. As a brief record of their endeavours in this regard, this history of the rise of the Dharma will instil faith among readers and dispel their doubts. Hold it in your heart!

1

The creation of the Universe, the Dharma-kings of India, and the life of Buddha Shakyamuni

In the beginning, there was boundless, empty sky, and from this arose the physical universe. Vapours from the ten directions began to stir, and mingling together, formed the Cross of Winds, a pale blue sphere of air, which is perfectly solid, 1,600,000 miles high and infinitely wide.[18] Above it, from a great body of water, there lies an enormous ocean, 1,120,000 miles deep and 1,203,450 miles wide. Above the ocean lies the Golden Ground, which is flat like the palm of a hand and 340,000 miles wide. Mt. Sumeru, King of Mountains, composed of many precious materials, appeared miraculously at the centre of the Golden Ground like the axle of a water-wheel. The eastern side of the mountain is made of silver, the southern side of lapis lazuli, the western side of ruby and the northern side of gold. It descends 80,000 miles into the ocean and rises 80,000 miles into the air. Seven golden mountains perpetually circle it: Yugamdhara, the 'Yoke', 40,000 miles high; Ishadhara, the 'Plough', 20,000 miles high, Khadiraka, the

'Acacia', 10,000 miles high; Sudarshana, 'Beautiful to Behold', 5000 miles high; Ashvakarna, the 'Horse's Ear', 2500 miles high; Vinataka, 'Subdued Form', 1250 miles high and Nemindhara, the 'Rim', measuring 625 miles in height. Around the seven mountains lie the Seven Playful Oceans, and in grottoes on the central mountain are the cities of the demigods. Above the grottoes is Trayastrimsa, the 'Abode of the Gods of the Thirty-three Realms'. The palace of the great god Indra, known as the Excellent Mansion of Victory, lies at the centre of the mountain. It too is constructed from various precious materials. Rising a further 80,000 miles is Yama, the 'Heavenly Abode that is Free from Strife'; 160,000 miles higher is Tushita, the 'Joyful Heaven'; 320,000 miles higher is Nirmanarati, the 'Heavenly Abode of Manifest Happiness'; and 640,000 miles higher is Parinirmitavashavartin, the 'Heavenly Abode of Those who Overpower the Manifestations of Others'. Everything below belongs to the Sphere of Desires, and everything above, including the Spheres of Form and Formlessness, rise one above another like the terraced steps of a stupa. The height and extent of each realm, and the lifespan, physical dimensions and amusements enjoyed by their respective inhabitants, may be found in the Abhidharma.[19]

To the east of Mt. Sumeru lies the continent of Purvavideha, together with its two subcontinents, all of which are shaped like half-moons. To the south is the continent of Jambudvipa and its two subcontinents, which are shaped like shoulder-blades. To the west is the continent of Godaniya and its two subcontinents, all of which are round. To the north is the continent of Uttarakuru and its two subcontinents, all of which are square.

In the sky, 40,000 miles above Mt. Vinataka, the sun, moon, constellations and so on rest upon the Sphere of Winds, which is clear, yet perfectly solid. The dimensions of the sun and moon, the extent and height of the constellations, the size of the four continents and their attendant subcontinents, and the entertainments, lifespans and physical proportions enjoyed by their inhabitants are also described in great detail in the Abhidharma.

Of all the continents, Jambudvipa is the most excellent. The subcontinents of Oddiyana and Suvarnadvipa and the two islands of

Singhala and Chandradvipa lie beside it, forming together the Continent of the South. The kingdom of India, which lies at the centre of Jambudvipa, resembles a silken canopy and is a land of treasures. Mongolia and Khotan resemble a horse-drawn carriage and are countries where all desires are satisfied. The lands of the Uighurs and the Chinese are like lotus flowers in full bloom and are places of great wonders. As to the kingdom of Tibet, the Land of Snows, it resembles an ogress lying upon her back. It is fraught with great ravines, it abounds in demons, ogres, dark mountains and rugged passes, and is indeed a benighted place. There are a further sixteen great lands, each enjoying prosperity and abiding in happiness.

In the beginning, the inhabitants of India were descended from the Prabhasvara gods and were endowed with boundless physical qualities. They lived forever by sustaining themselves upon the joy of deep meditation. They were born by magic, their bodies shone with light, and they travelled through the sky by miraculous powers. Then, because they consumed a white, honey-flavoured nectar known as 'Essence of the Earth', they lost their powers of flight, and the sustenance gained through deep meditation was lost to them. An orange substance known as 'Fat of the Earth' then appeared, and it, too, tasted like honey. When all of this had been eaten, a foodstuff known as 'Grove of Reeds' appeared. When all of this had been consumed, there appeared a species of grain called *salu*[20] that needed no cultivation. Whenever this food was required, people simply reached out and took what they desired. Some lazy persons, however, took the portion intended for the following morning and ate it that very day. Others did likewise, and before long, all the grain that required no cultivation was consumed.

After they began to practice agriculture, the produce of a field sown by one person was sometimes harvested and eaten by someone else. People therefore quarrelled and fought one another. The most outstanding person among them therefore divided the land into lots, over which each person had authority. In this way, he eliminated strife and the people were overjoyed. They agreed to nominate him as their leader and showed him respect. He was called Mahasammata, 'Honoured by Many', and was the first of the Indian kings.

Mahasammata's son was Rokha. His son was Kalyana. His son was Varakalyana. His son was Utposhadha. These are known collectively as the Five Early Kings. Utposhadha's son was Prince Mandhatar. His son was Charu. His son was Upacharu. His son was Karuka. His son was Charuman. These are known collectively as the Five Chakravartin Kings. Charuman's son was King Varada. During his time, a human lifespan was forty thousand years. Further, during his reign and that of his son, Buddha Krakucchanda appeared in India and taught the sacred Dharma. King Varada's son was King Mani. After three hundred royal generations had passed, a king known as Sadaprabha appeared. His son was King Chandha. At the time of this king, a human lifespan was thirty thousand years. During his reign and that of his son, Buddha Kanakamuni appeared in India and taught the sacred Dharma. After a further three hundred royal generations had passed, King Maharatna and his son King Krikin appeared. At that time, a human lifespan was twenty thousand years. During the reigns of these two sovereigns, Buddha Kashyapa appeared in the world and taught the sacred Dharma.

After a further two hundred royal generations had elapsed, a king known as Karnika arose and ruled the land of Potala. He had two sons; the elder was Gautama, and the younger was Bharadhvaja. The first was ordained; the second was made king, but as he had no son, heretical thoughts arose in his mind and he murdered his elder brother by impaling him upon a stake. In response to the exhortation of the people, Gautama shed a drop of semen upon a divan and it turned into two eggs. [Gautama shed his seed on account of his previous karma, and a spell cast by a black Brahmin caused it to change into eggs. In answer to Gautama's honest prayers, the Brahmin became gold in colour.] The eggs were placed in the shade of a clump of sugarcanes, and after a while, they turned into two infant boys. The name of one was Suryavamsha, 'Friend of the Sun', the other, Ikshvaku or 'Sugarcane Boy'. Suryavamsha had no children, but Ikshvaku became king and had many sons, who became known as the 'Ikshvaku lineage', and spread in all directions. After one hundred successive royal generations of descendants of the eldest son, King Virudhaka appeared. He had three sons and three daughters. They settled together incestuously on the banks of the Bhagirathi River. As a result of their cohabitation, their progeny multiplied and they became known as the Shakya ['How dare they!'] lineage, and they, too, spread in all directions. After fifty successive royal generations of descendants from the elder son, a king called Dasharatha arose. He had three sons: Mahashakya, Shakya Licchavi and Shakya Ridragpa. After twenty-five successive generations of royal descendants from the eldest son Mahashakya, King Aranemi appeared.[21] His son was King Anantapala. His son was King Dhanusthira. His son was King Singhahanu. He had four sons: King Shuddhodana, Shuklodana, Dronodana and Amritodana, and four daughters: Shuddha, Shukla, Drona and Amrita. Shuddha's son was Suprabuddha, Shukla's son was Mallika, Drona's son was Sulabha, and Amrita's son was Kalyanavardana.

King Shuddhodana had two sons, the Lord Buddha and his younger brother, Nanda. Shuklodana had two sons, Tishya and Bhadrika. Dronodana had two sons, Mahanaman and Aniruddha. Amritodana had two sons, Ananda and Devadatta. One son, Rahula, was born to the Lord Buddha. The Vinaya states that 1,150,100 royal generations elapsed between Mahasammata and Rahula.

First, the Lord Buddha cultivated excellent enlightenment. Secondly, he accumulated merit during three eons of incalculable duration. Then, in the ultimate sense, he was enlightened in the heavenly realm of Akanishta. In the conventional sense, however, he became the son of the god Shetaketu in Tushita, the 'Joyous Heaven' at the end of the Era of Conflict, when the lifespan of inhabitants of the world was one hundred years. Knowing that the time for subduing all sentient beings had arrived, he enthroned the reverend Lord Maitreya as his sacred regent in Tushita. He then cast his gaze upon his future natal city and the caste of his prospective parents, and descended in the form of an elephant from his heavenly abode to the royal palace of his father, King Shuddhodana, and entered the womb of his mother, Mayadevi, whereupon many auspicious signs appeared. Ten months later, on the eighth day of the last month of spring, under the constellation of Pushya, as his mother was resting before a bodhi-tree in the grove of Lumbini,[22] the Buddha was delivered between the ribs below her right armpit, unblemished by the defilements of the womb. Brahma and Indra received him into a length of *kashika*-linen,[23] and Nanda and Upananda bathed his body. The prince then took seven steps, each footprint became a lotus flower, and this the first eulogy was dedicated:

> When you, foremost among humans of every era, were born,
> You took seven steps upon the earth
> And said, 'I am the most excellent in the world'.
> I pay homage, O gifted one!

He was entrusted to the care of thirty-two nurse-maids, including his aunt Prajapati Gautami, who nurtured his development.[24] As the prince grew, he came to excel in the five fields of knowledge, including literature and mathematics. With his physical strength and martial skills, he overcame Devadatta and all the arrogant ones, and was without equal. At the age of twenty-nine, he took 84,000 wives, including Gopi and Yashodhara, and shouldered the affairs of state. Realising the futility of worldly actions, and perceiving that the city of Kapilavastu was surrounded by the unrelenting suffering caused by aging, disease and death, he determined to be ordained. His parents withheld their consent, however, so the Caturmaharajas, the four great guardian kings, bore him aloft into the sky above. He came before the Stupa of Purity, shaved his own head, and was thus ordained. For six or seven years thereafter, he underwent austerities by the Nairajnana River and elsewhere, and brought to perfection his profound meditation. At Varanasi and the grove of Rishipatana he turned the wheel of the Dharma of the Four Noble Truths to the Five Excellent Mendicants and other beings, who were adherents of the Lesser Vehicle. At Gridhrakuta, or 'Vulture's Peak', and elsewhere, he turned the Wheel of Dharma of the Extraordinary Vehicle for the myriad bodhisattvas and the sublime arhats. At Vaishali, Veluvana and elsewhere, he turned the Wheel of the Dharma of Ultimate Meaning for the retinue of bodhisattvas who had embarked upon the vehicle.

The Buddha arrived at Bodhgaya on the fifteenth day of the fourth month, that being the full moon. In the evening he subdued the maras, during the night he remained in meditative equipoise, and early in the dawn he attained complete enlightenment.

Having brought the Twelve Deeds to completion at the age of eighty, the Sage demonstrated the way to Nirvana at Kushinagara,[25] after which the sublime arhats arranged the collected precepts in three stages.

Four kings were born in their respective lands at the same time as the Lord Buddha himself, namely Prasenajit, son of Brahmadatta of Shravasti; Bimbisara, son of Mahapadma of Rajgir; Udayana, son of Shatanika of Kaushambi; and Pradyota, son of Anantanemi of Ujayani.

According to the school of Atisha, the Lord Buddha was conceived in a Wood-male-rat Year, was born in a Wood-female-ox Year, was enlightened in a Water-female-pig Year and attained Nirvana in a Wood-male-monkey Year. According to the Sakyapa school, the Buddha was conceived in a Fire-female-hare Year, was born in an Earth-male-dragon Year, was enlightened in a Water-male-tiger Year and attained Nirvana in a Fire-female-pig Year. Also according to the Sakyapa, 3455 years elapsed between the Lord Buddha's calculated year of birth in a Dragon Year, and Lama Tishri Kunga Lodro's ordination at the age of twenty-six in U in the Water-male-dog Year [1322].[26]

Among the ten 500-year periods during which the Teachings will endure, there are Three Periods of the Precepts of the Abhidharmacharya. Two years of the first of these three periods, the Sutracharya, have already elapsed, leaving 498 years. Added to the 500 years of the second period, the Vinayacharya, the resulting Age of Authentic Dharma will be 998 years. The duration of the third period, the Age of Dharma in Form Only, will also be 500 years. The Dharma will therefore endure for a further 1498 years, it is said.

[According to the *Illumination of Knowledge*, the Dharma-king Ashoka, who sponsored the second council on the teachings of the Buddha, appeared in India one hundred years after the Buddha attained Nirvana.]

As this is merely a summary, those who desire further details will find clarification in the Sutras and Vinaya. Those who are unable to consult these works directly should read carefully Buton Rinpoche's *History of the Dharma*, and the *Illumination of Knowledge* by Lama Chokyi Gyelpo,[27] which is in accord with Buton's descriptions.

This chapter,
concerning the creation of the
Universe, the appearance of the Dharma-
kings of India, and spread of the Holy
Dharma following the appearance on
earth of Buddha Shakyamuni,
is the first.

2

The creation and consecration
of the three images
# of Buddha Shakyamuni

ormerly, when the true Lord Buddha, surrounded by his four retinues, resided in the Grove of Jeta, the sublime Manjushri petitioned thus: 'At present, sentient beings may gaze upon your visage, make offerings to you and thereby accrue merit. After you have passed into Nirvana, however, beings will have no such basis on which to accumulate merit. Show us, therefore, a symbol by which we may do so'. After Manjushri had made his supplication, four rays of light shone forth from the smiling countenance of the Buddha. One struck the great god Brahma, one struck the *mahagraha* Vishnu, one struck Indra, King of Gods, and one struck the sculptor Vishvakarma, and each was invested with inspiration. Folding his hands in devotion, the great god Brahma said:

> From five precious materials
> I shall create an image of the Dharmakaya form
> Of the Victorious One, Protector of the World,

The sage whose infinite qualities defy the imagination,
In order that virtue and goodness may extend in every
    direction.

Then Vishnu folded his hands in devotion and said:

From precious materials
I shall create an image of the Sambhogakaya form
Of the foremost among humans, he who endows pure
    form,
The victor over the snowy ocean,
The treasure that fulfils all desires,
In order to alleviate poverty among sentient beings.

The King of Gods, Indra, folded his hands in devotion and said:

From five precious materials
I shall create an image of the Nirmanakaya form
Of the sage of sages, god of supreme gods,
That resembles a mass of gold, ornamented with the major
    and minor signs of greatness,[28]
In order that all beings may accumulate merit.

Then the sculptor Vishvakarma folded his hands in devotion and
said:

I shall be the sculptor
Who makes these three miraculous images
Of the teacher of gods and humans, the King of Shakya,
From the five precious substances,
In order that sentient beings may accumulate merit in
    future.

The 'Glorious Intangible Stupa'

The great god Brahma placed one great mound of precious sapphires, one of melted gold and other metals, and a third of melted crystal before the craftsman Vishvakarma, as materials for the creation of the symbol of the Lord Buddha in the Dharmakaya form. Vishvakarma then melted and refined these precious substances and cast the desired symbol in a mould. It was in the shape of a stupa, its size was equal to the breadth of Brahma's outstretched arms, and it was the colour of smoke. The Buddha himself consecrated it, strewed flowers upon it and blessed it. This image of the

Dharmakaya in the form of a stupa was borne to the realm of the gods and remained there. The dakinis of divine wisdom then transported it to the land of Oddiyana in the west, where it was suspended in the sky, without touching the ground. It therefore became known as the 'Glorious Intangible Stupa'. As it had been taken to the realm of the gods, it was also called the 'Stupa that Descended among the Gods'. On account of its colour, its other name was the 'Smoke-like Stupa'.

The 'Victor over the Snowy Ocean'

Vishnu then placed before Vishvakarma one great mound of precious sapphires, another of melted emeralds and a third of melted crystal, as materials for the creation of a symbol in the Sambhogakaya form. Having melted together these precious materials, Vishvakarma cast an image of the Buddha eighty miles in height, the essence of which was Vairochana, the Victor over the Snowy Ocean. Its two hands were in the attitude of meditation, it was blue in colour, and it had a crystal the size of a vase upon its forehead. As it was placed in the Great Outer Ocean, the half of the image below the navel was submerged in the water and benefited sea-creatures. The half of the image that was above the navel benefited those that inhabited the dry land. Birds perched upon its head and shoulders, and marked it with their droppings. As a result, although the image was originally blue, it gradually turned white. On the fifteenth day of the month, the rays of the full moon fall upon the crystal on its forehead, and it is anointed with signless water.[29] If a merchant who is seeking riches upon the Outer Ocean moors his vessel in the crook of the image's arm and makes offerings to it, he will receive all the wealth that he desires. Stairways ascend its front and back. The Buddha himself consecrated the image, strewed flowers upon it and blessed it.

As raw materials for the creation of a symbol of the Buddha in the Nirmanakaya form, Indra gathered the five precious celestial substances: *indranila*-sapphires, *indragoba*-cochinealstone, *tonka*-sapphires, great *tonka*-sapphires and *kodze* 'design-of-beauty';[30] and the five precious earthly substances: gold, silver, pearl, amethyst and coral, as well as other valuable materials. As he wished to create an image of the Sage at the age of twelve, the Buddha's nurse-maid Prajapati Gautami informed him, 'At the age of eight, he could encircle an object the height of the throne in the Lumbini Grove within the ring finger of his right hand. At the age of twelve, when he stood upon the threshold of the Great Shravasti Gate, his head touched the lintel'. Thus she described his height.

The craftsman Vishvakarma then cast these precious materials in a mould to create an image of the Buddha in the Nirmanakaya form at the age of twelve. Its hue was that of refined gold, its two hands were in the attitude of meditation and earth-subduing respectively, and it was ornamented with the major and minor signs of greatness. By simply gazing upon its countenance, diseases caused by the Three Poisons are dispelled and genuine fervent devotion is born.[31] It engenders every quality when seen, heard, contemplated or touched. After this image, indistinguishable from the actual body of the Sage himself, had been created, it became the glory of every god and human.[32] The Lord Buddha consecrated it, strewed flowers upon it and blessed it. It was then taken by the gods to their celestial realm, where it remained for 100 years, after which the dakinis of divine wisdom took it to the land of Oddiyana in the west, where it remained for 500 years. It was then borne into the air by magic and was transported to Bodhgaya in India, where it remained for a further 500 years. Thus the three images of the Sage, the fully enlightened one, were created. Having completed his works, the Buddha passed into Nirvana.

Not long after the Buddha left the realm of sorrow, in the land of Magadha, three sons were born to a certain Brahmin by the name of Mahapala the Householder and a reverend dakini of divine wisdom. The older two followed the heretical religion, but the youngest was wholeheartedly devoted to Buddhism. As the doctrines of the Brahmins and the Buddhists were irreconcilable, the three brothers quarrelled among themselves. Their mother declared, 'If you feel cold, wear clothes! If you are hungry, get something to eat! Why argue about religion?' But the youngest son said, 'We three brothers cannot reconcile the teachings of the Brahmins and Buddhists. Which is superior?' His mother replied, 'I shall send you to Mt. Kailash, home of the god Mahadeva, to ask this question'. She

placed a charm to guarantee fleetness of foot upon her three sons'
shoes, and putting the shoes upon their feet, she sent them on their
way. In an instant, they arrived at the summit of Mt. Kailash, where
they came upon a beautiful girl who was gathering flowers in a
precious vase. They asked the girl, 'Who are you and what will
you do with the flowers that you have gathered?' She replied, 'I
am a servant of the goddess Umadeva. On the fifteenth day of the
month, at the full moon, the sublime arhats, having risen into the
sky by magic, will come to our palace to teach the Dharma. I shall
give the flowers to them'.

Falling in with the girl, they proceeded to the palace of the god
Mahadeva. When they arrived, as it was the fifteenth day of the
month, they beheld the sublime arhats, who had travelled through
the sky by magic, seated upon a precious divan that had been set
out for them. Mahadeva and the goddess Umadeva strewed flowers about, invited the arhats to discourse upon the Dharma, and
offered prayers. After the teaching, the sublime ones departed into
the sky once more. The three brothers then asked Mahadeva which
religion was superior, the heretical or the Buddhist, to which he
replied, 'The Inner Teaching, Buddhism, is superior. I, too, desire
enlightenment on the basis of these teachings. Except for the mere
provision of temporary happiness, the heretical groups lack essence in the ultimate sense'.

Being firmly convinced, the three brothers returned to India, and
said to their mother, 'We shall adhere to Buddhism, the Inner Teaching'. To this their mother responded, 'It is good that you shall dwell
within this teaching! Now, each of you must build a shrine. The
oldest, Mahamase, shall build a shrine in Varanasi. The second,
Sibasame, shall build a shrine in the Grove of Jeta. The youngest,
Tratasame, shall build a shrine at Bodhgaya'. The two older brothers each constructed shrines, just as their mother had instructed,
and completed their task first. The shrine built by the youngest
son at Bodhgaya consisted outwardly of a stupa and inwardly of a
hall of worship. Sandalwood was ground to a powder and mixed
with clay to form a mound as the raw material for the image of the
Lord Buddha at the age of thirty that the youngest son wished to

create. The mother said, 'The sculptors and yourself, taking food and water, shall remain inside the shrine. Iron nails shall be driven into the door, and the construction of the image shall be completed in three months and three days'. After three months and two days had passed, the mother returned and demanded that the door be opened. Her son said, 'Only three months and two days have passed. One day still remains.' The mother replied, 'It matters not that one day remains, as I shall die tomorrow. There is nothing more important to me than to behold the face of the Buddha. If I do not see his likeness, no one else will be able to judge its accuracy. Open the door, for I must see the image'.[33] When her son opened the door, the sculptor, who was a manifestation, vanished like a rainbow.

This image of the Buddha at the age of thirty, ornamented with the major and minor signs of greatness, was most miraculous to behold. Those who came before it forgot their hunger and thirst, so that others had to ply them with sustenance. When those who had seen the image ventured to leave, being unable to turn away, they walked out backwards. If a person was suddenly taken ill, the mere sight of its countenance dispelled the malady. When someone was burning with anger on account of a quarrel, the mere sight of its countenance subdued completely these emotions and bestowed compassion and enlightenment-thought.[34]

Just as the mother had foretold, she departed from this world of sorrows the following day. When they examined the image to see what defect had arisen because she had entered the shrine one day too early, they discovered that the little toe on the right foot was missing!

The Sandalwood Jowo and the Jowo Shakyamuni resided at Bodhgaya for many royal generations, after which the Dharmaking Dharmapala arose in India. At the same time, an emperor known as Tritima Dzaya ruled in China. Although the two sovereigns had never seen nor met one another, they became friends. The emperor gave the Indian king three gifts, the last of which was a seamless garment of finest silks, decorated with the design of four eternal knots reaching up to the chest. The Indian king thought to himself, 'Surely the emperor has some great desire. What could it be?' Just then, a letter from the Chinese emperor arrived, and on opening it, the Indian king read the following:

> Dharma-protecting king of India, Possessor of the Teachings,
> The treasure of Dharma which is of boundless power and
>   glory:
> In India, a land more sublime than any other,
> By the power you have achieved as the result of merit
>   accrued in former existences,
> You enjoy every sensual pleasure
> And nurture your subjects with benefits and happiness.
> By the accumulation of merit, I have no such symbols for
>   worship.
> I, the emperor of this uncivilised land of China,
> Lack the precepts of the Victorious One and images of the
>   Sage.
> As there are no opportunities to hear the Dharma in this
>   land,
> I beseech you to bestow upon us, out of your kindness,
> The image of the Lord Buddha at the age of twelve,
> The five Sutras and four monks.[35]

As these were the contents of the emperor's letter, the Indian king thought to himself, 'In India, we have the Dharma of the Great Vehicle,[36] as well as the Buddha's mortal remains and relics, and shravakas and arhats. None of these are found in China. As the Dharma will not decline in India, and as it will certainly flourish in China, I will confer with the Lord Buddha himself and present these items to the emperor'. Returning to his palace, he came before the image of the Buddha, which usually faced south, but as it had turned to face the east, he thought, 'It seems that the Lord himself would gladly travel to China!' The image of Shakyamuni and the Three Jewels were then placed aboard a great vessel that had been constructed for the purpose, and fine silks and a marquee of precious materials were erected over them. The king then dispatched the vessel upon the great river that flowed from India to China, accompanied by unceasing music, innumerable flags and the like. He then made this reply:

O Emperor of China, heed my words!
The object of my veneration, this image of the Sage,
Was created at the behest of Indra, King of Gods,
From ten precious materials
By the sculptor Vishvakarma,
And was consecrated by the Buddha himself.
Whoever sees, hears, contemplates, touches or supplicates
This image of the peerless master of victory,
Will speedily attain Buddhahood.
Thus taught the Victorious Ones.[37]
Although I cherish the Jowo,
Which is endowed with such qualities,
As I do my own heart,
In response to your gifts and weighty request,
I give this object of veneration to you as an offering,
In order that you may lead the sentient beings of your land
    to virtue.
Be faithful and bow down devoutly before it!

Such was the message he sent. The Emperor of China rejoiced and was greatly pleased, and welcomed the vessel with music that defied the imagination. The Jowo and the Three Jewels eventually reached Emperor Dzaya's palace, all sentient beings were led to benefits and happiness, the barbaric land of China was subdued, and the sacred Dharma was caused to flourish.

This chapter,
in which the three images
of Buddha Shakyamuni
are created and consecrated,
is the second.

3

The spread of the Holy Dharma in China and Mongolia, and an enumeration of their kings

History of China

In regard to the arrival in China of the Jowo Shakyamuni and Sandalwood Jowo and the spread of the Dharma in that land, the history of the royal lineages recorded in the great Chinese annals states that the first emperor was called Zhou[38] [a contemporary of the Indian king Dhanusthira[39]]. Four royal generations after that sovereign, on the eighth day of the fourth month of the twenty-fourth year of the reign of an emperor known as Zhou Zhaowang (being a Wood-male-tiger Year), many miraculous signs, including lights and sounds, appeared in the west. [Other than identifying the date of this celebration of the Buddha's birth, the years do not tally, yet it is stated thus in the Chinese annals.] The Chinese astrologers performed a divination and thereby learned of the birth of the Lord Buddha.

The Buddha achieved perfect enlightenment at the age of thirty and proceeded to Tushita, the Joyful Paradise, to instruct his mother in the Dharma. During his absence, King Utrayana created the sandalwood image. It was consecrated when the Buddha descended again from the realm of the gods, after which he prophesied that the two images would serve to benefit sentient beings in the land of China, one thousand years after he passed into Nirvana.[40]

The thirty-six sovereigns in the dynasty of the first Chinese emperor known as Zhou each reigned for one hundred years. Thereafter, an emperor called Qin Shihuang and his son held the throne for seventy years. Then an emperor called Han Gaozong arose, and his royal descendants held the throne for twelve generations. Then a minister known as Wang Mang usurped the throne and reigned for eighteen years, after which a scion of the previous dynasty, Guang Wudi, being a descendant of Han Gaozong himself, appeared, slew Wang Mang and recaptured the throne. The eldest of Guang Wudi's five sons became the emperor known as Han Mingdi. His son became the emperor Han Xiandi. The throne was seized from Han Xiandi's hands by one of his nephew-ministers by the name of Cao Cao. This minister's descendants then reigned for five generations. The throne was recaptured from them by one of their own ministers by the name of Sima Zhao. The first emperor of the Hou Qin reigned after him. His eldest son, founder of the Dong Qin, took the throne. He was succeeded by his younger brother, founder of the Xi Qin. [In Buton's *History of the Dharma*, this emperor is called Tritim, but the same person is intended.] The Chinese annals also state that the Jowo Shakyamuni and the Sandalwood Jowo arrived in China at that time and the Holy Dharma was propagated. After this, a civilian minister called Cheng Xiang usurped the throne and the lineage was severed. The emperor known as Sui Yangdi and his son succeeded him. Thereafter, the emperors of the Tang dynasty arose.

Further, according to the Chinese annals, the Tang dynasty was founded and contacts with Tibet were established 2566 years after the Lord Buddha passed into Nirvana. It is said that the first Tang emperor was a contemporary of the Tibetan king Namri Songtsen.

The emperor's son Tang Gaozong succeeded him. Gaozong's son Emperor Taizong was a contemporary of the Tibetan king Songtsen Gampo. During Taizong's reign, his daughter Wencheng Gongzhu came to Tibet.[41] Taizong's seven sons each took the throne in turn. When Emperor Zhongzong, a descendant of the eldest son, took the throne, he represented the fifth generation of Tang emperors. He was a contemporary of the Tibetan king Me Agtsom, and his daughter Jincheng Gongzhu also came to Tibet.[42] Zhongzong's son, known as Tang Xuanzong, succeeded him. Thereafter, one of his ministers, known as Huang Chao, rebelled and seized the throne. Five lineages, including the one called Liang, held the throne for fifty years. Then an emperor known as Zhao Taizu arose.[43] He lost the throne to the Minyag.[44] Eight successive generations of his descendants up to Mentse Lhatsun arose at Bianliang.[45]

History of Minyag

As to the history of the fall of the Chinese throne to the Minyag, in former times, the entire kingdom of Minyag was under Chinese rule. On a mountain between Ganzhou and Xiazhou that was known as Monshri, there dwelt a malevolent naga by the name of Sehu. When propitiated, this naga could bestow nothing more than temporary benefits and happiness, yet when aggrieved, he instantly caused leprosy and delirium. Wicked in the extreme, this evil being manifested himself as seven horsemen, and entered the fortress of Ganzhou. There, the leader of the horsemen had intercourse with a woman of the race of flesh-eating demons, and after the usual number of months had elapsed, she gave birth to a son. A portentous star appeared in the heavens where previously none had been seen. The Chinese astrologers undertook a divination and discovered that a usurper of the throne had been born. They reported their finding to the emperor, who commanded them to carry out a thorough search for the infant. In spite of their efforts, they failed to find him. When the child became a man, he gathered together his young friends and dwelt in a forest, from where they rose in rebellion. An old spirit-woman from Ganzhou told them how to proceed: 'On the fifteenth day of this month, draw up an army, and cast many horse-whips and much horse-dung into the Machu River.[46] Do this, and you will hold the seal of the Chinese emperor in your own hands!' Thus she spoke.

On the fourteenth day of the month, the old woman mounted the wall of the fortress, beat her breast and wept. The emperor sent a messenger to inquire into the disturbance, and the old woman declared: 'By the prophesy of Indra, King of the Gods, the king of Minyag will be raised to the throne. If we do not surrender, not a single Chinese will survive. It is said that an army of unimaginable proportions will arrive tomorrow'. When they asked how she knew this, she replied, 'Look into the Machu River tomorrow: the water has been discoloured by whips and dung!' Thus she spoke.

When they went to look into the river early the following morning, it was indeed as the old woman had said, and they were terrified. They asked her how to appease the enemy, and she responded, 'Only surrender will placate him'. The emperor and his servants, seven in all, then set out to surrender the royal seal, but they came upon a multitude of horsemen who were the sons of the naga. The horsemen seized the seal, slew the emperor and dispatched the ministers one by one. Thus the Chinese empire came under the aegis of the Minyag. The naga's son, who was the king of the Minyag, therefore adopted his father's name and became known as King Sehu. In the sixth royal generation descended from him, there arose a king known as Gyelgo. The rule of the Minyag kings, from Sehu until Gyelgo, lasted for 260 years.

History of the Mongols

Bortechino, Son of the Sky, was the first king of the Mongols.[47] His son was Batachiqan. His son was Tamacha. His son was Qorichar-mergen. [It is said that Qorichar-mergen was the emanation of Padmasambhava.] His son was A'ujam-boro'ul. His son was Yeke-nidun. His son was Sem-sochi. His son was Qarchu. His son was Dobun-mergen. Alan-qo'a followed him. His son was Bolapa. His son was Bodonchar-mungqaq. His son was Qabichi. His son was Biker. His son was Menen-tudun. His son was Qaidu-qahan. His son was Bai-shingqor-dogshin. His son was Tumbinai-qahan. His son was Qabul-qahan. His son was Bartan-ba'atur. His son was Yisugei-ba'atur. His son was Chinggis Khan, known as Yuan Taizu. Until this time, Mongolia had been ruled by China and Minyag, and lacked the Teachings.

The Mongol emperor Chinggis Khan, blessed with longevity and the mandate of Heaven, a sovereign endowed with magical powers, arose 3250 years after the Buddha attained Nirvana.[48] Having conquered the whole of China and Minyag, he occupied the throne for twenty-three years and reigned over his realm. Chinggis Khan's younger brother was Emperor Urukai, and his four sons were the emperors Jochi, Chaghatai, Ogedei [who reigned for six years] and Tolui-noyan.

Emperor Jochi had eight sons. Emperor Chaghatai had nine sons. Emperor Ogedei's eldest son was Emperor Guyug [who reigned for half a year]. His younger brothers were Qadan and Qashi-qahan. Emperor Guyug [who reigned for six months] had five sons: Emperor Mongke-qahan [who reigned for nine years], Emperor Qubilai-Sechen-qahan [this is Emperor Sechen],[49] Hulegu [emperor of Upper Hor,[50] whose conquests were great], Sayin-Bugha and Ariq-Boke. Emperor Sechen took the throne 3258 years after the Sage passed into Nirvana and 3500 years after the Sandalwood Jowo was made. The Chinese annals and Lama Chokyi Gyelpo's *Illumination of Knowledge* are in agreement on this. [One of Emperor Sechen's younger daughters had eight sons: Hugechi, Oqruqchi, Qutlug-Temur, Esen-Buqa, Toghan, Kokochu and Dorje. The son of Oqruqchi was Emperor Temur-Buqa.]

Emperor Sechen reigned for thirty-five years and had four sons: Dorje, Jim-Gim, Mangqala and Nomoghan. Emperor Jim-Gim had three sons: Emperor Kamala, Darmabala and Emperor Oljeitu [who reigned for thirteen years]. Emperor Dharmapala and his consort Dahong Taihou had two sons: Emperor Kulug [who reigned for four years] and Emperor Ayur-Paribhadra Buyantu [who reigned for nine years]. Emperor Ayur-Paribhadra Buyantu had two sons: Emperor Gegen and Emperor Siddhipala. Emperor Gegen's son was Emperor Kamala. His son was Emperor Yesun-Temur Qinwang [who reigned for five years]. His son was Emperor Arjiba [who reigned for forty years]. Emperor Kulug had three sons:

Emperor Kushala [who reigned for one month], Emperor Kulug and Emperor Tog-Temur-Jagagatu. Kushala's son was Emperor Ratnashri [who reigned for eleven years]. His brother Emperor Toghan-Temur reigned for forty-eight years and ruled over the kingdom. [The throne was seized from him by the Chinese Tai Ming Emperor, it is said.[51]]

An expert in the records and annals of the Chinese and the Mongols, Sherab Yeshe, the Master of Instruction at Tsentse, translated these materials at Gungtang. The master of both worldly and spiritual affairs who excels in all qualities of his race and heredity, the Omniscient Tselpa, Situ Gewai Lodro, compiled these records into a single volume.[52] As the above account is merely a summary of his work, those who desire a deeper understanding of the records of the Chinese and the Mongols should consult the original text.

This chapter,
concerning the spread
of the Holy Dharma in the lands of
the Chinese and the Mongols
and the enumeration
of their kings,
is the third.

4

The birth of the sublime Avalokiteshvara from a lotus, and the qualities of the Six-Syllable Mantra

The birth of Avalokiteshvara

Now to the spread of the Buddha's teachings in Tibet, the Land of Snows. In former times, when the Lord Buddha dwelled in Veluvana, the Bamboo Grove, surrounded by his retinue of arhats who were seated about him, from the whorl of hair between his eyebrows shone forth a multicoloured rainbowlike ray of light. The ray extended to the snowy kingdom of Tibet in the north, the Buddha looked in the direction it had taken and smiled, whereupon the bodhisattva Sarvanivaranivishkambini inquired, 'What is the meaning of this?' [according to the *White Lotus Sutra*]. The Lord Buddha then replied:

> Son of your race! In this place where no being has been a candidate for conversion by the Buddhas of the Three Times, a

barbaric snowy realm filled with multitudes of demons and ogres, at some future time the Holy Dharma will spread and flourish like the rising sun, and sentient beings will be led to the enlightenment path of liberation. The spiritual guide who will tame this barbaric land shall be the sublime Lord Avalokiteshvara. Should you wish to know the reason for this, in former times, when Avalokiteshvara performed the deeds of a bodhisattva, having first prayed before the Thousand Buddhas, he made the following supplication: 'May I lead to the enlightenment road of liberation all sentient beings in the barbaric Land of Snows, a place untrodden by the Buddhas of the Three Times, by the power of the subduing precepts. May this wilderness be my field of subjugation. May I become like a mother and father to the demons, ogres and every other creature that dwells there. May I become a liberating helmsman for them all. May I become the lamp that dispels the darkness. May I cause the Teachings to endure, while spreading and expanding in that barbaric land the entire Dharma taught by the Buddhas of the Three Times and the other Tathagatas. Once these beings have taken refuge, having heard the names of the Three Excellent Jewels and thereby achieved a higher rebirth, may they enjoy the sacred Dharma.[53] While bringing about the maturation of each being by appropriate means, having liberated them, may I cause this wilderness to become a precious continent. May this all come to pass!' Based on the power of this prayer, as none of the Buddhas of the Three Times had subdued Tibet, Avalokiteshvara made it his own field of subjugation. Such is the explanation.

Thus spoke the Buddha. A ray of light, white like the flower of the lotus, then shone forth from his breast and illuminated all the world. When it reached Sukhavati, the Western Paradise, it was absorbed into the breast of Amitabha, the Buddha of Boundless Light. A second ray of light then shone forth from Amitabha's breast and vanished into the Lake of Lotuses, thus foretelling the appearance of a buddha-manifestation who would subdue the barbaric Land of Snows. In that realm of Sukhavati,

> As there is the chequered design upon the precious golden ground,
> Even the names of the elements 'earth' and 'stone' do not exist.

As the clear flame of wisdom is blazing,
Even the name of the element 'fire' does not exist.
As the river with eight qualities flows,
Even the name of the element 'water' does not exist.
Beautified by enlightenment-trees,
Even the words 'tree', 'shrub' and 'forest' do not exist.
Sustained by the nourishment of deep meditation,
Even the words 'hunger' and 'thirst' do not exist.
Clad in pure morality,
Even the word 'clothing' does not exist.
As beings are endowed with their own radiance,
Even the words 'sun' and 'moon' do not exist.
As all possess the power of forbearance,
Even the words 'struggle' and 'strife' do not exist.
Other than the greatest happiness,
Even the word for 'suffering' does not exist.
Other than Nirvana,
Even the word 'Samsara' does not exist.
Other than the three forms of the Buddha,
Even the word 'sentient being' does not exist.
Other than immortality,
Even the words 'aging' and 'death' do not exist.
Free from reincarnation in a body composed of the four
    elements,
Even the word 'sickness' does not exist.
Born miraculously from a lotus,
Even the names of the four kinds of birth do not exist.[54]

The Dharma-king known as Bhadraparam who dwelled in that realm of Sukhavati dispatched his attendants to the shores of the Lake of Lotuses to gather flowers as an offering for the Buddha. On arrival, they beheld upon the water a great lotus with stalks as thick as yokes and leaves as large as shields. Manifold rays of light shone forth from the ovary of the lotus, which was like a great pitcher set amid its thousand petals. Having witnessed this, they informed the king, who was greatly astonished.

A mighty vessel was built, and the king and his retinue, bearing diverse offerings, came before the lotus. They made offerings and said prayers, whereupon the ovary split in four and from within it appeared Avalokiteshvara, the spiritual guide who subdues the barbaric Land of Snows, the manifestation of miraculous birth. His legs were crossed in the lotus position, and he had a single countenance and four arms. His upper hands were folded in prayer at his breast, his lower right hand clasped a rosary of clear crystal, and his lower left hand held a white lotus that opened near his ear. This being was beautified with the major and minor signs of greatness, adorned with many precious ornaments and clad in raiments of fine silk of every kind. The hue of his body resembled sunshine upon a mass of snowy mountains. The *enaya*-deerskin upon his left shoulder covered his breast. Resplendent with his locks in five spiral coifs, his head was adorned with jewels. A smile graced his pleasing countenance, and rays of light radiated from his body in all directions.

King Bhadraparam and his retinue rejoiced in great exultation and conducted the deity to the royal palace to the accompaniment of music of every kind. The king then addressed the following words to Buddha Amitabha:

> From the ovary of a flower upon the Lake of Lotuses,
> Came a spiral-coiffed manifestation of miraculous birth
> Whose body possesses the hue of a snowy mountain.
> Adorned with precious ornaments,
> The sight of his beautiful and pleasing form captivates the
>   mind.
> Is this miraculous manifestation,
> Resplendent with the major and minor signs of greatness,
> A royal prince, a scion of our lineage?
> Or is he a manifestation who will strive for the sake of
>   sentient beings?

Such was the king's inquiry. Buddha Amitabha replied:

> On the lake with eight qualities where lotuses grow,
> Born from a flower, this princely manifestation
> Is the Great Compassionate One, the sublime
>   Avalokiteshvara,
> Whose hue is that of the white waterlily,
> And who is beautified with precious ornaments.
> It is beneath this most excellent of forms,

Endowed with the miraculous signs of greatness,
To be a scion of your royal lineage.
This manifestation is the Great Compassionate One
Who will strive for the sake of sentient beings
By means appropriate to individual needs
In that barbaric Land of Snows.

Thus he spoke. At that moment, the earth shook in six different ways and the gods caused flowers to fall like rain.

The Six-Syllable Mantra

Amitabha then placed his hand upon the head of Avalokiteshvara and said:

Son of your race! The sentient beings who dwell in the barbaric Land of Snows have not been subdued by any of the past buddhas, nor will they be tamed by any of the future buddhas. As it is difficult for the present buddhas to subdue them, based on the power of prayers that you made in former times, it is best that you become their subjugator. This is best!

Having beheld your sublime body and heard the sound of the Six-Syllable Mantra, may the sentient beings who dwell in the Land of Snows be saved instantly from rebirth in the three lower realms and acquire a higher rebirth. May the sight of your sublime body and the sound of the Six-Syllable Mantra completely pacify the mischievous thoughts entertained by all demons, ogres, evil fiends, flesh-eating *pishachi*-spirits and other creatures who steal the radiance of life, as well as those that cause death. May these beings be endowed with benefits, happiness, compassion and enlightenment-thought. May the sight of your sublime body and the sound of the Six-Syllable Mantra completely pacify the wicked thoughts of tigers, leopards, tawny bears, red bears and other cunning wild animals that possess ruthless minds, those whose fierce roars alone instil fear, and those who kill their prey, feast upon flesh and drink blood. May they abide in loving-kindness by regarding one another as their own father and mother.

May the mere sight of your sublime body and the sound of the Six-Syllable Mantra cause the nectar of nourishment to fall like rain upon all sentient beings in the Land of Snows whose bodies are tormented by hunger and thirst or who are wracked with suffering, thereby satisfying all their hearts' desires and assuaging completely their anguish.

Having merely beheld your sublime body and heard the sound of the Six-Syllable Mantra, may those sentient beings in the Land of Snows who are wicked, blind, diseased, disabled, and those who are unprotected, having lost their refuge, be free forever from all disease. May they be endowed with perfect faculties and extraordinary powers.

When sentient beings in the Land of Snows behold your sublime body, may their lives be prolonged. Having become a great physic for their afflictions, may you save them from all illness. May you become the protector of those that have none. May you become the refuge of those that have none. In the barbaric Land of Snows, the tutelary deity that they deserve is the Great Compassionate One. With you, their tutelary deity, as the foundation, innumerable buddhas and bodhisattvas will appear in this wild land at some future time, and the teachings of the Buddha will spread and flourish. As to the Dharma that they deserve, it is the Six-Syllable Mantra. With this essence as the foundation, the entire Dharma taught by the Buddha will spread and flourish, and beings will enjoy the sacred teachings.

OM MANI PADME HUM! These six syllables are the quintessence of all the buddhas' thoughts; the sole essence of the eighty-four thousand heaps of Dharma collected together; the essential *dharani*-mantra distilled from each of the seed-syllables of the five buddha-families and wrathful Guhyapati deities; the source of all virtue, goodness and qualities; the root of all miraculous accomplishment of benefits and happiness; and the great path to paradise and salvation.

OM MANI PADME HUM! With one glimpse of these six syllables, which are the essence of all Dharma and the most excellent speech, one may achieve the Irreversible Stage and become a captain in the salvation of beings.[55] By hearing these words, one may achieve a higher rebirth and become a leader in the liberation of sentient beings. If an animal, even an ant or worm, hears this mantra beside its ear at the time of death, once it is liberated from its body, it will be reborn in Sukhavati, the Western Paradise. Thinking of the mantra, like the sun shining upon a snowy mountain, the misdeeds and obscurations of their adverse karma accumulated since beginningless time will be purified in entirety, and they will be reborn in Sukhavati. By touching the Six-Syllable Mantra, the empowerment of innumerable buddhas and bodhisattvas is achieved.

A single meditation upon the mantra is equivalent to hearing, contemplating and meditating. All phenomena will appear in the Dharmakaya, and the mine of altruistic activity will be cast open. If one wears the mantra upon one's person, one's human form will be transformed into a relic of the Buddha. The four hundred and four diseases will not harm one, nor will fire, water, poison, weapons or the upper and lower classes of demons. When these six syllables are inscribed upon a precious material, or upon cloth, paper, bark or even soil or rock, the eighty-four thousand heaps of Dharma are invested in that inscription. Having enjoyed happiness in this life, have no doubt that the result of Buddhahood may be achieved in a single lifetime and in a single body!

One might weigh Sumeru, the King of Mountains, upon a set of scales. One might wear away a diamond by rubbing it once every hundred years with a cloth of the softest *kashika*-linen. One might discover the number of drops of water in a vast ocean. One might count each atom, shrub or tree in the Land of Snows. One might accomplish all of these, yet no one can calculate the amount of merit earned from a single recitation of the Six-Syllable Mantra. One might remove, load by load, all the sesame seeds that fill a building one hundred miles long. One might haul, load by load, all the water that would accumulate if it rained day and night without interruption for twelve months. One might accomplish all of these, yet no one can calculate the amount of merit in a single recitation of the Six-Syllable Mantra.

As it is thus, Son of your race, and as there is no need to describe these qualities at length, one might estimate the amount of merit in the veneration paid to the ten million Tathagatas like me, yet no one can calculate the merit in a single recitation of the Six-Syllable Mantra.

OM MANI PADME HUM! The syllable *Om* alleviates the sufferings of birth and death among the gods. *Ma* assuages the pain of warfare and conflict among the demigods. *Ni* eases the miseries of birth, aging, disease and death in the realm of humans. *Pad* dispels the suffering of servitude experienced by animals. *Me* frees hungry ghosts from the torments of hunger and thirst. *Hum* eases the agonies of heat and cold among the denizens of the hellish realms.

Praised by all the buddhas,
The concentrated essence of all Dharma
Appears as the glory of all beings.
The empowerment of the Six Syllables is now bestowed.
I invest the essential initiation of all the buddhas
In you this day.
Having assembled together, all the buddhas
Bestow the initiation of the King of Knowledge Mantras.

Om is the perfection of generosity.
O Lord Buddha, who is without avarice,
The Dharmakaya of the embodiment of all assembled
    buddhas,
Grant the blessing of empowerment.

Ma is the perfection of patience.
O Lord Buddha, who is without anger,
The Sambhogakaya of great bliss,
Grant the blessing of empowerment.

Ni is the perfection of moral conduct.
O Lord Buddha, who is free from the faults of emotional
    afflictions,
The Nirmanakaya of three spontaneously accomplished
    forms,
Grant the blessing of empowerment.

Pad is the perfection of meditation.
O Lord Buddha, who is free from distraction,
The omniscient body of Sarvajnanakaya,
Grant the blessing of empowerment.

Me is the perfection of diligence.
O Lord Buddha, who is free from sloth,
Whose omniscient and compassionate teachings envelop all
    beings,
Grant the blessing of empowerment.

Hum is the perfection of wisdom.
O Lord Buddha, who is the embodiment of all activity,

Whose mind is the quintessence of extraordinary
    capabilities,
Grant the blessing of empowerment.

The words of the Six-Syllable Mantra are the sound of the
    dorje[56]
Blessed by all the buddhas,
The peerless essence of the Dharma.
Grant the blessing of empowerment.

By bestowing this empowerment, impurities are cleansed and
the overflowing water becomes Amitabha, who adorns your
head.

Om is endowed with the five classes of wisdom.[57]
Ma envelops everything in compassion.
Ni serves as guide to the six classes of beings.
Pad alleviates all suffering.
Me burns up all sins and obscuration.
Hum assembles all qualities.

By the blessing of the Six-Syllable Mantra,
May sentient beings in the Land of Snows
Be led to the path of liberation.
This essence of all essences,
Blessed by all the Victorious Ones,
Is the source of all benefits and happiness,
The root of all miraculous accomplishment,
The stairway to heaven,
The gate that seals the path to the three lower realms,
The ferry-boat through Samsara,
The lamp that dispels the darkness,
The hero that vanquishes the five poisons,[58]
The blaze that consumes misdeeds and obscurations,
The hammer that strikes at suffering,
The spiritual guide that subdues barbarity,
The Dharma that the Land of Snows deserves.

The essence of all essences
Of study, contemplation and meditation
Upon the Sutras, Tantras and oral treatises collected together
Is this all-satisfying precious king.
Recite the Six-Syllable Mantra!

By the blessings of this essential *dharani*-mantra
Sentient beings in the wilderness of the Land of Snows
Are led to the path of maturation and liberation,
And the sacred Dharma will spread and flourish.

Thus prophesied Buddha Amitabha.

This chapter,
concerning the birth of
the Sublime One from a lotus
and the qualities of the
Six-Syllable Mantra,
is the fourth.

The sublime bodhisattva of compassion and protector of Tibet, Avalokiteshvara

5

The sublime
Avalokiteshvara leads
sentient beings in the Land of Snows
to maturation and
liberation

The sublime Avalokiteshvara turned his thoughts to benefiting sentient beings in the Land of Snows and generated the enlightenment thought before the Buddha Amitabha. He knelt upon his right knee, folded his palms and prayed:

> May I lead to happiness all six classes of beings in the Three Spheres.[59] In particular, may I lead to the path of happiness all beings in Tibet, the Land of Snows, who are difficult to subdue. Until I have brought them to the path of liberation and enlightenment, though I be fatigued and weary, may I contemplate neither rest nor happiness for a single moment. Should such thoughts arise, may my head crack into ten like a cotton boll, and may my body split into a thousand like the petals of a lotus!

Having made this oath, Avalokiteshvara descended into the hell realms, where he expounded upon the Dharma of the Six-Syllable Mantra, led the denizens of the hell realms to benefits and happiness and assuaged the infernal suffering caused by heat and cold. He then proceeded to the realm of the hungry ghosts, where again he taught the Dharma of the Six-Syllable Mantra, led the hungry ghosts to benefits and happiness, and dispelled the suffering caused by hunger and thirst. Then he came to the animal realm, where he taught the Dharma of the Six-Syllable Mantra, led all animals to benefits and happiness and dispelled the suffering of servitude. Next he proceeded to the human realm, where he taught the Dharma of the Six-Syllable Mantra, led human beings to benefits and happiness and dispelled the suffering caused by birth, aging, sickness and death. Then he went to the realm of the demigods, where he expounded upon the Dharma of the Six-Syllable Mantra, led the inhabitants of that realm to benefits and happiness, and eased the suffering brought about by warfare. Next, he proceeded to the realm of the gods, where he expounded upon the Dharma of the Six-Syllable Mantra, led the gods to benefits and happiness and eased the suffering caused by death and fall from privilege.

Avalokiteshvara then came to the untamed Land of Snows, where he perceived that the upper region of Ngari Korsum resembled a pool, and was a land abounding in deer. There he taught the Dharma of the Six-Syllable Mantra and led all beings to benefits and happiness. He perceived that the lower region of Amdo, Kham and the Three Ranges resembled fields and were lands abounding in many birds. Here, again, Avalokiteshvara taught the Dharma of the Six-Syllable Mantra and led all beings to benefits and happiness. Between these two regions lay the four districts that comprise U and Tsang. These resembled an irrigation canal and were lands abounding in wild beasts. Here, too, he taught the Dharma of the Six-Syllable Mantra and led all beings to benefits and happiness.

Then at last Avalokiteshvara arrived at the summit of Marpori, the 'Red Hill', in Lhasa. Gazing out, he perceived that the lake on Otang, the 'Plain of Milk', resembled the Hell of Ceaseless Torment. Myriads of beings were undergoing the agonies of boiling, burning, hunger and thirst, yet they never perished, but let forth hideous cries of anguish all the while. When Avalokiteshvara saw this, tears sprang to his eyes. A teardrop from his right eye fell to the plain and became the reverend Bhrikuti, who declared: 'Son of your race! As you are striving for the sake of the sentient beings in the Land of Snows, intercede in their suffering, and I shall be your companion in this endeavour!' Bhrikuti was then reabsorbed into Avalokiteshvara's right eye, and was reborn in a later life as the Nepalese princess Tritsun.[60] A teardrop from his left eye fell upon the plain and became the reverend Tara. She also declared, 'Son of your race! As you are striving for the sake of the sentient beings in the Land of Snows, intercede in their suffering, and I shall also be your companion in this endeavour!' Tara was also reabsorbed into Avalokiteshvara's left eye, and was reborn in a later life as the Chinese princess Kongjo.[61]

The Sublime One then proceeded to the shores of the lake, where he expounded upon the Dharma of the Six-Syllable Mantra, and by his boundless compassion, uttered these truthful words:

> May I lead to the continent of emancipation and liberation
> Those who are tormented by all kinds of unbearable
>   suffering
> In this great, bottomless hell,
> On account of the adverse karma that they have accumu-
>   lated since beginningless time.
> May the rain of benefits and happiness perpetually cool
> Those who have no refuge and cry out in anguish
> While boiling in this seething lake of poison,
> Licked eternally by the fires of hell.
> May the myriad denizens of this lake,
> Tormented by heat, cold, hunger and thirst,
> Having forsaken their present bodies,
> Be reborn among beautiful races which possess the Dharma
> In my own realm. OM MANI PADME HUM!

Once Avalokiteshvara had spoken thus, the denizens of the hells were freed from the sufferings of heat and cold. They were endowed with healthy bodies, their minds were released from torment and they were led to the enlightenment path of liberation.

Avalokiteshvara led to happiness by various means the six classes of beings in the Three Realms, including the inhabitants of the Land of Snows, who are difficult to subdue, and his mind was greatly fatigued. He therefore reposed in profound meditation of restfulness and equipoise. When he gazed down again from the summit of Mt. Potala, however, he beheld that not even one hundredth of the sentient beings in the Land of Snows had been led to happiness, and he fell into deepest despair. At the very instant at which a yearning for rest and happiness arose, by the power of the prayer that he had previously made, his head split into ten and his body ruptured into a thousand fragments. He then prayed to Buddha Amitabha, who appeared in a trice, bound the fragments of Avalokiteshvara's shattered head and body into a bundle with his own hands and spoke these words:

> All Dharmas arise on the basis of causes and conditions,
> And rest firmly on the root of motivation.
> Whatever prayer is made will be granted.
> By the efficacy of the power of the prayers that you have
>   offered,
> They are highly praised by all the buddhas.
> By the truth of this,
> Your prayers will be answered in an instant.

> Son of your race, intercede in suffering! As your head has split into ten, you shall be blessed with ten visages, corresponding to the Ten Perfections. Accompanied by Amitabha above them, you will be blessed with eleven visages in all.

> Amitabha will dwell among the eleven countenances.
> Homage and praise to the reverend Avalokiteshvara,
> Who fulfils the activities of peace, increase, power and force!

> As your body split into one thousand pieces like the petals of a lotus, you will be blessed with one thousand arms. Each arm will be a sovereign that turns the Wheel of Dharma, and their thousand palms will be blessed with a thousand eyes.

> The thousand eyes are the Thousand Buddhas of the glorious aeon.
> Homage to the Sage who subdues by means appropriate to
>   each candidate,

The reverend Avalokiteshvara!
Exquisitely eulogised by the Thousand Buddhas,
It is prophesied that you, the Victorious One, will tame
    barbarity.
Homage to the reverend Avalokiteshvara,
Who subdues each candidate by appropriate means and
    strives to benefit beings!

Thus spoke the Buddha Amitabha. Avalokiteshvara manifested himself in many forms for the sake of subduing the denizens of the Land of Snows, and thereby led all beings to spiritual maturity and liberation.

This chapter,
in which the Sublime One
leads sentient beings in the Land of Snows
to maturation and liberation,
is the fifth.

6

Avalokiteshvara manifests himself as the King of Horses and strives to benefit sentient beings

The sublime Lord Avalokiteshvara strives to benefit sentient beings in many ways. In order to provide examples of adherence to virtue and rejection of misdeeds, in this episode from the *Zamatog Sutra* Avalokiteshvara manifests himself as Changshe Balaha, the King of Horses, and proclaims his intention to toil for the sake of beings.

Now, a company of merchants from the south of India, whose fortunes had declined, set sail in a great vessel upon the Outer Ocean to search for riches, each with his own copious provisions for the voyage. After seven days, however, an adverse wind rent their craft asunder:

> At noon, black clouds descended like fog
> And blotted out the sunlight, cloaking all in darkness.
> A terrifying tempest shook the earth
> And cast down all the trees and forests.

Upon the ocean, waves sprang like lions.
Pounded by the surge, heaven and earth seemed to crash
    together.
The merchants clung to one another,
Each calling aloud the names of his dear ones and weeping.
Seized by panic, they cried for salvation.
Helpless and exhausted, they shed bitter tears.
At that moment, their ship was wrecked!

The merchants clung fast to the timbers of their shattered vessel, and driven together by a great wind, they were cast upon the shores of an island known as Singhala,[62] which was the abode of ogresses. Calling one another by name, the merchants eventually reached dry land. The ogresses sensed their arrival, and having manifested themselves as young women of great beauty, came before the merchants, bearing copious food and drink. They consoled the castaways, saying 'You must be exhausted!' 'How terrifying for you!' and so forth. Not realising that they were ogresses, the delighted merchants beheld only beautiful women, and conversed gaily with them. Then the ogresses said as one, 'O merchants! Do not venture to the head of the valley!' and each woman then led one of the men to her own house to be her husband. They begat children and indulged in many pleasures, but a voice was heard to say:

Tormented by adverse karma,
Merchants borne by contrary winds,
Fell into the hands of the Lord of Death,
Like deer caught in a net.
Now these deluded beings have no escape.
Having lost their senses, they cling to ogresses as their wives
And are deceived by their goddess-like appearance.
Sated upon the food of deceitful seduction,
The merchants have forgotten, like a dream, their former
    sufferings,
And their carefree thoughts have caused them to become
    complacent.

The great captain of the merchants, realising that Singhala was an island of ogresses, was filled with suffering and despair: 'How can this happiness that we now enjoy come to an end?' With these

thoughts, he fell into deepest despondency. He then asked himself, 'Why are we forbidden from entering the head of the valley?'
and one night, after his mistress had fallen asleep, he stole away to
investigate. In the forbidden valley, he heard murmurs issuing from
a doorless iron building. 'Who is this?' he thought, and listening
closely, he discerned that the voices were those of another party of
Indian merchants. The captain scaled a tree that grew in front of
the prison and called out, 'Who is within?'

'We are merchants who lost our way', the inmates replied.

'How long have you been held here?'

'Like you, our ship was blown here by adverse winds. The
women took us in, but not realising that they were ogresses, we
became their husbands, begat children and indulged in many pleasures. When you arrived on this island, we were cast into this
doorless prison of iron. Now they are devouring us one by one.
Consider our suffering and our fear of death and flee this instant!
Now is the time to make your escape. Once you are locked inside
this iron prison you will have no refuge. There is no way out!'
Thus they replied. 'But, in truth, we cannot escape!' said the captain. The prisoners went on: 'There is a way. We also considered
escaping, but were held back by our ties to sensual pleasures. Renounce your attachment to all things and flee! This is how: to the
north of yonder low pass, amid the golden sands, there lies a turquoise spring surrounded by tender grass like lapis lazuli. On the
night of the full moon, Balaha, King of Horses, who is able to carry
on his back one hundred men, will descend from the sky upon a
moonbeam. He will drink at the turquoise spring, graze upon the
lapis lazuli grass and roll three times in the golden sands. Having
shaken himself, he will declare in the language of humans, "All
Indian merchants stranded on the island of ogresses, ride upon
my back, and I shall deliver you to your own land!" Such will be
the words of this manifestation, the most excellent of horses, who
will come to that place. Having mounted the horse, renounce attachment to sensual pleasure, and your families here, close your
eyes, and you will reach safety.'

'We must do as they say', thought the captain as he returned
to his house. When he came to the bed where his ogre-wife lay

sleeping, she sensed his plot and said, 'The merchant whose thoughts are evil will cause his own downfall. If you allow your mind to wander, it will be your undoing! Where have you been? You feel cold!'

'I merely went outdoors to relieve myself', lied the captain. He then assembled the other merchants in secret, and after he had described in detail all that had taken place, they agreed that they should flee. On the night of the full moon, they gave a narcotic to their ogre-wives which caused them to fall into a deep sleep. The captain led his band across the low pass to the northern regions, where, amid the golden sands, they found the turquoise spring surrounded by the lapis lazuli meadow, by which they awaited the arrival of Balaha, the King of Horses.

Indeed, before long, Balaha descended from the sky upon a rainbow-moonbeam. He drank from the turquoise spring, grazed upon the lapis lazuli meadow and rolled three times upon the golden sands. Having shaken himself, he declared in the language of humans: 'All merchants who are trapped on this island of ogresses, ride upon my back! Renounce all attachment to the ogre-women, their offspring and the pleasures you enjoy here, close your eyes, and I shall deliver you to your own land!' The captain replied:

> O, manifestation who is the most excellent of horses
> And liberator of beings!
> We merchants journeyed together
> To islands in the Great Ocean to search for riches.
> As our luck ran out, the vessel was wrecked at sea,
> And unfavourable winds drove us to this island of ogresses.
> We are trapped in the ogre-land of Yamas of adverse
>   karma.[63]
> As we have no other means of escape,
> Most excellent of horses, O Compassionate One, grant us
>   refuge!

The captain then mounted the horse's neck and grasped its ears, while his fellow-merchants rode upon its back. 'Renounce all attachment to the ogresses' homes, your children and the pleasures that you enjoyed here. Close your eyes until we reach the other side of the ocean!' With these words, the most excellent of horses bore the merchants into the sky. The ogresses, however, sensed their departure, led forth their children and cried:

> Would you abandon a lofty fortress?
> Would you abandon your dearly beloved spouse?
> Would you abandon children who are your own flesh and
>   blood?
> Would you renounce delicious food and drink?
> What evil and shameless men!

So saying, some of the ogre-women raised their infants into the air, while others angrily brandished items of clothing.[64] When the company of merchants heard this, it was as if arrows had pierced their hearts, and believing that the ogresses had spoken the truth, with the exception of the captain, they all looked back. A sense of attachment arose in them, and when they turned around, they slipped off the horse's back and fell to the ground, where they were seized by the ogresses, who had shed their former beautiful countenances and now appeared in their original forms: their heads bristling with hair, and their breasts flung over their shoulders. The ogresses bared their fangs and devoured the entire company without a moment's delay.

When Balaha reached the other side of the ocean, he told the captain to open his eyes and dismount. The captain looked around and saw that none of the merchants remained upon the horse's back. Smitten by deepest anguish, he asked through his tears, 'Oh! King of Horses, what has become of my companions?' The most excellent of horses pawed the ground with his hoof. He, too, shed a tear and replied:

> Your merchant-companions, whose good fortune had
>   expired,
> Forgot their own homelands in the continent of
>   Jambudvipa,[65]
> And were undone by their attachment to the island of
>   ogresses, whose karma was unfavourable.
> Forgetting their fathers, mothers and bosom-friends,
> They were undone by their attachment to the ogresses'
>   youthful faces.
> Forgetting their relatives and their own sons who could be of
>   service to them,

They were undone by their attachment to the seductive
    ogresses' children.
Alack and alas! How pitiful are sentient beings!

If a disciple murders his Vajra-master[66]
And is condemned to the Hell of Unceasing Torment,
Even though the lama's compassion is great, what can be
    done?
If children whose views have become perverse
Are carried away by the adverse winds of misfortune,
Even if their parents love them dearly, what can be done?
Ignoring good advice and helpful words,
Your fellow-merchants fell to earth when they looked back.
Although the most excellent of horses has great skill in flight,
    what could be done?
Weep not, merchant captain, but attend to me again:
Well-being and suffering in this life are but a dream, an
    illusion,
Like a waterfall on a precipitous mountainside, or lightning
    or clouds in the sky.
Do not form attachment to happiness in Samsara!

Thus Balaha expounded upon the Dharma of the Four Truths.
By the time the captain had dried his tears, he was within sight of
his own home, and the horse then vanished like a rainbow in the
sky. When the captain reached his door, his parents and all his relatives gathered about, embraced him and wept for joy. Then other
merchants' parents and relatives came forward, saying 'Where is
my father?' 'Where is my uncle?' and 'Where is my nephew?' Each
one cried out a name and wept. The captain gathered them together and described the sea voyage, the loss of the vessel in the
terrible storm, and how they were driven by adverse winds to the
island of ogresses. He told of their union with the ogresses in ignorance of their true nature, and the subsequent birth of their children. He described how, once they had recognised the ogresses,
they sought a means of escape, how the inmates of the iron prison
had advised them, and how the other merchants, ignoring the
words of the King of Horses, fell when they looked back. As a result of the captain's detailed description of these events, his audience, saddened by the sorrowful state of Samsara, came to have

faith in the causes and effects of karma, and were thereby led to the sacred Dharma.

Just as this example shows, those who commit misdeeds and exhibit attachment to things in this life, like the merchants who fell from the horse when they looked back, will wander in Samsara, having no opportunity to escape from the three lower realms. Those, like the captain, who renounce attachment and practice the sacred Dharma, having won the happiness of rebirth in the higher realms, will achieve enlightenment.

This chapter,
in which Avalokiteshvara
manifests himself as the King of Horses
and strives to benefit
sentient beings,
is the sixth.

7

The descent of the Tibetan race from a monkey and a rock-ogress

The sublime Avalokiteshvara, having conferred layperson's vows upon a magical monkey, dispatched him to meditate in the snowy realm of Tibet. There, beside a black rock, while he was devotedly contemplating loving-kindness, compassion, enlightenment-thought and the profound Dharma of emptiness, a rock-ogress, suffering on account of her karma, approached him, and before she departed, made manifold indications of her carnal desire for him. Later, disguised as a woman, the ogress said to the monkey, 'Let us be married!' But the monkey replied, 'As I am a disciple of the sublime Avalokiteshvara, it would contravene my vows to become your husband'. 'If you reject me, I will kill myself!' exclaimed the rock-ogress as she threw herself at the monkey's feet. On rising, she addressed these words to him:

Alas! Great Monkey King!
Think of me a little and hear my plea.
By the power of my karma, I was born among the race of
    ogres.
As my lust grows, I have become enamoured of you.
Driven by my desire, I have come to make this request.
If you will not marry me
I will take a rock-ogre husband.
Every day we will slay ten thousand living beings,
And every night we will devour a thousand creatures.
I will bear countless ogre-children
And this snowy realm will be filled with ogre-cities.
Every living creature will become an ogre's prey.
By comparison, is it not better to think of me
And show your compassion?

As these plaintive words caused her tears to flow, the
Bodhisattva-monkey thought to himself, 'It would contravene
my vows to marry this ogress, but if I do not, it will prove to be
an even greater misdeed!' With these thoughts, he appeared in
an instant before the Sublime One on Mt. Potala and made this
supplication:

Alas! Compassionate Protector of Beings:
I have protected my vows as I would my life.
An ogress from the race of devils, smitten by lust,
Poured forth her varied laments,
And while encircling me, came to rob me of my vows.
What can I do to protect them?
Oh! Compassionate Protector of Loving-Kindness, consider
    my plea.

After the monkey had spoken, Avalokiteshvara responded,
'Marry the rock-ogress!' and voices of the reverend Bhrikuti and
the reverend Tara resounded from the sky: 'Excellent indeed!' The
Sublime One then blessed the marriage of the monkey and the rock-
ogress in order that this snowy land of Tibet might possess three
qualities: that at some future time, the teachings of the Buddha
might spread, flourish and endure; that spiritual friends might arise

in unbroken succession; and that precious treasures might be discovered, so that benefits, happiness, virtue and goodness might
increase in all ten directions.

The monkey and the rock-ogress, being united as husband and
wife, bore six monkey-children of differing dispositions, one reborn from each of the six classes of beings.[67] The monkey-child
reborn from among the denizens of the hell realms had a stern
countenance and could withstand great hardships. The child from
the realm of the hungry ghosts had loathsome features and an in-
satiable appetite. The one reborn from the animal realm was stu-
pid and vulgar. The monkey-child from the human realm was endowed with increasing wisdom and sensitivity. The one from the
realm of the demigods was aggressive and jealous, and the monkey-child from the realm of the gods was patient and virtuous.

The Bodhisattva-monkey led his six children to the Forest of
Assembled Birds, which abounded in fruit, and they dwelled there
for three years. At the end of that time, the monkey-king returned
and saw that by virtue of his karma, his children had increased to
five hundred in number. As they had devoured all the fruit and
had nothing else to eat, and although neither mother nor father
could succour them, they cried, 'Father, what can we eat? Mother,
what can we eat?' The monkey-children threw up their hands, pit-
eous and impoverished. The Bodhisattva-monkey then thought to
himself, 'This cannot be the result of my own defilements. These
monkey-children have become so numerous because I followed
the instructions of the Sublime One'. Thinking this, he appeared in
a trice upon Mt. Potala and supplicated Avalokiteshvara with these
words:

> Alas! Not realising that married life was a prison,
> Not knowing that I had been deceived by a she-devil,
> I am mired in the Samsaric mud of offspring.
> Not recognising that sensual desires are poisonous leaves,
> My compassion turned to lust, and I was deceived.
> Bound by carnal urges, I am oppressed by a mountain of
>   suffering.
> Having swallowed the poison of defilements,

I am afflicted by the epidemic of adverse karma.
Accumulated woes torment me:
Alack! Alas! Compassionate Protector of Loving-Kindness,
How can I succour my children?
I am in this predicament at the Sublime One's behest.
We now resemble a city of hungry ghosts;
In the next life we will no doubt be reborn in the hell realms!
I therefore beseech you to protect us with your compassion.

As the monkey besought him thus, the Sublime One replied, 'I shall protect your progeny'. Avalokiteshvara then arose and took from a crevice on Mt. Sumeru barley, wheat, peas, buckwheat and rice, and cast them upon the earth. The place where they fell then became filled with crops that required no cultivation. The Bodhisattva-monkey led his monkey-children thither and showed them the food. Tradition holds that the monkey then said '*Zotang* – Eat!' and the place became known as Zotang Gongpori.[68] Once they had sated themselves upon these crops, the monkey-childrens' hair and tails grew shorter, they learned to speak and they became human. They ate the crops that required no cultivation and began to wear garments fashioned from leaves.

Thus the inhabitants of this snowy land of Tibet, being the descendants of a monkey-father and rock-ogress mother, form two lineages. As to the monkey-father's lineage, they are those who are patient, faithful, compassionate, diligent, those who delight in virtue and those who are eloquent. These are of the father's lineage. As to the rock-ogress mother's lineage, they are those who are lusty, angry, mercenary, profit-seeking, greedy, competitive, garrulous, strong, courageous, active, restless, scatterbrained, daring, those whose minds suffer from an excess of the five poisons,[69] those who enjoy hearing about the faults of others and those who are tempestuous. These are of the mother's lineage.

At that time, the mountains of Tibet were clad in forests, and every valley was filled with water. Having dug ditches and channels, all the water was drained away, the plains became fields and many cities were built. It is said that shortly thereafter, Nyatri Tsenpo arrived to become king of Tibet, and the distinction between sovereign and subject arose.

This chapter,
concerning the descent
of the Tibetan race from a monkey
and a rock-ogress,
is the seventh.

8

The rise of the
first Tibetan kings

Nyatri Tsenpo

As to the successive generations of Tibetan kings, these include the Seven Tri from the Sky, the Two Teng from Above, the Six Intermediate Leg, the Eight De of the Earth and the Three Tsen from Below. Thus, counting each one, there were twenty-seven generations from King Nyatri Tsenpo to Lhatotori Nyenshal,[70] who was the manifestation of the sublime Samantabhadra and was the first to introduce the teachings of the Buddha to Tibet.

According to the *Testament of the Pillar*, the twin kings Kyabding and Shatanika were descended through successive Dharma-kings from Ashoka, himself a descendant of the Indian king Shakya Ridragpa. When disagreement over government arose, the youngest of Shatanika's three sons, who bore the marks of greatness, being unable to seize the reins of power, fled to Tibet disguised as a woman, as had been prophesied by the deities.[71]

King Nyatri Tsenpo is carried down from the mountain

On the other hand, Buton Rinpoche's *History of the Dharma* states that the person who bore the marks of greatness was the son of King Pradyota, or perhaps a fifth-generation descendant of either King Prasenajit of Kosala or King Bimbisara. In any case, both sources agree that the person with the marks of greatness became King Nyatri Tsenpo.[72]

The Tibetan annals state that Nyatri Tsenpo first descended upon the peak of Lhari Rolpo, but looking about him perceived that Mt. Yarlha Shampo was higher and the region of Yarlung more pleasing.[73] He therefore lit upon the mountain at Tsentang, where he was seen by herdsmen who were tending their flocks. When they approached and asked him whence he had come, he simply pointed to the sky. 'He must be a celestial prince from the heavens', they cried. 'Let us make him our king!' They bore him down from the mountain on a throne that they carried upon the napes of their necks, and he was therefore called King Nyatri, 'Nape-throne'.[74] [This took place two thousand years after the Buddha had passed into Nirvana.] Nyatri Tsenpo was the first Tibetan king.

King Nyatri Tsenpo undertook the construction of the Umbu Langkhar Palace.[75] His son was Mutri Tsenpo. His son was Dingtri Tsenpo. His son was Sotri Tsenpo. His son was Metri Tsenpo. His son was Dagtri Tsenpo. His son was Sibtri Tsenpo. These kings are called the Seven Tri from the Sky. It is said that when each of these successive princes was old enough to ride a horse, his father ascended a magical sky-rope and disappeared into the heavens like a rainbow. The tombs of the Seven Tri were built in the sphere of the sky, and their celestial bodies left no corpse, but vanished rainbow-like. So it was.

Trigum Tsenpo

Sibtri Tsenpo's son, Trigum Tsenpo, had three sons, Shatri, Nyatri and Jatri. Trigum Tsenpo was possessed by a demon, and said to a minister by the name of Long-ngam Tadzi the Equerry, 'You must face me in battle!' Long-ngam replied, 'Why, O King? It is improper for me, a subject, to do battle with my own sovereign'. In spite of this entreaty, and as he was powerless to resist, the equerry was compelled to do battle with the king, and the fourteenth day of the fourth month was chosen for the duel.

Now the king had a dog named Khyimo Nyengyi Na Sangma, 'She-dog who Hears All', which was the manifestation of a deity, and he sent this dog to eavesdrop on Long-ngam. Realising this, Long-ngam said, 'In two days' time, the king will come to slay me. If he does the following I will be unable to withstand him: if he comes without a military escort; if he wears a headband of black silk and attaches a mirror to his forehead; if he carries a dead fox on his right shoulder and a dead dog on his left shoulder; if he brandishes his sword above his head; and if he brings a red ox bearing a sack of ashes'.

The dog subsequently revealed everything to the king, who exclaimed, 'I shall do precisely as he says!' Two days later, having done as Long-ngam had said, King Trigum Tsenpo set out to kill him. The red ox, however, was disturbed by the grinding of the king's teeth, the sack was rent asunder and clouds of ashes blinded the king's eyes. The dead fox enfeebled the king's war-spirit, the dead dog weakened his masculinity-spirit,[76] and when he brandished his sword above his head, he accidentally severed his magical sky-rope. Minister Long-ngam took aim at the mirror fastened on the king's forehead, loosed an arrow and slew him.

Rulakye

Trigum Tsenpo's three sons fled to the regions of Kongpo, Nyangpo and Powo. Minister Long-ngam usurped the throne, and Trigum's queen was set to work tending the horses. One day when the queen had taken the horses out to pasture, she fell asleep and dreamed that she had intercourse with a man whose body was entirely white and who was the emanation of Yarlha Shampo.[77] On awakening, she saw a white yak rise from her pillow and gallop away. After eight months had passed, she gave birth to a ball of blood that was the size of a human fist and that could quiver at will. She felt compassion for it because it was of her own flesh and blood, and she did not throw it away. It had neither eyes nor a mouth by which the queen might succour it, so she placed it inside a warm wild-yak horn and rolled the horn in the hem of her trousers. Several days later, she inspected the horn and found that it contained a baby boy. He became known as Janggibu Rulakye, 'Son of Jang, Born in a Horn'. At the age of ten, the boy said to his mother, 'Where

King Rulakye's mother sleeps with a magical white yak near Mt. Yarlha Shampo

are my father and older brothers?' When she told him of the events of the past, he contrived by various means to exhume the body of his father from Nyangchu Kyamo and built a tomb for his remains on the Plain of Dartang in the region of Ching. He executed Minister Long-ngam and visited his three older brothers to invite them to return, but Shatri and Nyatri declined, as they had become kings of Kongpo and Nyangpo respectively, where their descendants are still found to this day. Rulakye also invited Jatri to return from the region of Powo, and Jatri settled in Yarlung, where he built the Jing-nga Tagtse Palace.

The former queen took her son Jatri by the hand and made a vow before the gods, whereupon a voice from the sky proclaimed, *'Bu de kun le gyel* — This son of yours will vanquish all!' Although the precise words were *bu de kun le gyel*, he became known as *Pude Gunggyel*. He subsequently took the throne and appointed Rulakye as his minister.

The rise of Bon

During the time of these kings, the religion of Swastika Bon arose, and the sage known as Shenrab Miwo was born at Olmoi Lungring in Persia.[78] All the Bon scriptures, including the *Eight Great Realms*, were translated from the language of Zhangzhung, and underwent further development. Bon evolved into nine sects: the four sects of the Cause School and five of the Effect School. The Swastika Vehicle was the foremost of the five sects of the latter school, all of which focussed on the desire to attain a glorified body. As to the four sects of the Cause School, they were the Nangshen Belto, Trulshen Beltson, Chashen Jutig and Durshen Tsoncha.

The Nangshen Belto summoned up good fortune and blessings by means of invocations and sought efficacious remedies from the spirits. They caused wealth to increase through virtue, goodness and the generation of happiness. The Trulshen Beltson made use of ghost-traps, established a hierarchy and shrines and could dispel negative influences, both present and future. The Chashen Jutig showed the paths of good and evil, cleared away doubts about 'is' and 'is not' and practiced clairvoyance into mundane affairs. The Durshen Tsoncha removed obstacles for the living, located suitable gravesites using divination, overcame minor malevolent spirits, observed the heavenly constellations and subdued earth-demons. Proponents of all traditions beat drums and tambourines, and used parables and riddles to guide the affairs of state.

[According to the Tibetan histories, Bon spread during the reign of King Nyatri Tsenpo but was suppressed under King Trigum Tsenpo. It spread again at the time of Pude Gunggyel and suffered further suppression under Trisong Detsen. A Bon lama by the name of Nyachen Lishokara then brought the embers of Bon from Kham to U and Tsang. He revealed all the hidden Bon scriptures and established the Bonpo monasteries of Rizhing, Darding, Geding, Entsakha, Zangri, Yogtang and others. It is therefore said that he brought about the increase of Bon. Like the Dharma, the teachings of Bon also underwent the three stages of early, intermediate and late transmission.]

At this time, charcoal, the essence of burnt wood, and glue, the essence of boiled leather, both came into use. Iron, copper and silver ores were discovered, and these were smelted over charcoal fires to produce their three respective metals.

> Holes were bored though timber spars to make ploughs and
>   yokes.
> Pairs of oxen were put to the yoke, and the plains were tilled
>   to make fields.
> Water from lakes was diverted into channels, and crops were
>   sown.

Prior to this, no crops had ever been raised in fields. Trigum Tsenpo and Pude Gunggyel, father and son, are known as the Two Teng from Above. The tomb of one was located on a rocky mountain, the other in a meadow. The construction of both tombs was supervised by Rulakye.

Descendants of Pude Gunggyel

Pude Gunggyel's son was Asholeg. His son was Desholeg. His son was Tisholeg. His son was Guruleg. His son was Drongzherleg. His son was Isholeg. These are known as the Six Intermediate Leg.

> The tombs of the Six Leg were built where the rocky
>   mountains meet the meadows,
> And resembled rainbows rising above the sward.

Isholeg's son was Zanam Zinde. His son was Detrulnam Zhungtsen. His son was Senol Namde.[79] His son was Denolnam. His son was Denolpo. His son was Degyelpo. His son was Detrintsen. These were the Eight De of the Earth.

> The tombs of the Eight De were built upon a riverbank
> And resembled drifts of snow by the water.

King Detrintsen's son was Tritsennam. His son was Tridra Pungtsen. His son was Tride Togtsen. These three are known as the Three Tsen from Below.

> The tombs of the Three Tsen were built on Gangkartse,
>   'Snow Mountain Peak',
> And resembled mist arising above the snow.

Lhatotori Nyenshal

The son of Tride Togtsen was known as Lhatotori Nyenshal. He was an emanation of the sublime Samantabhadra and ruled the kingdom until he reached the age of eighty. Lhatotori dwelled atop the Umbu Langkhar Palace, the great residence which had appeared miraculously without the aid of human hands. In accordance with the prophesy made in former times by the Lord Buddha at the Bamboo Grove, several objects descended from the sky upon a sunbeam and landed on the roof of the royal palace as precursors of the spread of the Buddha's teachings in Tibet. These were the *Zamatog*, *Essence of the Six Syllables*, *Pangkong Chaggyapa*, a silver stupa measuring one cubit high, a mould for making votive stupas known as Chittamani and an object called Mudra Chaggya. The following prophesy then resounded from the heavens: 'In five generations' time, there will arise a king [Songtsen Gampo] who will understand the meaning of these objects'.

Although Lhatotori appreciated that these items were most miraculous, he had no inkling of their significance. He therefore named them the Secret Antidotes,[80] set them upon a precious throne and made offerings to them. By virtue of these acts, he became a young man again and lived to be one hundred and twenty years of age. He became known as 'the one who achieved two lifetimes in one body'. King Lhatotori was the first to bring to light the sacred Dharma.

*The Secret Antidotes descend upon a sunbeam
to the roof of the Umbu Langkhar Palace*

His tomb was built in his own dominion,
At Dartang in the region of Ching.
A tumulus that resembled a nomad's yak-felt tent rose
above it.[81]

As Lhatotori's son, Trinyen Zungtsen, made offerings to the Secret Antidotes, the extent of his realm increased.

His tomb, built at Donkhorda,
Was inconspicuous with a gently sloping tumulus.

His son, King Drang-nyen Deru, took as his queen Chimza Lugyel, the Princess of Chim [a female naga], from the land of Dagpo. She bore him a blind son who became known as Mulong Konpatra, 'Blind Rare Intelligence'. At first, Queen Lugyel was very beautiful, but as time passed she grew pale and emaciated. The king therefore said to her, 'Formerly you were very beautiful. Are you unwell? What ails you?' 'There is a particular food in my homeland that is unavailable here; this is why I am ailing', she replied. 'That being the case, by all means fetch this food hither and eat it!' commanded the king. A serving-woman with a pure heart was then dispatched to acquire the foodstuff. She fried a great number of frogs in butter, and as there were many loads of the food, she concealed it in a storeroom. Lest anyone observe her, the queen devoured the frogs in secret. She thus regained her former beauty and her countenance became radiant once more. 'This food has miraculous qualities', thought the king to himself. 'I too must try it!' Taking advantage of the queen's absence, he opened the door of the storeroom. Upon entering, he beheld the many sacks filled with great quantities of frogs. His mind was filled with doubt, and as a result, he contracted leprosy.

The king and queen entered their tomb while still alive, and passed on to their son a testament that proclaimed, 'Worship the Secret Antidotes, our ancestral tutelary deities. Summon a physician from the land of Hachi, and take the throne when your sight has been restored!'

> Drang-nyen Deru's tomb was built at Zhangda,
> And became known as Sonche Dumpo, 'Circular Sign of the
>   Living'.

So it was. As Mulong Konpatra devotedly worshipped the Secret Antidotes and summoned a physician, his sight was indeed restored. The first thing he saw was a wild sheep on Tiger Mountain in Kyisho, and he therefore became known as Tagri Nyenzig, 'Beheld a Sheep on Tiger Mountain'.

> Tagri Nyenzig died at the age of forty.
> His tomb, built at Donkhorda,
> Lay to the left of Trinyen Zungtsen's.
> It was also inconspicuous with a gently sloping tumulus.

Tagri Nyenzig's son was Namri Songtsen. During his reign, the sciences of medicine and astrology arrived from China, China and Gilgit were subdued, salt was discovered in the north of Tibet, and the palace known as Tritsig Bumdug was built. Namri Songtsen died after he had ruled the kingdom for sixty years.

> His tomb was built at Donkhorda,
> To the right of Trinyen Zungtsen's.
> It had a great outer wall shaped like a scapula.
> It is said that the tomb was called Gangri Sogkha,
> 'Snowy Mountain Shoulder-blade'.

So it was. It is truthfully said that the foundation on which all benefits and happiness arise, that is, the royal Tibetan line from King Nyatri Tsenpo to Lhatotori Nyenshal, consists of twenty-seven generations that span 500 years. As none of these kings had any connection with the Dharma, their histories have not been related in detail. Lhatotori Nyenshal, during whose reign the Dharma was first revealed, reached the age of 120, and during the four subsequent generations, up to the time of Namri Songtsen, a further 111 years elapsed. Such is the account in the *Great Samye Record of Edicts*. [According to the *Illumination of Knowledge*, King Nyatri Tsenpo appeared in Tibet 2000 years after the Buddha passed into Nirvana, and Lhatotori appeared 2500 years after this event.]

As this is merely a summary, those who desire a more detailed account may consult the *Great Samye Record of Edicts*, the *Testament of the Pillar* and the *Wish-fulfilling Tree of the Royal Lineage*.

This chapter,
concerning the rise of the
first royal Tibetan lineage,
is the eighth.

PART II

THE REIGN OF
KING SONGTSEN GAMPO

The great Dharma-king Songtsen Gampo

9

Four rays of light emanate from the body of the sublime Avalokiteshvara, and the Dharma-king Songtsen Gampo is born

he sublime Avalokiteshvara realised that the time was ripe for the religious conversion of sentient beings in the snowy land of Tibet, and four rays of light emanated from his body. The ray that arose from his right eye reached Nepal and illuminated everything in that land, including the king, Amshuvarman, and his naga-palace in the city of Kathmandu. The ray of light then gathered as one and entered the womb of King Amshuvarman's consort. After nine months had passed and the tenth month had begun, an especially exalted princess was born. None in the whole world was as sublime as she: her skin was white, her complexion tinged with red, from her mouth wafted the scent of *hari*-sandalwood and she was accomplished in all fields of knowledge. This then was the Nepalese Princess Tritsun.[82]

The ray of light that emanated from Avalokiteshvara's left eye reached China and illuminated everything in that land, including the emperor, Taizong, and his palace Trashi Trigo in the city of Zimshing.[83] The ray of light then gathered as one and entered the womb of the emperor's consort. After nine months had passed and when the tenth month had begun, an especially exalted princess was born. None in the whole world was as sublime as she: her skin was blue, her complexion tinged with red, from her mouth came the scent of the blue *utpala*-lotus and she was versed in all fields of knowledge. This then was the Chinese Princess Kongjo.

The ray of light that arose from the mouth of Avalokiteshvara fell upon the Chu-gyagpa Precipice of Dragla[84] in the snowy realm of Tibet and became the aspect of the Dharmakaya, the mystical antidote that subdues barbarity: this then was the Six-Syllable Mantra.[85]

The ray of light that arose from the heart of Avalokiteshvara reached Tibet and illuminated everything in the Land of Snows, including the Jampa Mingyur Ling, the 'Palace of Immutable Loving-Kindness', in Nondra Totsel, and King Namri Songtsen himself. The ray of light then gathered as one and entered the womb of the king's consort, Driza Tokarma, Princess of Dri, and auspicious signs appeared in all directions. After nine months had passed and when the tenth month had begun, in the Fire-female-ox Year [617], an especially sublime son was born. Upon his head was Amitabha, the Buddha of Boundless Light. His hands and feet bore the sign of the Dharma-wheel and his hair was heaped up in a spiral coif. The buddhas blessed him, the bodhisattvas made auspicious pronouncements, the deities caused flowers to fall like rain and the earth shook in six different ways.

Three different perceptions of this event arose: to the Buddhas of the Ten Directions, it appeared that the sublime Avalokiteshvara, having planned the liberation of sentient beings in the snowy land of Tibet on the basis of the power of prayers in former times, shining like a brilliant lamp in the darkness of this wild region, had cast his gaze upon the precious continent. In the perception of the Bodhisattvas of the Ten Stages, it appeared that Avalokiteshvara, with the intention of leading the sentient beings of this wild and snowy realm to the Dharma, manifested himself as a king who would strive to benefit beings by means appropriate to each.

In the perception of the common black-headed people, it appeared that a son of unsurpassed wonder had been born to the king.

By the time this royal prince attained his majority, he excelled in the arts, astrology, physical pursuits and the five fields of knowledge, and he was endowed with many fine qualities. The ministers exclaimed, 'This sovereign of ours possesses every quality, and his mind is truly profound [*gampo*]!' and he therefore became known as Songtsen Gampo. When he was thirteen years old his father died, and he took the throne.

The Dharma-king Songtsen Gampo meditated upon the following question: 'Whither in this snowy land should I go to strive for the sake of sentient beings?' and eventually reached this resolution: 'As my forefather Lhatotori Nyenshal, the emanation of the sublime Samantabhadra, resided upon the summit of Marpori, the Red Hill, in Lhasa, I shall follow in his footsteps and remove to that place, which is set about with pleasing, auspicious trees, to strive for the benefit of sentient beings'. Having spent one last night at Nondra Totsel, the king and his retinue broke their fast the next morning and travelled as far as Yamtrang, where they unloaded their baggage at the foot of the Precipice of the Six-Syllable Mantra. They sent their animals out to pasture and made camp, and the king bathed himself in the river. When Minister Nachenpo beheld in the water a scintillating multi-coloured ray of light, he exclaimed, 'What is this, O King? It is most wondrous that such a light should appear in the river!' The king replied, 'Great Minister, heed well! The Six-Syllable Mantra has appeared upon these rocks in this wild and snowy land. The mantra is the path that leads all beings to liberation; the collected essence of the thoughts of every buddha; the source of all benefits, happiness and qualities; the antidote that subdues barbarity; the Dharma that this snowy land deserves; the quintessence; the mystical six syllables that are the words of the Dharmakaya; the most excellent speech. These lights themselves will benefit the multitude of beings!' As soon as the king made offerings to the rock, varied rays of light arose and struck the cliffs on the opposite side of the gorge. As both sides were linked by rainbow-coloured lights, this place was named Jandang, 'Rainbow-light'. Images of the deities also appeared spontaneously on

the rocks at that time. [These images of Avalokiteshvara, Khasarpani, Hayagriva and so on were carved again in relief by Nepalese
sculptors at a later date.] Songtsen Gampo eventually reached
Lhasa, built a palace on Marpori and dwelt there.

This chapter,
in which four rays of light
arise from the body of the sublime
Avalokiteshvara, and the
Dharma-king is born,
is the ninth.

10

Minister Tonmi
brings the alphabet from India,
and King Songtsen Gampo creates
the Laws of the Ten Virtues

Tonmi Sambhota and the Tibetan alphabet

As Tibet had no alphabet for facilitating the creation of royal Dharma-laws based on the Ten Virtues,[86] or for increasing the five sensual pleasures,[87] or for promoting the exchange of gifts, or for issuing the pronouncements of the Dharma among the subjects under the king's dominion, Songtsen Gampo dispatched seven talented ministers to India to study the art of writing.[88] Having encountered the three species of demon that inhabit the borderlands, however, they were forced to return. A great amount of gold was then given to the son of Tonmi Anu, known as Tonmi Sambhota,[89] an honest man endowed with sharp intelligence and many other qualities, and he was sent to India to study the alphabet. The minister journeyed to the south of that continent, which was said to be the abode of a certain Brahmin by the name of Lijin, who was skilled in the art of letters. When Tonmi reached the Brahmin's residence, he prostrated himself devotedly and made this request:

> You are of the Race of All-increasing Compassion, who are
>   manifestations of the deities!
> You were born into the class of Brahmins, who are endowed
>   with many qualities!
> By the power of qualities practiced in former lives,
> You have mastered the language of the race of Holy Ones.
> You are the great Brahmin of perfect learning and accom-
>   plishment in knowledge.
> I beg you to hear my plea and consider my plight!
> I am a minister from the wild land of Tibet,
> And my sovereign is the Great Compassionate One himself.
> Having taken power at the age of thirteen,
> While seated upon his precious throne,
> He entrusted these many gifts to me
> And dispatched me to your country to study the alphabet,
> Because my homeland lacks the art of writing.
> For the consolation of his retinue and subjects by means of
>   the Dharma,
> And for the creation of royal laws based on the Ten Virtues,
> I beg you, skilled savant, to teach me
> Grammar, logic and the entire accumulation of knowledge.

Having made this petition, he offered the gold into Lijin's hands. The great Brahmin accepted the gift and made this reply:

> Heed well, O son of a fortunate race!
> Gifted minister by the name of Tonmi,
> A great man who has realised the meaning of the Two
>   Truths:[90]
> The art of writing, poetry and the like,
> And all miraculous qualities,
> These I shall impart to you, O great minister.
> You will console the inhabitants of the wild realm of Tibet
> With the wisdom of the sages and the precepts,
> Using the grammar and the logic of the alphabet.

Thus he spoke. The Brahmin then led Tonmi into his precious celestial mansion, and by instructing him in the form of the letters, Minister Tonmi honed the faculties of his mind. Holding aloft the

Minister Tonmi Sambhota journeys to India to learn the art of writing

lamp of wisdom, he studied the alphabet. As there were many classes of letters in the Devanagari script, such as the *ga* and *ta* groups, that could not be translated into Tibetan, he invented the vowel signs. He arranged the letters of the Lantsa script of the gods and the Vartula script of the nagas to form the entire miraculously accomplished Tibetan alphabet.[91]

> The fifty letters of the Indian alphabet
> Consist of the thirty principal letters,
> The ten prefixes and the ten suffixes.
> No letter of the Indian alphabet,
> Apart from its own inherent function,
> Can be joined to every other letter.
> All the letters fall into the above classes.
> With this alphabet as a basis,
> The Tibetan script was refined as its quintessence,
> And the form of each respective letter
> Was crafted most excellently.

The twenty primary letters are *ka, kha, ca, cha, ja, nya, ta, tha, pa, pha, tsa, tsha, dza, wa, zha, za, ya, sha, ha* and *a*. The sole dispensable letter is *wa*. The five prefix letters are *ga, da, ba, ma* and *'a*, and the ten suffixes are *ga, da, ba, ma, 'a, nga, na, la, ra* and *sa*. The five letters of greatest importance are *ga, da, ba, ma* and *'a*. The nine with descenders are *ka, ga, ta, da, na, nya, zha, sha* and *ha*. The six letters that lack equivalents in the Indian alphabet are *ca, cha, ja, zha, za* and *'a*.

The sixteen 'son' letters are *ka, ga, nga, da, ta, na, pa, ba, ma, ca, ja, nya, tsa, dza, la* and *ha*.[92] The seven 'mothers' are *ka, ga, ba, za, ra, la* and *sa* [the latter three are mothers of all subjoined letters]. For *la*, there are four special mothers: *ka, ga, ba* and *za*. These are all the mothers of *la*. [These four letters are only subjoined by *la*.]

> *La* has two special sons:
> *Ca* and *ha* are the two sons of *la*.
> *Tsa* and *dza* are the two sons of *ra*.
> Being neither prefixes nor suffixes,
> And being neither mother nor son,
> Are the ten letters that are complete unto themselves:
> *Kha, cha, tha, pa, tsha, wa, zha, ya, sha* and *a*.

Ga and *ba* may accompany any letter. [They are both mother and son, and prefix and suffix.]

Superimposed, like hats, are the three 'suspended letters': *o*, *i*
and *e*.
These may be joined to all other letters.
Placed below, like seats, are the three 'beautiful letters': *ya*, *ra*
and *u*.

Ya may be subjoined to seven letters, forming *kya*, *khya*, *gya*, *pya*,
phya, *bya* and *mya*. *Ra* may be subjoined to eleven letters, forming
kra, *khra*, *gra*, *pra*, *phra*, *bra*, *mra*, *sra*, *shra*, *dra* and *hra*. *U* may accompany any letter, as well as both subjoined *ya* and *ra*, forming, for
example, *kyu*, *khyu*, *kru* and *khru*. Thus the concepts of subjoining
letters and spelling arose in Tonmi's mind.

Furthermore, based on the Lantsa script, which resembles the
alphabet of the devas, the 'headed' *uchen* Tibetan script was created. [The use of *ha* and *'a* as sons with other letters, and the reversed *na*, *sha*, *tha* and so on, were invented at a later date by pandits
with profound understanding of the letters when the dharani mantras were being translated from Sanskrit into Tibetan.] Based on
the Vartula script, which resembles the alphabet of the nagas, the
'angular' *zurchen* Tibetan script was created.

As this is merely a summary, those who desire a more detailed
account may consult the following of Tonmi's works: *The Creation
of the First Letters*, *The Development of the Thirty-Letter Alphabet*, *Foundation for the Art of Spelling*, and *Tonmi Dodzi's Treatise on Language*.

Moreover, having studied all the teachings on writing under the
pandit Devavidyasinha, Minister Tonmi became skilled in the five
fields of knowledge and translated into Tibetan the *Pinnacle of the
Precious Collection*, the *Zamatog Sutra* and the twenty-one Sutras
and Tantras of Avalokiteshvara. One historical work states that he
also translated the *One Hundred Thousand Verses on the Perfection of
Wisdom*. In short, Minister Tonmi became skilled in all aspects
of learning. Finally, on his departure for Tibet, he addressed the
Brahmin:

> You have taken me into your heart, O Victorious Prince!
> Great are your kindness and wondrousness.
> Bless me, O Compassionate One.
> In the unblemished sky of your perception,
> The dual constellations of skilful means and wisdom are
>   rising,

And the pure clouds of prayer are gathering.
Writings on grammar and logic rise like the sun and moon,
Dispelling the darkness of ignorance among living beings.
Above the ocean of your mind of happiness and clarity,
Fed by tributary streams of the intelligent mind,
Pure water-birds of prayer are soaring.
There dwell the jewels of compositions on grammar and
    logic,
Dispelling poverty and misfortune among living beings.
Upon the stainless tree of the illusion body
Grow the twin branches of skilful means and wisdom,
The flowers of scholarship, discipline and knowledge bloom,
And the fruits of writing ripen.
All that you have given to me, the minister Tonmi,
I shall hold dearly in my heart.
I came to the land of India,
And met you, the Wise and Accomplished One.
Writing is the foundation of qualities;
I have embraced it all within the compass of my mind.
I shall return to U in the land of Tibet,
Where the king will hold a great celebration.
He guards his kingdom as dearly as the Dharma itself.
He will cause the art of writing to spread
Among ministers and subjects, himself at their head,
And will cause it to flourish among them all.
You have taken me into your heart, O Victorious Prince!

Having spoken thus, he touched the Brahmin's feet with his forehead, and set out for Tibet with many of the teachings of the
Mahayana Dharma. On his arrival in Tibet, a celebration that defied the imagination was held to welcome him. When King
Songtsen Gampo reached the site of the festivities, Minister Tonmi
had grouped together words with rhyming vowels and presented
him with this sample of writing:

Your clear visage bears a rosy complexion of perfect beauty!
Your profound oral instructions are complete and free from
    contradictions.
You dispel all adverse karma and habitual tendencies:
You, the perfectly pure and sacred sublime Maitreya!
The wisdom of the Enlightened Ones is certainly true:

Beholding the peace itself achieved by practice of deep
   meditation.
Most excellent defender who vanquishes the accumulation
   of negativities,
Overcome the evil of the Three Poisons and subdue all![93]

[This sample of Tonmi's writing was carved upon a rock in the
stone shrine of Dzinkhogna.]

Heart-son of Lord Avalokiteshvara,
The Dharma-king by the name of Songtsen Gampo,
To you I pay homage!

Thus he eulogised. The king was greatly pleased, and thinking of
the precious teachings of the Buddha, he bowed down with great
reverence and paid respect to Tonmi. When the Songtsen Gampo
did this, the other ministers, motivated by jealousy, proclaimed
that it was improper for a sovereign to behave in this way towards
one of his subjects. In order to counter their competitiveness, Minister Tonmi spoke these words:

I, the kind-hearted Minister Tonmi,
Journeyed to the distant land of India
And endured hardships of extreme cold and heat.
My reverent mind brought me to venerate
The learned Brahmin Lijin.

I offered him gifts of precious jewels and gold;
He instructed me in the form of letters whose meaning is
   difficult to fathom.
Pointing to them one by one, he clarified uncertainties and
   doubts in my mind.
I mastered the concepts of words and vowels,
And established the thirty Tibetan letters,
On the basis of the fifty letters of the Indian alphabet.
I became firmly convinced of my own gifts
And immediately comprehended all knowledge.
The present is joyous and future lives will be blissful.
There has never been an educated person
In this wild land, the kingdom of Tibet:
I am the first.
I am the lamp that dispels the darkness.

The sovereign, the king, shines like the sun and moon.
None of you, my minister-friends, is my equal.
Have I, Tonmi, not shown great favour
To the people of the snowy land of Tibet?

[This is known as 'The Pride of Tonmi'.] As he spoke in this way, the other ministers stared mutely at one another, and their jealousy abated.

Songtsen Gampo's ministers

At that time, the Three Hundred Ministers of Renown included the Sixteen Famous Ministers; the Four Indispensable Ministers, [who were] attendant upon the king's body, speech and mind; the Inner, Outer and Intermediate Ministers; and the Sixteen Ministers Descended from Bodhisattvas. Further, there were the Six Mighty Outer Ministers, the Six Excellent Inner Ministers and the Four Ministers Who Relay Commands.

The One Hundred Inner Ministers attended upon the king and managed all internal affairs. These included the Six Excellent Inner Ministers: Trulgyi Nachen Rigzang [of Trandrug], Zhangpo Gyelgyi Tramzang [of Hor], Chogro Rigpai Kezang [of Chogro], Lharzig Shogpo Tenzang [of Kham], Kai Nyagton Pelzang [of Gyama Yarton] and Be Chang Pelgyi Legzang [of Kyetag Ringmo in Be, it is said].

The One Hundred Outer Ministers managed external affairs. These included the Six Mighty Outer Ministers, Khyungpo Buna Zangtsen [of Khyungpo in the north], Lamtri Delhag Tritsen [of Yarto], Mutri Dorje Namtsen [of Gyel in Penyul], Tinggi Jangchub Chogtsen [of Je], Tarpa Lui Peltsen [of Chonggye], and Rongpo Trulgyi Detsen [of Son in Yarlung].

From China in the east and from the region of Minyag, examples of handicrafts and astrological reckoning were obtained. Dharma and the art of writing were imported from India in the south. From the lands of the Mongols and Nepalis in the west came material wealth and treasures. Model laws and administration were brought from the lands of the Uighurs in the north. In short, while conquering lands in all four directions and enjoying their wealth, Songtsen Gampo became king of half the world.

The One Hundred Intermediate Ministers equalised differences among the people. These included Tonmi Sambhota [of Raga in Tonlung], Gar Sangtsen Yulzung [of Rampa in Tolung], Dri Seru Gongton [of Drigung], Nyang Trizang [of Nyangser] and Yangton. [The names of the Outer, Inner and Intermediate Ministers were assembled from the *Record of Royal Commands*.]

Laws of the Ten Virtues

In accordance with commands issued by the king, the Laws of the Ten Virtues were drafted:

> The good shall be rewarded, the evil punished.
> Those above shall be constrained by the law,
> Those below protected.
> Four regiments of guards shall be established.
> Streams in the upper valleys shall be dammed for reservoirs.
> Rivers in the lower valleys shall be used for irrigation.
> A system of measures and weights shall be established.
> The fields shall be apportioned.
> Writing shall be taught to the people.
> Horses shall be tamed.
> Worthy customs will be introduced for emulation.
> Those who quarrel shall be punished.
> Murderers shall pay blood-monies, great and small.
> Thieves shall repay the price of goods stolen,
> Plus eight times the value; nine times the value in all.
> Adulterers shall have their limbs severed and shall be
>   banished to another land.
> The tongues of those who lie shall be cut out.
>
> Furthermore, while taking refuge in the Three Jewels,
> Be faithful and devoted.
> Acknowledge the kindness shown by your parents, and
>   respect them.
> Do not offend the sensibilities of those who bestow favour:
>   one's father, uncles and elders. Repay goodness.
> Do not criticise those of noble qualities and honourable
>   descent,
> But revere and accept them.
> In all your actions and deeds, follow the example of those of
>   noble qualities.

Apply your mind to the Dharma and to writing, and strive to
grasp their meaning.
Have faith in the causes and effects of karma,
Refrain only from unvirtuous action.
Help intimate friends and neighbours, show them no ill-will.
Be straightforward and sincere.
Eat and drink in moderation. Behave with modesty.
Repay debts on time. Do not falsify weights or measures.
Be disinterested and do not involve yourself in unsolicited
activities.
In conversation, pay no heed to women.
Adhere firmly to your own views.
When disputes over 'is' and 'is not' arise, take oaths,
With local deities and Dharma-protectors as witnesses.

Based on the model of the Ten Virtues, the Twenty Laws of Tibet
were established at Shomara in Kyisho. The king and ministers
affixed their seals, and the laws spread across the land like the
light of the sun and moon.

As a result, the sovereign and his subjects rejoiced.
While the Teachings flourished, the realm expanded in all
directions.
With the creation of the Dharma-laws, the people obeyed the
king's commands.
With a deity serving as sovereign over the people, the whole
kingdom lived happily.
Men were heroic, horses swift, and entertainments rivalled
those of the gods.
With faith in the Dharma, both this life and the next were
filled with bliss.
Forsaking quarrels and strife, all beings were recognised as
parents.
By teaching the art of writing to everyone, the doctrines of
the Buddha spread.
Shunning unvirtuous friends and relatives,
The jewel of the Ten Virtues was discovered.
Each person bore this jewel upon their heads, and the sun of
happiness arose.
As king and ministers were manifestations, there were no
taxes or forced labour.

In the expanse of the sky, the Eight-spoked Wheel appeared.
On the ground below, the Eight-petalled Lotus bloomed.
On the mountains between, all Eight Auspicious Signs were
    seen.
Wish-fulfilling trees shaded gardens of bliss,
Where all the birds sang for joy,
The earth shook in six different ways
And the gods caused flowers to fall like rain.

In the pleasant and auspicious grove of Draglhatsel,
In the cool shade of wish-fulfilling trees and walnut trees,
The great Dharma-king was seated upon a throne,
Attended by the heroic and magical assembly of ministers,
And surrounded by a retinue of Tibetan subjects.
Many-hued rainbows formed a canopy,
Which revolved like a parasol in the sky above the king.
The sovereign and his retinue ate their fill
Of treacle, sultanas, candies and other foods
Of one hundred flavours.
For the amusement of the great Dharma-king,
Players in masks of the snow-lion, yak and tiger,
Drummers, dancers, actors,
Each offered up performances for the king.
The great celestial drum, guitars,
Cymbals and other instruments paid homage.
That finest of medicines, *agaru*, sandalwood
And sweet incense wafted through the air.
Umbrellas, victory banners, pennants, streamers
And silks of many colours filled the skies in honour of the
    king.
Sixteen beautiful girls of pleasing disposition,
Wearing fine ornaments and carrying flowers,
Entertained the king with song and dance.
When the joyous laws were made,
All the Tibetan subjects rode upon their horses,
Fine silks were hoisted to the top of every tree,
And the great and holy drum of the sacred Dharma sounded.
The royal laws were made on the foundation of the Ten
    Virtues,
And entertainments in accord with the five sensual pleasures
    increased.

In this snowy kingdom of Tibet,
The royal laws shone like the sun and moon
And spread across the land.

This chapter,
in which Minister Tonmi
brings the alphabet from India, and
Songtsen Gampo creates the
Laws of the Ten Virtues,
is the tenth.

11

Songtsen Gampo's tutelary deities are brought from India and Nepal

The 'snake-heart' sandalwood image from India

The great manifestation-king Songtsen Gampo thought to himself, 'In striving to benefit sentient beings in this wild land of Tibet, I must create an image of my tutelary deity. As to the materials for this task, if precious gold or silver are used, at some future time when merit among beings is at a low ebb, I fear that it may be plundered. Clay and stone cannot be used, as they are inferior substances. If the image is made from wood, it may eventually crack. Which material, then, is best?'

Early the next morning, after the king had supplicated the Sublime One, the buddhas and bodhisattvas, the sublime shravakas and the sons and daughters of the gods appeared like gathering clouds in the sky before him. The sublime Manjushri and Samantabhadra, holding precious vases filled with nectar, bestowed empowerment upon the king and anointed him. All the buddhas

gave their blessings and all the bodhisattvas made auspicious pronouncements. The sons and daughters of the gods appeared among
the clouds, paid homage with every kind of celestial music and
caused flowers to fall like rain. At that moment, a many-hued ray
of light fell upon the body of the king, and rays of light also covered the whole of this wild and snowy land. Each of the manifestations benefited sentient beings by whatever appropriate means and
transformed this barbaric realm into the semblance of a precious
continent. Then the gods addressed the king in a single voice,
saying:

> O Manifestation-king Bodhisattva!
> You who are sovereign over all the black-headed throng:
> On the basis of merit accrued through your devotion,
> If you desire an image of your tutelary deity,
> In the south of the land of India
> On the shores of the Ocean of Singhala,
> Behind a self-created statue of Khasarpani,
> Beneath the sand where elephants sleep,
> Lies a miraculous, complete, self-created image of
>   Avalokiteshvara
> Made from 'snake-heart' sandalwood.
> This, then, shall be the royal tutelary deity.

Having spoken, they disappeared. The king then thought to himself, 'As no mortal could ever locate this image, I must dispatch a
manifestation'. At that instant, from the whorl of hair between the
king's eyebrows there appeared a manifestation-monk known as
Akaramatishila, who bore Amitabha, the Buddha of Boundless
Light, upon his head. The king then dispatched Akaramatishila to
procure the image of the deity.

Using his magic powers, the manifestation-monk reached the
south of India and came to the city known as Magadha, wherein
dwelt a king named Utpala-Gesar. Although members of the royal
lineage had been Buddhists in the past, they had subsequently
embraced the religion of heretics,[94] and every day five goats were
sacrificed as an offering before an image of Vishnu. To the left of
the royal palace was the so-called Stupa of the Lotus Wheel, which
had been consecrated by the former buddha Krakucchanda.

The manifestation-monk, seated in the cross-legged lotus position, levitated through the air around the stupa at the level of its vaselike central portion. The king witnessed this feat from the roof of his palace and was amazed, but when he invited Akaramatishila into his presence, the monk declined. The king continued to press him, but the monk replied, 'If you agree to do whatever I say, I will come to your palace, but otherwise I will not'. Utpala-Gesar then agreed to follow Akaramatishila's bidding, so he descended to the palace and became the king's personal chaplain.

Akaramatishila then said to King Utpala-Gesar, 'In former times, it seems that your people were Buddhists, but as you have adopted this heretical religion, you must now return to the Buddhist ways and seek refuge in the Three Jewels'. After the monk had spoken, the king promised most sincerely to comply. Again Akaramatishila addressed Utpala-Gesar, 'O King, you shall now build one hundred and eight shrines and place images made from "snake-heart" sandalwood and "cow-head" sandalwood in each one'. The king replied, 'It is beyond my capability to obtain "snake-heart" sandalwood, because it is only found in Akanishta, the Eastern Heaven. Nor can I obtain "cow-head" sandalwood, as it is found only to the north of Malaya[95] beneath the coils of a venomous cobra. The construction of one hundred and eight shrines must therefore suffice'.

Again Akaramatishila said to the king, 'As I have knowledge of "snake-heart" sandalwood, I shall fetch it. Send a retinue and servants with tools to accompany me!' The king and his retinue then accompanied the monk to the shores of the Ocean of Singhala, where, behind the self-formed stone image of Khasarpani, lay a great herd of sleeping elephants. The monk then said, 'Among these elephants is one that faces the east. It has a red trunk and a tassel of the leaves of the medicinal herb *giwang* upon the nape of its neck. Beneath this beast is the "snake-heart" sandalwood tree'. 'How did it come to be under the elephant?' asked the king. Akaramatishila replied, 'In the heat of the summer, the air is cooler wherever the sandalwood grows. Even its leaves can dispel the torment of the heat. Therefore, whenever the weather is hot, knowing where the tree may be found, the elephants lie down upon it'.

They then roused the elephants, and digging in the sand where the beasts had lain, they came upon the 'snake-heart' sandalwood tree.

Again the king spoke: 'As such a tree has never been seen in the realm of humans before, how did it get here?' The monk replied, 'When the former buddha Krakucchanda was in this world, an arhat shravaka travelled by magic to Akanishta, the Eastern Heaven, where he acquired a stalk of the "snake-heart" sandalwood tree, which bore four seeds. He made an offering of three seeds to Buddha Krakucchanda, and the fourth he offered to Lord Khasarpani, who placed it upon the crown of his head. A gust of wind blew the seed away, and it fell behind Khasarpani's back. There, buried in the soil, dakinis moistened it with nectar on the night of the full moon, and the seed began to sprout. When Buddha Kanakamuni was in this world, it put forth flowers. At the time of Buddha Kashyapa, its fruit ripened. At the time of Buddha Shakyamuni, it became a mighty tree, and when he passed into Nirvana, it fell and was covered by sand'.

Having retrieved the sandalwood tree from beneath the sand, the branches were cut off, and innumerable rays of light shone forth from four fissures in the wood, illuminating every land in the world. The light was then reabsorbed into the tree, and the words 'Cut me slowly' resounded from within it. In the centre of the four pieces into which the tree had split, there arose an image of the sublime Avalokiteshvara, the Wish-fulfilling Jewel, with three placid and seven wrathful visages, ten in all, accomplishing the enlightened activities of peace, prosperity, power and force. Amitabha appeared above its ten faces. The image was endowed with ten primary hands, each with its own symbolic implements. Light and rays of light radiated from it in all directions. The remaining sandalwood was then divided into one hundred and eight pieces, from each of which was fashioned an image for the one hundred and eight shrines.

Further, in order to obtain the 'cow-head' sandalwood, Akaramatishila displayed a piece of musk at the appropriate time,[96] and having won the wood, it, too, was made into one hundred and eight images.

Akaramatishila then retrieved a full *dre*-measure of relics of the seven historical buddhas from the central lotus-vase portion of the Stupa of the Lotus Wheel, after which the structure was resealed. He then proceeded to an island in the middle of the ocean, where he beheld a buddha seated on every blade of grass, and of this grass he gathered a bunch. Finally, he ventured to the banks of the Nairajnana River, where he beheld a buddha seated upon every grain of sand, and of this sand he gathered a *dre*-measure.

Akaramatishila brought from India the image of Avalokiteshvara that arose from the 'snake-heart' sandalwood tree. He also brought the following substances: the 'cow-head' sandalwood, a branch of the Bodhi Tree, sand from the Nairajnana River, a bunch of *kusha*-grass, soil from the Eight Great Hermitages and so on. When he reached Tibet, he offered all of these to the king, who rejoiced greatly.

The *hari*-sandalwood image from Nepal

Songtsen Gampo then thought to himself, 'At the present time in the southern land of Nepal, there is a hidden manifestation which will miraculously benefit sentient beings in the future'. With these thoughts, he supplicated his tutelary deity, and from the breast of the self-formed image there arose a ray of light that extended to Nepal. Looking in the direction of the light, he perceived in a great forest on the borders of India and Nepal the self-created images known as the 'Four Divine Brothers' arising from a *hari*-sandalwood tree that also radiated light in all directions. The king then sent the manifestation-monk Akaramatishila to fetch them. When the monk reached the city of Mangyul, he beheld many people dying from pestilence. He proceeded from Mangyul to the city known as Kathmandu, where he saw many dying from leprosy. Next he travelled from Kathmandu to the border between India and Nepal, where a malevolent demon was causing many deaths among the inhabitants.

At this latter location, a herdsman was tending many buffalo in a forest. One of these beasts, endowed with karma and good fortune, entered the forest during the day and circumambulated the *hari*-sandalwood tree that stood there, whereupon milk flowed from her udders. That evening, the buffalo's owner said to the herds-man, 'You have been milking my beast!' The herdsman denied the accusation, saying, 'I have done no such thing. During the day the buffalo were wandering in the forest'. The next day, the herdsman, accompanied by the owner, proceeded into the forest to investi-gate. There they beheld the buffalo circumambulating the *hari*-san-dalwood tree that radiated light in all directions, the milk flowing from her udders, and the two were amazed.

Knowing that the sandalwood image of the king's tutelary de-ity would arise from this tree, the manifestation-monk split it open with an axe, whereupon voices resounded from each of the four pieces thus created. The voice from the uppermost piece declared, 'Hue me carefully and place me in the city of Mangyul', and from this piece arose the image known as the Sublime Wati. A voice from the second piece said, 'Hue me carefully and place me in the city of Kathmandu,' and from this piece arose the image known as the Sublime Ugang. A voice from the third piece said, 'Hue me carefully and place me on the border of India and Nepal,' and from this piece arose the image known as the Sublime Jamali. A voice from the final piece of sandalwood then said, 'Hue me carefully and I shall go to the snowy kingdom of Tibet to become the tute-lary deity of King Songtsen Gampo'.

The Sublime Wati was placed in the capital of Mangyul,[97] Ugang was placed in Kathmandu, and Jamali was placed on the border of India and Nepal. Through the blessing of these images, each of the three locations was freed from the threefold fears of untimely death described above.

The manifestation-monk then placed the image of the sublime Avalokiteshvara upon the summit of Mt. Potala, and bringing the image of Khasarpani with him, he offered it to the Dharma-king Songtsen Gampo when he reached Tibet. The king was overjoyed, and having beheld the image of his tutelary deity, he thought to himself, 'Now all efforts for the benefit of sentient beings will proceed without impediment!' This manifestation-monk known as Akaramatishila once more dissolved into light and was reabsorbed into the whorl of hair between Songtsen Gampo's eyebrows.

This chapter,
concerning the procurement
of the king's tutelary deities
from India and Nepal,
is the eleventh.

12

The Nepalese princess Tritsun is invited to Tibet

The manifestation-king Songtsen Gampo thought to himself, 'As I shall propagate the teachings of the Great Vehicle in this snowy land of Tibet, there is an image of the Lord Buddha in India, one in Nepal, and a third in China. Because the teachings of the Great Vehicle have flourished in these lands that are graced by the presence of such images, I shall therefore bring one of these to Tibet by whatever means are appropriate'. After the king supplicated the self-created sandalwood image, two rays of light arose from its breast; one shone towards the east, the other to the west. Looking in the direction of the western ray of light, he perceived that there dwelt in the land of Nepal a princess known as Tritsun, daughter of King Amshuvarman. Her body was white with a pinkish hue, from her mouth wafted the fragrance of *hari*-sandalwood and she excelled in all fields of knowledge. He further perceived that if he invited Tritsun to Tibet, she would bring with her an image of the Lord Buddha at the age of eight, together with all the teachings of the Great Vehicle.

Looking in the direction of the ray of light that shone towards the east, he perceived that there dwelt in the land of China a princess known as Kongjo, daughter of Emperor Taizong. Her body was blue in colour with a pinkish hue; from her mouth came the scent of the blue *utpala*-lotus and she was accomplished in every field of learning. He further perceived that if she were invited to Tibet, she would bring with her an image of the Lord Buddha at the age of twelve, together with all the teachings of the Great Vehicle.

Surpassing this mundane world, the king then entered into meditation and behaved as if he were in a dream. Next morning, all the ministers came before him, paid homage and inquired with one voice, 'Mighty One, are you indisposed or in good health? Is your mind blessed with happiness?' 'With the greatest happiness!' he replied. 'Last night I dreamed that I took as my wife one beautiful girl who was the daughter of the king of Nepal in the west, and another who was the daughter of the emperor of China in the east'. Minister Gar said, 'We ministers shall bring these two princesses to Tibet by whatever means, but do not divulge this dream to others! Let us assemble early tomorrow morning before the royal throne at the foot of the wish-fulfilling walnut tree on the Draglha meadow. Further, let the Inner, Outer and Intermediate Ministers, who are the Six Foremost Men, each bring barley beer and a joint of meat for our repast'.

The following morning, when the six ministers assembled, each had brought a joint of meat for the feast: two had brought hind legs, two had brought forelegs, one had brought a chest section and one brought the loins. When the joints were laid out, they formed a complete carcass. Tonmi exclaimed: 'The existing preconditions are excellent! As we came to this meeting and our actions harmonised without prior discussion, whatever we wish will be achieved. Let us not restrict the scope of our deliberations!' To this Minister Gar responded, 'Indeed, the scope of our deliberations will not be restricted. Let us invite the two beautiful daughters of the kings of Nepal and China to become consorts for our sovereign. He is now sixteen years old and is eminently capable of ruling the kingdom'. To this the ministers voiced their unanimous approval.

Six ministers feast on joints of meat and beer

Minister Gar came before the king and said, 'Grant that I might first invite the princess from the land of Nepal'. Assenting, the king gave him five gold coins and said, 'Let these be a token of our invitation'. The king also gave Gar a precious lapis lazuli helmet studded with rubies and commanded, 'Give this as the bride-price for the princess. The king of Nepal will ask three questions. On each occasion do not fail to give him one of these'. So saying, he handed Gar three boxes, each containing a pronouncement. Provisions for the journey, clothing, ornaments and the like were also given to the minister, and a great caravan of horses, mules, camels and other beasts of burden was dispatched. 'Wherever the path grows perilous, offer prayers to the reverend Bhrikuti as you go', commanded the king. Minister Gar then paid homage to his sovereign, and bearing the dispatches and provisions, he set off for Nepal with one hundred ministers on horseback and all the beasts of burden.

They eventually arrived in the city of Kathmandu in the precious land of Nepal and came before the gates of the Naga Palace, which was the residence of the king, Amshuvarman. Making their suit in the presence of the sovereign, Minister Gar offered the five gold coins as a token of his invitation, and placing the precious ruby-studded lapis lazuli helmet before the king, he said, 'Great King! This helmet possesses limitless qualities. Whenever people or livestock are smitten by pestilence, if you circumambulate the city while wearing it, the diseases will abate. Whenever frost or hail are immanent, if you circumambulate the fields while wearing it, the danger will be averted. If you wear it in battle, you will be victorious! As there is nothing in the world more valuable than this, it is impossible to estimate its worth. I offer it to you as the bride-price for the princess. Command that your daughter might become the consort of our Tibetan king!' To this the king of Nepal replied, 'Is your king possessed by demons? He is mad! I am the scion of an unbroken royal lineage that reaches back to the time of Buddha Kashyapa. Our families can never be joined in matrimony! Although you have come from a distant land, return now and ask your king if he can establish royal laws based on the Ten Virtues of the Dharma. If he is able to do so, I will give you the princess, otherwise I will not'.

Gar then took the first of the three boxes containing Songtsen Gampo's pronouncements and placed it in the king's hands. Opening it, the king beheld the following words in the language of the Nepalis inscribed in golden letters upon blue paper: 'You, the king of Nepal, have laws based on the Ten Virtues, but I, king of this wild land of Tibet, have no such laws. While taking delight in your legal system, if you give me your daughter, I shall create five thousand manifestations of myself, and then I shall be able to create these laws in a single morning. Is this not miraculous? If you still withhold your daughter after I have done this, I shall dispatch an army of fifty thousand manifestations. You will be slain, the princess will be seized and all your cities captured!'

As this was the message, the king of Nepal was terrified, but despite this, he concealed his fear and retorted, 'Your king is boastful in the extreme! Go now and ask him if he has the capacity to build shrines in Tibet. If he can, I will give you the princess, otherwise I will not'.

Gar then placed the box containing Songtsen Gampo's second pronouncement into the king's hands and said, 'O King, it will be impossible to conclude this business if I have to travel back and forth on the long road between Nepal and Tibet in response to each of your inquiries. Therefore read this message, which is a reply to your words'. The king read the following: 'You, the king of Nepal, are able to build shrines, but I, ruler of a barbaric land, am not. While you take delight in the construction of shrines, if you give me your daughter, I shall create five thousand manifestations of myself to build one hundred and eight shrines, all the doors of which will face you. Is this not miraculous? If you still withhold your daughter after I have done this, I shall dispatch an army of fifty thousand manifestations, you will be slain, the princess seized and all your cities captured!'

As this was the response, the king grew even more afraid, but again he concealed his fear and said, 'Your master is being extremely boastful again. Can the five sensual pleasures be entertained in Tibet? If they can, I will give you the girl, otherwise, I will not. Go now and ask your king'.

Then Gar placed the box with the third pronouncement into the hands of Amshuvarman and said, 'It is inappropriate that I should return to Tibet every time you ask a question. Here is the answer. Read it!' The king opened the box and read the following: 'You, the king of Nepal, possess great wealth, yet I, king of the uncivilised land of Tibet, have nothing of the kind. While enjoying your prosperity and splendour, if you give me your daughter, I shall emanate five thousand manifestations of myself to create limitless wealth, including precious jewels, gold, silver, fine silks, clothing, ornaments, food, drink and the like. And especially, by conducting trade at the four points of the compass, treasures from the borderlands will accumulate at my door, and I shall become wealthy. Is this not miraculous? If you still refuse to give me your daughter after I have achieved all this, I shall dispatch an army of fifty thousand manifestations, you will be killed, your daughter seized and all your cities captured'. As this was the response, the king of Nepal thought to himself, 'This has been the Tibetan king's consistent reply. Perhaps this is the truth after all!' Then, with a great sadness upon his heart, he finally promised to send his daughter to Tibet.

'What troubles you, Father?' inquired the princess of the king, who was sitting in deepest despondency. Her father replied, 'It seems that you must become the consort of the king of Tibet'. The princess exclaimed, 'I will never go to such an evil, distant land! It has no Dharma, no amusements and I will be unable to see my family'. Her father replied, 'Do not say such things. You have no choice in the matter. The king of Tibet is a manifestation who seems to possess clairvoyance and other magical powers. His minister produced a letter in reply to whatever questions I asked him, without even returning to Tibet. If the king discovers that you have refused his invitation, an army of fifty thousand manifestations will descend upon us. I will be killed, you will be seized and every city in the kingdom will be captured. You must go!'

The princess then said to herself, 'Turning my back on my homeland, I must depart for the wild and wicked land of Tibet, a distant country that has no Dharma. I will never see my family again. Yet

I cannot disobey my father's command'. Weeping, she addressed these words to the king:

> Alas, my only father, O Great King!
> The Land of Snows is a wild and barbaric place.
> Untouched by Dharma, Tibet is a continent of darkness
> Whose inhabitants are an evil breed, a race of flesh-eating
>   outcasts.
> Famished and impoverished, it resembles the realm of
>   hungry ghosts.
> If I, your daughter, am compelled to go to such a place,
> Give me the object of your veneration,
> The image of Akshobhya-vajra, the deity who fulfils all
>   needs and desires,
> Whose qualities when seen, heard, contemplated or touched
> Are beyond imagination.
> Give me, too, the image of Maitreya, Wheel of Dharma,
> Precious protector of loving-kindness, regent of the Sage,
> Excellently endowed with the major and minor signs of
>   buddhahood,
> A treasure that is the source of all benefits and happiness.
> Give me the sandalwood image of the reverend Tara, the
>   Compassionate One,
> To dispel hindrances and interferences.
> Give me the precious herbs *tagshade* and *ratnade*[98]
> To alleviate poverty in the land of Tibet.
> Give me the lapis lazuli begging-bowl,
> That precious source of delights that satisfies all desires
> And is the basis for enjoyment of the glory of the ambrosial
>   nectar that is food and drink.
> As the Land of Snows is a place of hunger and thirst,
> Give me many precious treasures.
> It is a realm of freezing cold;
> Give me, therefore, sufficient clothing for a lifetime.
> In the wild land of Tibet
> How should I behave?
> Only father, O King, advise me!

The princess's lament caused her tears to flow as she petitioned her father. Words of kindness then sprang from the depth of the king's heart, and he made this reply:

You, O daughter, who is as dear as my own heart:
This especially blessed land known as Tibet
Has towering mountains, unsullied soils,
And snowy ranges that resemble a wild sheep's nape.
Cool and beautiful, it is the abode of gods, a celestial
    mansion.
Miraculous and marvellous, it is the foundation on which all
    benefits and happiness arise.
It is the source of the four great rivers[99] and is beautified by
    shrubs and forests.
The five grains thrive,[100]
And the various precious materials abound.
Animals prosper, and the populace enjoys an annual bounty
    of butter.
The sovereign is a deity; his retinue are bodhisattvas.
Although the sacred Dharma has yet to reach Tibet, it has its
    royal laws.
It is to such a place, my daughter, that you must go.
My tutelary deity, Akshobhya-vajra,
And the reverend Maitreya, Wheel of Dharma,
Were cast by manifestation-sculptors
From a mound of accumulated precious materials of various
    kinds
As a tutelary deity for the Indian Dharma-king Krikin,
And were consecrated by Buddha Kashyapa himself
When a human lifespan was twenty thousand years.
First, the Lord Maitreya, Wheel of Dharma, was created.
Next the image of Akshobhya-vajra was cast,
A creation of boundless wonder.
Ornamented with the major and minor signs of greatness,
It is the source of benefits and happiness,
A symbol for the faithful
Whose qualities on being seen, heard, contemplated or
    touched are beyond imagination,
An image without comparison in the world
For the accumulation of merit by future sentient beings.
It was revealed by prophesy
That this was to be the Teacher of Gods and Humans,
King of Shakya, at the age of eight.
When these images were made, the world was filled with
    light,

And the gods caused flowers to fall like rain.
Although this excellent symbol,
Endowed with such qualities,
Is as dear to me as my own eyes,
I give it to you, my beautiful daughter.
This image of the reverend Maitreya, Wheel of Dharma,
I give to you to lead all beings to virtue.
This self-created sandalwood image of the reverend Tara
I give to you, my beautiful daughter,
To increase goodness, having thoroughly pacified
The Eight Fears and other hindrances.
The precious herbs *tagshade* and *ratnade*
I give to you to ease the pain of poverty.
The great lapis lazuli begging-bowl,
A precious treasure that satisfies all needs and desires,
I give to you in order that ambrosial food and drink may fall
    like rain
To assuage the suffering of thirst and hunger.
Precious gold and silver, fine silks and ornaments,
A caravan of elephants, camels and mules,
Provisions for the journey, and food and clothing:
Whatever you desire, I give to you, my daughter.
I will send ten handsome girls of good birth and pleasing
    disposition
As a retinue to befriend you in your sorrow.
Alas, my daughter from whom I am loath to part!
Hold this, my final testament, in your heart:
In the royal palace of the Land of Snows,
When associating with the Tibetan ministers or commoners,
Behave in the following way....

So saying, the king gave her boundless essential advice on worldly affairs and social customs. He then presented gifts to the Tibetan ministers and held a celebration that defied the imagination.

As it was impossible to transport the images of Akshobhya-vajra and Maitreya by carriage, the king desired to place each upon the back of a beast of burden, but no animal was capable of the feat. Only a pair of white manifestation-*dzomo* could carry them, and one of the images was then placed upon the back of each beast.[101] Together with the many loads of treasures, Princess Tritsun then set off for Tibet, mounted upon a white mule and surrounded by the ten handsome girls and the Tibetan ministers. The Nepalese ministers, with their retinues and servants, accompanied the princess all the way to the capital of Mangyul.

In the narrow defiles where the waters raged against the rocks, the beasts of burden were unloaded and the treasures were carried forward one by one. It is even said that the two images walked over the rocks upon their own legs! The baggage was then reloaded on the mules, camels and elephants, and with each of the statues riding again upon a *dzomo*, the caravan finally reached Tibet, where it was welcomed on a grand scale by the ministers and commoners, bearing all manner of musical instruments.

When King Songtsen Gampo arrived at the place of the festivities and met Princess Tritsun, three different perceptions of the event arose. To the Buddhas of the Ten Directions, it seemed that the king and queen were striving for the benefit of sentient beings by means of the Twelve Deeds.[102] To the Bodhisattvas of the Ten Stages, it appeared that the sublime Avalokiteshvara and the reverend Bhrikuti, having manifested themselves as the king and the queen respectively, were working to benefit beings. To the black-headed commoners, it appeared that the royal couple were offering drinks to one another while spinning yarn together.

The royal palaces

After the royal couple, accompanied by the assembly of ministers, had taken up residence in the palace, the king never ventured beyond its confines, but remained before the image of his tutelary deity, giving offerings and praying. Princess Tritsun thought to herself, 'As the king is beautified by his race, physique and glories, the fear of foreign armies must be the cause of his reluctance to leave the palace. I shall therefore find a way to quell his uneasiness. If I supplicate the lapis lazuli begging-bowl, untold quantities of food and drink will arise. I shall give these to the people of Tibet and set them to work in order to build a mighty fortress'.

She then petitioned the king and consulted the Inner and Outer Ministers and all the members of the cabinet. The lapis lazuli begging-bowl, filled with samples of every kind of sustenance, was

The Nepalese princess Tritsun negotiates a dangerous gorge
on her journey to Tibet

placed upon a precious throne, and prayers were offered to it. All manner of food and drink that could be desired then arose and was distributed to the Tibetan people, and the foundations of the fortress were laid in the Wood-female-sheep Year [635].[103] It was of great height, having thirty stories. Each side was one *gyangdrag* in length, its great gate faced the south and it contained nine hundred apartments.[104] Including the king's personal residence at its summit, there were one thousand apartments in all. The entire fortress was beautified with precious embossed beam-ends, parapets, eaves, roofs and the tinkling of bells and chimes.[105]

As regards its grandeur and the beauty of its design, it resembled the Victorious Celestial Mansion of Indra, King of Gods. One could never tire of the sight of it, as it was ornamented with all manner of precious materials and silk furnishings of various sizes. It was indeed most pleasing to the eye. As regards the terror it inspired, it resembled Langkapuri, the City of Ogres. Weapons and ten red lances with pennants were displayed upon every turret, and silk banners were suspended from them. As to its defence, five people alone could defend it from attack by a foreign army. Furthermore, to the south at Chagpori, the 'Iron Hill,' a pit ten fathoms deep was excavated, planks of wood were laid across it and these were covered with bricks. Thus, if a single horse were to gallop across the pit, the sound of ten would result.

To the south, Tritsun's personal residence, a nine-storeyed palace known as the Celestial Auspicious Mansion of Draglha, was constructed on the model of the Fortress of Bricks. It was spacious, of a goodly height and beautified with many designs. An iron bridge, adorned with silks, yak-tails, bells and chimes, linked the residences of the king and queen, and they would walk back and forth across it. The sovereign and his ministers held a great celebration to mark the completion of the matchless, marvellous and exquisite palace.

This chapter,
in which the Nepalese princess
Tritsun is invited to Tibet,
is the twelfth.

13

The Chinese
princess Kongjo is
invited to Tibet

inister Gar came before King Songtsen Gampo and said, 'Command me to invite a Chinese princess to Tibet'. Assenting, the king handed him seven golden coins and said, 'Give these coins as a gift to accompany our invitation'. He then handed Gar a suit of precious armour studded with rubies and said, 'Give this armour as the bride-price for the princess'. He also gave him a full *dre*-measure of gold dust and said, 'Spend this gold as the need arises. The Chinese emperor will ask three questions in succession. On each occasion, give him one of these'. So saying, he handed the minister three letters in the form of scrolls.

Many loads of necessities for the journey, clothes, ornaments and the like, were loaded onto camels, mules and other beasts of burden, and were dispatched to China. 'By day or night, and wherever the paths or precipices grow difficult, make supplications to the reverend Tara as you proceed', commanded the king. Gar then took the loads containing all the gifts that the king had given him, and together with one hundred horsemen, set out for China on the eighth day of the fourth month of the Fire-male-monkey Year [636], which coincided with the constellation of Pushya.

The caravan eventually arrived at the gate of Trashi Trigo, the palace in the city of Zimshing where the Chinese emperor Taizong resided.[106] This city embraced a hundred thousand households, each side was the length of a day's journey, and it had four great gates: it was terrifying to behold! By coincidence, the ministers of the Dharma-king of India, the warrior-king Gesar,[107] the Persian king of wealth and the king of the Uighurs[108] had also arrived, each accompanied by one hundred horsemen, and each desiring the hand of the princess. Thus, suitors of five races with five hundred horsemen arrived simultaneously before the Chinese emperor.

The Indians were located at the eastern gate, Gesar's ministers were in the south, the Persians in the west and the Uighurs were at the northern gate, but the Tibetan ministers remained at the northeast corner of the city. The others presented their gifts and had audiences with the emperor, but when the Tibetan ministers requested an audience, they were instructed to wait. Seven days passed, and when the emperor and his retinue came out of the palace, Gar offered the seven gold coins as a token of his invitation. He then placed the precious ruby-studded lapis lazuli armour before the emperor and said, 'Great Emperor, this armour is endowed with many qualities. Whenever pestilence afflicts people or livestock, if you circumambulate the city while wearing this armour, all pestilence will abate. When frosts or hail threaten, if you circumambulate the fields while wearing it, disaster will be averted. If you wear it in times of conflict, you will be victorious. No one in the world can estimate its value. I offer it to you as the bride-price for your daughter. Grant that your wise princess may become the consort of the Tibetan king'. Thus he petitioned.

The emperor fixed Gar with a daggerlike gaze, and he and his retinue let forth great peals of unbecoming, scornful laughter. The emperor replied, 'Such an impossible request is astounding in the extreme. I am the scion of an unbroken royal line that stretches back from the present day to the first Chinese emperors. Your Tibetan king can never be my equal in strength or wealth. Even though you have come from a distant land, return now and ask your king if he is able to promulgate royal laws based on the Ten Virtues. If he is able to do this, I will give him my daughter. But if he fails, I will not send her'. Thus he spoke.

Minister Gar then replied, 'If I were to make the round trip between China and Tibet each time you ask a question, it would be impossible for us to conclude this business. In reply to your inquiry, our Tibetan king sent this'. So saying, he presented the first scroll to the emperor. The emperor opened the letter and read the following message, written in golden Chinese characters upon blue paper: 'You, the Emperor of China, have laws, yet I, the king of Tibet, still lack the Dharma-law. While rejoicing in your royal laws based on the Ten Virtues, if you give me your daughter, I will create five thousand manifestations of myself, and I will be able to establish laws based on the Ten Virtues in a single day. Is this not miraculous? After I have done this, if you still refuse to give me your daughter, I will dispatch an army of fifty thousand manifestations. You will be killed, the princess seized and your entire realm vanquished'.

As these were the contents of the letter, the emperor became very afraid, and although he was terrified, he concealed his fear and said, 'Your Tibetan king is boastful in the extreme. Can he build shrines in this land of Tibet? If he can, I will give him my daughter, but if he cannot, I will not release her. Go now and ask your master.' Thus he spoke. Gar then placed the second scroll into the emperor's hands and said, 'It is not feasible for me to travel to Tibet on account of every question. Here is the reply to your question; please read it'. The emperor opened the letter and read the following: 'In your land of China, the Dharma has been promulgated and you are able to construct shrines. As I, the king of Tibet, am unable to construct shrines, while you rejoice in such work, give me your daughter and I will create five thousand manifestations of myself to build one hundred and eight shrines, the doors of which will all face towards China. Is this not miraculous? After I have done this, if you still refuse to give me your daughter, I will dispatch an army of fifty thousand manifestations, you will be killed, the princess seized and your entire realm vanquished'.

As these were the contents of the letter, the emperor grew very afraid, and although he was afraid, he again concealed his fear. 'Your Tibetan king is brazen in the extreme. Does entertainment for the five sensual pleasures exist in your country? If so, I will give you my daughter, otherwise I will not. Go now and ask'. Thus he spoke. Having placed the final scroll into the emperor's hands, Gar said, 'As it is impossible to travel to Tibet for every question, and as this is the reply to your words, please read it.' Thus he replied.

Having opened the letter, the emperor read the following: 'You, the Emperor of China, possess great wealth. Although I, the king of Tibet, lack such riches, if you, rejoicing in your wealth, give me your daughter, I will emanate five thousand manifestations of myself to create riches in the form of gold, silver, grain, fine silk, clothing, ornaments and foods. These will be comparable to the wealth of the gods. Moreover, having opened trade routes in each of the four directions, all the treasures of the borderlands will be accumulated effortlessly at my gates, and I will become rich. Is this not miraculous? If I do this and you still refuse to give me your daughter, I will dispatch an army of fifty thousand manifestations, you will be killed, the princess seized and your entire realm vanquished'.

As these were the contents of the letter, the emperor grew even more terrified and thought to himself, 'Although there are many who desire my daughter, in the end I may have no choice other than to give her to the Tibetan king!' With these thoughts, he returned to the palace with a heavy heart.

Then the princess's father the emperor, her mother the queen, her brother the prince and the princess herself all consulted together. Her father said, 'The Dharma came from India, and on account of this great boon conferred upon us in former times, I will give my daughter to the Indian Dharma-king.' Being obsessed with riches, her mother said, 'Let us give her to the Persian king of wealth.' The prince, who delighted in athletic prowess, said, 'Give her to the king of the Uighurs.' The princess who prized physical beauty, said, 'The appearance of one's lifelong companion, one's spouse, is the most important'. Having said this, she felt inclined towards the warrior-king Gesar. No one, however, came forward in favour of Tibet. The emperor said to his daughter, 'I am impartial towards your suitors, and I will give you to the one with the sharpest wits. Let us therefore test their intelligence'.

Trials of Minister Gar

Now the emperor had a life-protecting piece of turquoise, known as Zhaggormo, which was about the size of a small shield and possessed a wondrous lustre. It had a hole at one end, another in the centre, and between these two holes, it was hollow like a piece of bamboo. The emperor handed a silken thread to the five ministers, saying, 'I will give my daughter to whomever can thread the silk through the hole in the piece of turquoise'. Being physically stronger than Gar, the other ministers snatched the turquoise first, and trying various means to draw the thread through the ornament, they passed it from hand to hand for many days. As none succeeded, they finally gave it to Minister Gar: 'We have failed, despite all our efforts. See for yourself if you can do it'. So saying they gave him the turquoise and silken thread. Now Gar, being a man of intelligence, had succoured a Chinese ant with food and milk from the outset. The ant now climbed onto Gar's thumb, and he tied the thread around its waist. Holding the ant securely, he placed it into one of the holes in the turquoise. With the ornament in his hand, he blew into one hole, and propelled by his breath, the ant finally emerged from the other hole. Minister Gar then untied the thread from the ant's waist, and gripping the thread tightly, pulled it right through the turquoise. 'As it was I who succeeded, give me the princess', Gar said to the emperor, but the emperor replied, 'I wish to test your intelligence again'. He treated the Tibetans with contempt and refused to relinquish his daughter.

The next day the emperor gave each of the ministers five hundred sheep and said, 'I will give my daughter to whomever can slaughter and butcher all the sheep, consume all the meat and process all the hides by tomorrow'. Each of the Tibetan ministers then slaughtered a sheep and butchered it, and the meat was heaped together on one side and the hides on the other. The meat was then cut into pieces the size of a thimble and was arranged on a bed of salt. The ministers then dropped each morsel straight down their throats. By eating it in this way, all the meat was consumed. As to the hides, the Tibetan ministers sat in a row, each one worked a hide, and then passed it to the next person. When the hides reached the end of the row, they were ready to be treated with oil. Each minister then applied the oil, worked the hides again and passed them back along the line. By the time the hide arrived back at the beginning of the row, it was finished. When the Tibetans looked around at the other ministers, they saw that they had not completed a single hide. Gar then said to the emperor, 'As it was I who succeeded where the others failed, give me the princess', but the emperor replied, 'I wish to test your intelligence again', and refused to relinquish the girl.

The emperor then gave each group of suitors one hundred pitchers of barley beer and said, 'I will give the princess to whomever can drink all the barley beer before noon tomorrow, without spilling any and without getting drunk'. Gar then set a small bowl before each of the Tibetan ministers and served a little beer to each. By taking one mouthful at a time from the very beginning, they soon drank all the barley beer. None was spilled, nor did they become drunk. Having done this, they looked around at the other ministers, who had filled large cups with barley beer, and fearing that they might be unable to finish it, had gulped it down. They had became drunk, vomited and spilled the beer. Gar then said to the emperor, 'As it was I who succeeded where the others failed, give the princess to me!' but the emperor replied, 'I wish to test your intelligence again'. He treated the Tibetans contemptuously and still refused to relinquish the girl.

The emperor then gave the ministers one hundred mares and one hundred foals and said, 'I will give the princess to whomever can determine which foal belongs to which mare'. The other ministers were confounded, but Gar separated the foals from the mares, and for a whole day gave them fodder but no water. The next day, he sent the foals back to the mares, whereupon each young one found its own mother and was suckled by her. Thus Gar discovered which beasts belonged together. 'As I succeeded where the others failed, give me the princess', he said, but the emperor replied, 'I wish to test your intelligence again', and still refused to relinquish the girl.

The next day, the emperor presented the ministers with one hundred hens and one hundred chicks and said, 'I will give the princess to whomever can determine which hen and which chick belong together'. The other ministers were again at a loss, but Gar scattered brewing barley on the ground. The birds faced the grain and ate it together in pairs. Those that ate with their necks close to the ground and behaved aggressively were the chicks, and those that did not were the hens. Thus Gar determined which was which. 'As I succeeded and the others failed, give the princess to me,' he said, but the emperor replied, 'I wish to test your intelligence again', and still he refused to relinquish the princess.

The emperor then gave the ministers one hundred logs of *sam*-wood[109] and said, 'I will give the princess to whomever can determine which end was nearer the crown of the tree and which to the foot'. The other ministers were unable to tell the two ends apart, but Gar took the logs to the riverbank and threw them in. The ends that had been at the foot of the tree were heavier and sank, and those that had been at the crown were lighter and floated. 'As I succeeded where the others failed, give the princess to me', Gar said, but the emperor replied, 'I will test your intelligence yet again', and he still refused to relinquish the princess.

One evening, a great drum was beaten in the palace, and the other ministers proceeded thither. The hostess of the Tibetan ministers said, 'The other ministers have gone to the palace. Are you not going also? It would surely be best if you do'. Gar replied, 'But I was not invited, nor do I understand the significance of this drum'. The hostess replied, 'If the other ministers have gone, even though you have not been invited, you should go anyway!' Thus she spoke.

Then Minister Gar, filled with suspicions on account of the drum, led the Tibetan ministers from their residence to the palace, but as he passed each doorway, he marked it with the sap of the indigo plant. Thus they eventually reached the palace, where the other ministers had already assembled. That evening, after the emperor had entertained them, and as the night was dark, he said, 'You ministers shall now return to your lodgings. I will give my

The Chinese emperor entertains the Tibetan ministers

daughter to whomever can find his way back successfully'. Thus he spoke. Gar borrowed a butter-lamp from the palace, and leading the Tibetans past each doorway in turn, proceeded by observing the marks that he had made earlier and was thus able to relocate his lodgings. At dawn the following day, the Tibetans went to see how the other ministers had fared: some had entered the wrong houses, and others, failing to find their quarters, had slept in the street. Gar then said to the emperor, 'I found my lodgings, but the others failed. I therefore request the princess', but the emperor replied, 'In three days' time, on the plain before the eastern gate, three hundred bright and beautiful girls, adorned in their finery, will be arranged in a row with the princess among them. I will give her to whomever can identify her'.

The final test

At that time, Gar was cohabiting with his hostess, and he behaved lovingly towards her. Having seduced her with food and drink, they were conversing happily: 'A year has passed since we ministers arrived in China. My wits are the sharpest, but every time I win the princess, the emperor behaves with contempt and refuses to relinquish her. Although I have never seen the miraculous Kongjo, she is as famous as the Blue Turquoise Dragon. As you and the princess seem on the most intimate terms, you must tell me exactly how to recognise her. This is of the greatest importance, because in three days' time, Kongjo will be placed amid three hundred girls standing in a row on the plain at the eastern gate. The emperor has said that he will give the princess to whomever can identify her. On account of their superior strength, the other ministers will make their selection first. It is possible that any one of them will recognise her and therefore win her. That will make it very difficult for me. Even if they fail and I succeed, it is still possible that the emperor will behave contemptuously again and refuse to relinquish her. Moreover, if I have the good karma to win her, as I do not know what she looks like, you must describe her carefully. I will become your husband and remain here with you. I can send the princess to Tibet with the other ministers'. So saying, he gave her a gift of a full *dre*-measure of gold dust.

The hostess replied, 'You Tibetan ministers are in the right, and the emperor is indeed biased against you. But he is not alone; not a single person is favourably disposed towards Tibet. It is said that your country is like the realm of the hungry ghosts. The princess is hoping that she will be won by one of the other ministers, and if they outwit you on a single occasion, she will be given to one of them. As the princess, this miraculous Kongjo, is my mistress, I know her intimately. She is skilled in Chinese astrology, and if she uses this means to discover that it was I who betrayed her, I will be put to death. I therefore dare not tell you how to recognise her'.

Then Gar said, 'I know a way for you to tell me that will never be revealed by astrology!' Having closed all the doors inside the house, he arranged three large hearth-stones on the floor and placed a great cauldron filled with water upon them. Next, he scattered the feathers of various species of birds on the water and covered the cauldron with a red shield. He seated his hostess on the shield and covered her head with a pot which was itself covered with a net. He bored a hole in the pot and inserted a copper trumpet into the hole through the net. 'Even if it is revealed by astrology that you told me about the princess through this trumpet, no one will ever believe it! Now, describe her carefully.' Then the hostess spoke:

> Great Minister, heed well:
> The miraculous Princess Kongjo
> Is no taller than the other girls.
> Nor is her natural form more beautiful.
> Nor are her ornaments or clothes finer.
> As for her characteristics:

> Her body is blue, tinged with pink, and from her mouth wafts the scent of the blue *utpala*-lotus. Her body is so fragrant that a turquoise honeybee circles about her. On her right cheek is a design like the spots on a die, and her left cheek bears the mark of a lotus. Above the vermilion spot in the centre of her brow is an image of Tara, the size of a grain of barley. On her teeth are beauty spots, and there are marks of loveliness upon her neck. Princess Kongjo will not be at the end of the row of the three hundred assembled girls, nor will she be in the centre. She will be near the sixth girl from the left. As the body and raiments of the princess are taboo and no part of them may be touched,

take an unused arrow with a length of silk attached. She will
be wearing five layers of silken garments with an attractive
scent. Catch the collar of her clothes with the notch of the arrow and lead her out.

Gar then dismantled the structure. His body and mind were both
brimming with happiness, and he said: 'In former times, we Tibetan ministers always enjoyed success. Now we must succeed
again. We did not come to China to conduct trade, nor did we come
to protect an ally. If we can bring this princess to Tibet, we will
have succeeded. But we must study the situation well: in three
days' time, it is certain that the princess will be given to whomever recognises her among the three hundred girls. We must therefore discern wisdom from foolishness!'

Three days later, three hundred girls adorned in their finery were
lined up on the plain at the eastern gate, and all the people of China
had assembled for the spectacle. Then the emperor spoke: 'Let the
ministers make their selections in the same order as before'. First
the ministers of the Dharma-king of India came forward, and from
the centre of the row they eventually chose two finely dressed and
beautiful girls. 'If this one is not the princess, the other one certainly is, so they will do', they said as they departed, angrily grinding their teeth. Next, the ministers of the Persian king of wealth
came forward, they too led out two beautiful girls, and repeating
the Indians' words, they also departed. Then the ministers of the
warrior-king Gesar did the same, as did the Uighur ministers.

Minister Gar saw this, and knowing that none of the girls who
had been selected was the princess, rejoiced greatly and smiled to
himself. With the arrow in his hand, he led the Tibetan ministers
towards the lefthand end of the row. To the first girl, Gar said:

> This girl looks like a butcher's daughter:
> Her hands are so red!
> The next looks like a potter's daughter:
> Her hands are so cracked!
> The next looks like a carpenter's daughter:
> Her clothes are so grey!
> The next looks like an armourer's daughter:
> Her upper garments are so dark!
> The next looks like a tanner's daughter:

Minister Gar selects Princess Kongjo from the assembly of three hundred girls

She wears so many leather straps!
The next looks like a blacksmith's daughter:
The hem of her gown is so black!
The next is probably the daughter of a silk weaver:
Does she not wear fine silks?
But the next is without doubt Princess Kongjo.
Her body is blue, tinged with pink,
From her mouth comes the scent of the blue *utpala*-lotus,
So sweet that a turquoise honeybee circles her.
On her cheeks are the marks of dice and the lotus.
On her forehead is the sign of the reverend Tara.
Her teeth are perfect and bear beauty spots.
This miraculous girl is lovelier than the others.

Gar enumerated these and other qualities, and as he led her out by
her collar with the notch of the arrow, the weeping princess followed the ministers.[110] Gar, rejoicing in his heart, then sang the
following song to the princess, accompanied by Tonmi Sambhota
and Dri Seru Gongton:

Aha! Miraculous!
You, Princess Kongjo,
Heed my words:
Delighting in auspicious experience,
In the royal palace
Built of five precious materials,
In the kingdom of Tibet,
Is a god who is the ruler of his people:
Songtsen Gampo,
Made majestic by his race, complexion and glory.
Once you behold him, your heart and mind will be
    captivated.
Great is his compassion;
His kingdom is governed in accordance with the Dharma;
His subjects obey his commands.
The king, ministers, retinue and subjects
Sing songs of joy.
The sun of Dharma shines.
The lamp of heroism is held aloft.
The mountains are clad in trees of every kind.
On the broad earth,

The five types of grain flourish in great profusion.
Gold, silver, copper, iron
And many other precious materials are found.
Yaks, horses and sheep all prosper.
Such is the happiness there.
Aha! Miraculous!
Princess Kongjo, listen!

Thus they sang. 'If this is true, then Tibet is similar to our own country', thought the princess as she wiped her tears away and followed the minister. Gar placed her upon a horse and led her to the marketplace saying, 'We Tibetans are superior to both the Indians and the Uighurs. I will take the princess, while all the other ministers remain behind, sucking on their fingers!'

The people of China poured forth laments and wailed, 'Our wise princess has been taken by the evil Tibetans'. The emperor said to the other ministers, 'As you are our relatives by marriage, take the girls whom you have chosen and return to your respective lands'. Minister Gar then told the princess to prepare for the journey to Tibet and sent her away.

Kongjo's departure

The princess returned to the palace, and her father the emperor said, 'You must now go to Tibet to become the Tibetan king's consort'. The princess replied, 'I shall never go to such a distant place, devoid of Dharma. It is an evil land where I cannot see my family'. Her father said, 'Do not speak so. You have no choice. The Tibetan king seems to be endowed with powers of clairvoyance and magic. Whatever questions I posed, his minister gave a reply without returning to Tibet. Once he learns that you have refused his invitation, an army of fifty thousand will descend on us, I will be killed, you will be seized and our land and fortresses captured. What can we do? Just look at his minister's way of doing things! It is best that you go'. The princess prostrated herself before her father and made this supplication:

Are these the instructions given by my only father, the
    emperor?
Are they given by my mother?

Have these words been forced from my brother?
Alas! Impossible! How strange!
I am to be sent to this country of Tibet,
To this Land of Snows,
A rugged place of freezing cold,
Abounding in evil deities, nagas, demons and ogres,
Where the snowy mountains resemble the fangs of a
    ferocious beast
And the rocky ranges are like the horns of a wild yak.
The inhabitants' thoughts are unvirtuous; their minds are
    miserable.
No grain grows there; it is a land of famines.
The Tibetans are flesh-eating outcasts, a race of ogres.
Their behaviour is coarse; they are a barbaric people.
It is an uncivilised place, untouched by the feet of the
    Buddha.
Lacking the Dharma, it is a continent of dimmed intelligence.
Having no objects or places of worship,
It lacks symbols for the accumulation of merit.

If I must go to such a place,
I request my father's object of veneration, the tutelary deity
    Shakyamuni.
The snowy land is a realm of hunger:
I request precious supplies.
The snowy land is freezing cold:
I request clothes to warm me for a lifetime.
In Tibet, the outcasts do not distinguish between clean and
    filthy:
I therefore request maidservants to console me in my grief.
In such a barbaric land,
Tell me how I should behave
When I keep company with the people of Tibet.

Having wiped away her tears, she made this request. Her father then gave her these kindly instructions:

You, my daughter, who are as dear as my own eyes:
Tibet, the Land of Snows,
Is especially exalted compared with other countries:
A place where snowy mountains form natural stupas,

Where the Four Lakes are laid out like a turquoise
    mandala,[111]
A continent where miraculous flowers of gold are found,
A cool and beautiful abode of gods, a celestial mansion,
The source of the Four Rivers, beautified by forests.
The five types of grain all thrive there, and precious
    materials of many kinds are found.
Animals abound in every place,
And the inhabitants enjoy an annual bounty of butter.
In this holy land of such miraculous qualities,
In a palace beautified with precious adornings,
The ruler of the people, a god who serves as king,
Is the true, sublime Great Compassionate One.
He is a sovereign endowed with skill and compassion,
Abstaining from the Ten Unvirtuous Acts,
Abiding by the laws of the Ten Virtuous Acts.
Enjoying power, glory and all desires,
He is a king of infinite qualities, scion of the gods.
His all-courageous, all-wise retinue consists of bodhisattvas.
You, my daughter, are going to such a place as this.
As the basis for your accumulation of merit, my beautiful
    one,
Here is my object of worship, this image of Shakyamuni,
Made at the behest of Indra
By the divine craftsman Vishvakarma
From ten precious materials,
And consecrated by the Buddha himself.
The Victorious One has said
That Buddhahood will be attained swiftly
By seeing, hearing, recalling, touching or praying to this
    matchless image.
Although I hold this Jowo, source of beneficence and joy,
As dear as my own heart,
I give it to you, my beautiful daughter.
Many precious supplies and a treasury of jewels
I give to you, my beautiful daughter.
Many valuable materials that are dear to me
I give to you, my beautiful daughter.
A great document case made from gold and turquoise

With the three hundred and sixty volumes of knowledge
And many varied ornaments of gold and turquoise
I give to you, my beautiful daughter.
Many recipes, foodstuffs
And methods for preparing drinks,
A golden saddle, a turquoise saddlecloth and more
I give to you, my beautiful daughter.
A mattress of fine silk with the design of eight lions, birds,
    magic trees, dice and jewels,
I give them to you to engender wonder in the king.
Chinese astrological tables and the three hundred fields of
    knowledge,
A mirror which shows good karma and bad
I give to you, my beautiful daughter.
The discipline of architecture, by which buildings are
    beautified,
Pleasing ornaments of special sublimity
And the sixty artistic disciplines
I give to you, my beautiful daughter.
Remedies for the four hundred and four diseases,
One hundred examination procedures,
Five investigative techniques and six diagnoses,
Four ways to concoct medicines and more, I give to you.
Fine silk clothes and glossy silks to warm you for a lifetime,
Ornamented garments of many colours,
Twenty thousand of these I give to you, my daughter.
Twenty-five girls of race and complexion that are a delight to
    behold,
Of sympathetic mind to console you in your grief;
I give them to you as a retinue.
Alas! You, my daughter, from whom I am loath to part:
As these are my final kindly words to you, hold them in your
    heart.
In order to subdue the people of the Snowy Land,
Your actions and behaviour should be like this:
Maintain a broad perspective, be skilful in your actions;
Be wise in all your thoughts and deeds;
Lay a good foundation with kind and thoughtful words.
Show reverence to your lord and loving-kindness to your
    retinue;
Be chaste, modest and conscientious.

He gave these and countless other pieces of advice necessary for the conduct of worldly affairs. Although her father held her in his arms as if unable to part with her, he knew that the princess had to go to Tibet, and he bade her countless farewells. The princess, accompanied by her maidservants, came before Minister Gar and said, 'The Jowo Shakyamuni will be taken to the land of the Great Minister. We will also travel to Tibet with untold wealth. Are there fertile soils, *dosinzen*-plants, tree-roses, *tsadrema*-grass or turnips in your homeland?'[112] To these questions, Gar replied, 'As we have everything except the last, bring some turnip seeds and radish seeds as well'. The Jowo Shakyamuni was then placed upon the carriage that was to be used to transport it. The task of drawing the wagon was entrusted to the two strongest men in China, Lhaga and Luga.

Moreover, multitudes of horses, mules, camels and so on, laden with precious items, fine silks, clothing, ornaments and necessities for the journey, were dispatched, and innumerable gifts were given to the Tibetan ministers. Princess Kongjo, wearing many precious ornaments and accompanied by her retinue of twenty-five beautiful girls, each mounted upon a horse, were escorted on their way by her father and mother and their retinue of ministers. After both of Kongjo's parents, with heavy hearts, gave her countless weighty and beneficial words of advice on worldly affairs, she finally set off for Tibet.

Among those who had come to see her off, the Tibetan minister named Dri Seru Gongton, being jealous of Gar, said, 'If one intelligent minister remains here in the princess's stead, there will be harmony between China and Tibet'. Having spoken, he turned his gaze upon Minister Gar. The emperor said, 'Since this beautiful princess of mine has been won by you Tibetans, Gar must remain with me in her stead'. Realising that Seru Gongton was jealous of him, Minister Gar said, 'I will create harmony between China and Tibet. I will remain'. Gar then led Tonmi Sambhota and Nyang Trizang to one side and said to them, 'I will only stay in China for five months, during which time I will unleash my evil designs. At the end of this period, send me a messenger disguised as a beggar'. Then all the ministers, surrounding the Jowo and the princess, proceeded to Tibet.

Lhaga and Luga transport the image of Buddha Shakyamuni to Tibet

Minister Gar's revenge

As Gar remained in China alone, the emperor gave him a woman and an excellent residence as a salary. But as he was deeply sorrowful and his mind was filled with sadness, Gar did not approach the woman, and as he did not eat, he grew pale and emaciated. The minister placed a rotting hide under his bed, and his body took on its repugnant odour. He applied vermilion to his right cheek and indigo to his left cheek, and coated the surroundings of his bed with phlegm that was stained with pus and blood. Thereupon his Chinese mistress said, 'Great Minister, I smell a strong odour on your body, and your complexion is pale. What ails you?' Gar replied, 'I have contracted a disease caused by the heat. Have you not noticed?'

She then informed the emperor, who, being worried, went to see him. 'Great Minister, what has happened?' he asked. Gar replied, 'I have contracted a disease caused by the heat'. So saying he vomited phlegm that was stained with pus and blood. Noticing the strong odour of Gar's body, the emperor commanded, 'Send a skilled physician here tomorrow', and with that, he departed. Then Gar said to his Chinese mistress, 'Woman, your defilements are so great that tomorrow when the physician arrives, he will be unable to read my pulse. Go and sleep at the house of a neighbour'. So saying, he sent her away. Gar then built a tall throne of bricks and tied one end of a cord to a beam on top of the throne and tied the other end to his penis. Placing the crown of his head on the ground, all his pulses became disturbed.

The next day, the emperor brought the physician to him. Having examined his pulse, this skilled physician said, 'As all the pulses of your body have become disturbed, it is difficult to diagnose your illness. It is not caused by wind, bile, phlegm or a combination of these. It is not a disease caused by the eighteen great *chipaidon* infant-harming sprites. It is not one of the one thousand and eighty diseases brought on by *gegrig* obstructive sprites. Nor is it a disease caused by *chungpoidon* goblins.[113] It appears to be a malady brought upon the centre of your heart by the unhappiness of your mind. It would indeed be difficult for any medical science or religious observances to help you'. Thus he spoke. Then the emperor

said, 'Let this physician come tomorrow and the day after and ex-
amine him again'.

Before the physician returned the following day, Gar concealed
a cat in his armpit and tied a string to its leg. When the physician
felt the pulse at the end of the string, he said, 'Your pulse is like
that of the lowliest wild animal!' So saying, he departed. The next
day, Gar hid a rooster in his armpit and tied a string to its foot. The
physician felt the pulse at the end of the string and said, 'Your
pulse is like that of the basest fowl!'

The emperor was greatly alarmed and said, 'Great Minister, as
you are a person of intelligence, do you know a remedy for this
disease? I will do whatever is required'. When the emperor had
said this, Gar thought to himself, 'Now I have an opportunity!'
'Great Emperor, this disease of mine is caused by the displeasure
of the divine guardians of Tibet at your seizure of me. It would
help if I were go to the summit of a high mountain from which the
ranges of Tibet are visible. There I shall supplicate the gods. Following this, I will require a sack filled with the ashes of fine silk; a
paunch filled with blood from the spleens of slaughtered sheep; a
lance-shaft made from charcoal, three fathoms long and free of
cracks; and a yellow horse with a red head. Each of these things
will be difficult to find, let alone to gather all together. It will even
be difficult for the emperor to hear about them. In truth, it is likely
that I shall die. Upon my death, eighteen evil omens will arise.
China and Tibet will be divided. As the king of Tibet has the power
of clairvoyance, once he learns of my demise, an army will be dispatched to destroy the whole of China. I came to this distant place
only to be abandoned by my fellow ministers. My body has been
wracked by disease, and although I think about my king, family
and friends, there is nothing I can do. Possessions, wealth, food,
drink, entertainment: how can they benefit me now? This life is no
more than a dream'. Having said this, he covered his head and fell
asleep. Again the emperor was terrified. 'I will do whatever I can
to help you. Sleep well', he said as he departed.

The emperor then set fire to all the forests, but no charcoal lance-
shaft was found. He burnt all his fine silks, but not even half a sack

of ashes resulted. He slaughtered all the sheep, but the blood of their spleens did not fill half a paunch. He did succeed in finding a yellow horse with a red head. The emperor then said to Gar, 'Although I failed with the other things, I have located the horse that you required.' To this the minister replied, 'If the other items are not found, there is nothing that can be done for me. Let the yellow horse with the red head be my corpse-bearer and set me upon it. Load food and clothing for these remains of mine on a good Chinese steed, and I shall go to a place from which the mountains of Tibet are visible in order to supplicate the gods'.

As preparations for Gar's journey were being made, the emperor said, 'Great Minister, since you are an intelligent person and as it is spring, the time for sowing crops, what should we do? Please advise us'. The minister replied, 'In my homeland of Tibet, the seeds are all roasted in an iron pan until they resemble hailstones. When these are sown, the harvests are greater and the plants taller, yet the crops ripen in only three months'. The emperor commanded, 'Do as the Tibetans do!' and the great court drum was struck. Everyone then roasted their grain and sowed the puffed cereal in the fields.

Minister Gar then cured his own body of its diseases, and as he was making preparations for his journey to supplicate the gods, the messenger disguised as a beggar who was sent by the other Tibetan ministers arrived. Gar addressed him with these cryptic words:

> One cannot recognise a distant billy-goat by his beard.
> Remain silent and forsake noise.
> The grain and the iron castle have come together.
> Fill the upper valley and the lower valley with 'foal-sticks'.
> Roll up the white silk and wave the black silk.
> The moon will arrive before the sun.

Once Gar had spoken, the beggar returned to Tibet and delivered the message to the ministers, but they could not comprehend it. Princess Kongjo understood, however, and explained it thus: 'It appears that Minister Gar has caused great mischief in China. "One cannot recognise a distant billy-goat by his beard" means "Do not talk to a bearded man with a moustache".[114] "Remain silent" means that I am to explain this message to you Tibetan ministers. "The grain and the iron castle have come together" means that having roasted their seed-grain, the Chinese were made to sow them. "Fill the upper valley and the lower valley with 'foal-sticks'" means "Put many arrows into quivers". "Roll up the white silk and wave the black silk" means that we should rest during the day and travel at night. "The moon will arrive before the sun" means that I should hasten to Tibet and reach it before you'.

Minister Gar then set out on the yellow horse with the red head for a place from which the mountain peaks of Tibet were visible in order to supplicate the gods. Another horse carried food, clothing and copious dried meat that was preserved in brine. Having escorted the minister on his way, the emperor sent four strong men to guard him.

After Gar had departed, the emperor said, 'It is certain that someone betrayed the identity of the princess. Let an astrological divination be carried out!' Having performed the divination, the following prognosis was given: 'Above three mountains is a great lake with various species of birds resting upon it. Above the lake is a pink plain on which sits a woman whose head and body are of equal size. Both her head and body are covered with eyes. The one with a beak of copper betrayed the princess!' The emperor did not believe the prognosis and promptly burned it. As the *Eighty-Chapter Astrological Treatise* had been sent to Tibet, no further copies were left in China.

Gar's escape

Minister Gar eventually arrived at a place from which the mountains of Tibet could be seen. Having secretly procured and concealed a large amount of barley beer, he now gave his guards the delicious dried meat to eat. 'It will be beneficial to my illness if you eat this', he said and made supplications to the gods. The four strong men became unbearably thirsty, and when he gave them great draughts of barley beer, they became drunk and fell down insensible. The minister hamstrung the four guards' horses and broke their weapons. Mounted upon the yellow horse with the red head and leading the other steed, he spoke these words:

> Let the ashes of the fine silks burnt on the fire
> Be the clothes of the emperor who was biased against us.
> Let the grainless ears of corn which turned to black dust
> Be the food of the miserly queen.
> Let the charcoal lance-shaft from the incinerated forest
> Be the weapon of the athletic prince.
> For the slaughter of the sheep whose spleens held no blood,
> I offer prayers of confession before the gods.
> Lying on my bed although I was not ill,
> What need was there to invite a doctor to my pillow?
> I will not tarry here; let me hasten to my own land!

With that, he whipped his horse and was gone. In China, the ears of corn then turned black, and the people lamented, 'The ears of corn have no grains within them! The evil Tibetan minister compelled us to burn all our fine silks and slaughter our sheep. Our forests were set on fire and as he made us roast all our seeds and plant them, there is no grain. Our wise princess and Jowo Shakyamuni have been taken by the Tibetans. He has done these wicked deeds! Alas! Alack! What can we do? We cannot allow him to return'. When the emperor heard it said that Gar might escape to Tibet, he feared that this might be true, so he dispatched one hundred Chinese horsemen of great prowess to seize him.

Minister Gar's four guards eventually awoke from their drunken stupor and thought, 'There are no horses for us to ride, nor do we have any weapons, and it would be shameful to return to China!' Fearing the emperor's punishment, they followed the minister. When the party reached the bend in the Great River, the horsemen who had been sent by the emperor also arrived nearby.[115] Gar engaged the four strong men as servants, and they covered the riverbanks with horse dung and hoofprints. Antelope horns were hardened in the fire and made into bows. Gar ordered them to loose some arrows, and they removed the feathers from the shafts of others and scattered them about.[116] When their pursuers saw these, they said to one another, 'The Tibetan horsemen who have come to meet Minister Gar are many, and their prowess is great. We will be unable to withstand them. It is better that we should return!' So saying, they turned back.

In the meantime, the Chinese princess and the other Tibetan ministers arrived at Denmadrag, where an image of Maitreya, seven cubits high, and two copies of the 'Good Action' invocation were carved upon the rock. They waited there for one month, but Minister Gar failed to arrive. They proceeded to Pungpori, where they ascended the pass by a transverse route. There they captured deer and milked them. Again the minister failed to arrive. They came to Pemashang in Kham where they sowed crops and established a water mill. They waited there for two months, but again the minister did not come. Then they proceeded to the gate of Godong, and as China's good fortune and blessings had been exhausted, the gate was obstructed by the power of the guardian deities of that country, and the party remained there for two months. When Minister Gar finally arrived, and he realised that the obstruction of the gate of Godong was caused by the displeasure of the protector deities of China, he sent aloft great clouds of smoke of various timbers and made offerings of food and libations of drink. Such were the prayers he offered up:

> We beseech, beseech, beseech. We beseech the deities.
> We beseech the deities of the emperor of China.
> We beseech the deities of the city of Zimshing.
> We beseech the deities of the royal queen.
> We beseech the deities of Trashi Trigo.
> We beseech you to raise this forest on high.
> We beseech the deities of the Tibetan ministers.
> We beseech the deities of the Land of Snows.
> Come and welcome the Chinese princess Kongjo!

While they all prayed together in this way, the forest in its entirety was raised aloft during the night, and they were able to proceed. They circumvented the icy surfaces of the Nine Sandy Passes, and in dark of night, they held butter-lamps aloft. The Forest of Sengdeng was raised up to the right, and the Forest of Lawa was raised up to the left. The party eventually reached Tibet without further obstruction.

Kongjo reaches Lhasa

A messenger was sent into the presence of King Songtsen Gampo with this request: 'As we the ministers of Tibet are about to arrive with the Jowo Shakyamuni, the Chinese princess Kongjo and the others, we request that a grand celebration be held to welcome us'. The king replied, 'It is a great miracle, because this princess appears to be the manifestation of the reverend Tara! Although we do not know the direction from which she will arrive, let us prepare a grand welcome'. Apparitions of the princess were seen in all four directions. Those in the east say that the princess came from the east, and for this reason, the name of the noble family is Gyamorab, 'excellent Chinese woman'. Those in the south say that she came from that direction, and at that time a saying arose to the effect that the glacier at Dribkyipu resembled a right-whorled white conch. Those in the west say that she approached from that direction. Some hold that an adage arose at that time to the effect that a protector image was built at Belpatsel because a rock there resembled a boar's snout.[117] Those in the north say that the princess came from the north, and because she and the Jowo were greeted there, it is said that the village was called Lhasu, 'Welcome the deity'.

In fact, having come from the north via the Gola Pass, they arrived at the Ramoche Plain, where the carriage sank into the sand, and as the two strong men, Lhaga and Luga, were unable to draw it any further, there it remained. A pillar was erected on each side of the Jowo, a curtain of fine white silk was drawn around it and offerings were made. The following day, Princess Kongjo, wearing garments of fine silk of various kinds and many ornaments of gold and turquoise, together with the twenty-five beautiful girls also wearing fine silks and various precious ornaments, arrived at the festivities on the Neutang Plain at Draglha to the accompaniment of guitar music. The ministers and all the Tibetan people assembled for the spectacle, and there was singing and dancing that defied the imagination.

The Nepalese princess was observing the festivities from the roof of the Auspicious Celestial Mansion at Draglha. When she beheld the Chinese princess and her servants adorned in their finery on the Neutang Plain, she was seized by unthinkable, passionate jealousy, and spoke these words:

> Alas! You, the Chinese princess Kongjo,
> Now you are here with your servants and retinue.
> After great difficulty, the go-between has brought you here.
> The distance was great, but you have arrived in Tibet.
> Although you are the daughter of the Chinese emperor,
> The difference between us is vast:
> I was the first to cross the threshold.
> I am the princess of the king of Nepal.
> Since I was the first to see the body of the king,
> I am the great and noble senior consort.
> If the senior consort is not regarded as great or noble,
> Then the religions of the world are without truth and
>   falsehood.
> As senior consort, I am the king's queen.
> The junior consort is the queen's servant.
> However, if you came with thoughts of the king,
> Let senior and junior consorts compete:
> Compete in praising the sublime Supreme Being;
> Compete in constructing shrines
> Which are the foundations on which religion and the
>   Supreme Ones rest;
> Compete in serving the king above;
> Compete in practicing the sacred Dharma through faith
> And in protecting the sinners and wretched ones below us;
> Compete directly in our inheritance and wealth
> And in raising crops in the fields;
> Compete in the greatness of our families in their own lands
> And in the value of our dowries.
> If you do not dare to compete in these things
> Do not dare to hope for the king.
> Do not presume to see yourself as queen.
> If a shrine the size of a quart-measure
> Is too small for the great senior consort,
> Then even a shrine the size of a single handful
> Is too big for the lesser, junior consort.

Thus she spoke. The Chinese princess then thought to herself,

> How mischievous! Having left behind my own family, glory and wealth, I have just arrived from a distant land. I am without lodgings or station, nor have I beheld the face of the king, or attained the title of queen, or met the ministers of external or internal affairs. In a place such as this, these challenges fuelled by jealousy are unfitting. We two came together from distant lands to be the king's consorts. Trusting one another and sharing our pleasures and our pains, two minds meeting as one, we should serve the sovereign and protect the people. If the association between the senior and junior consorts in thoughts and deeds proceeds correctly, we will be as sisters in this life. Having just arrived, I find the situation is otherwise. If she wishes to compete with these challenging words of jealousy, then in what ways are our two families, dowries, ourselves, our worldly actions—all of these—unequal?

With these thoughts, she replied:

> Alas! How strange! I feel like laughing.
> Before I have even found a place to stay,
> Before my two feet have crossed the threshold,
> Before my eyes have beheld the face of the king,
> You, O Queen, have made this untimely challenge.
> The feather of the bird that soars in the sky
> And the bamboo that grows in moist, warm places,
> Although each is equal in its necessary functions,
> By the power of their karma, they come together in an arrow
>   before the archer.
> The notion of primary and secondary is only a difference in
>   their names.
> The flower which grows in the marsh at the confluence of
>   three high valleys
> And the hollyhock which grows in the grove in the three low
>   valleys,
> Although they are equally splendid to behold,
> By the power of dependent causes, they come together as
>   offerings before the deity.

The notion of upper and lower is only a difference in their
    names.
Both Tritsun, who came from the capital of Nepal,
And I, Kongjo, who came from China,
Although our families and dowries are equal,
By the power of prayer, we came together before the king.
The notion of senior and junior consorts is a difference in
    name only.
Like melodious minstrels, if the senior and junior consorts
Associate harmoniously, they will be closer than sisters in
    this life.
If there is competition between them,
The outcome will depend on who is the most astute.
In the distant lands of China and Nepal,
The two kings, our only fathers, are each dwelling in their
    respective realms:
If we deign to flaunt our families in their lands, then let us
    compete.
The foundation on which all benefit, happiness and piety
    arise,
Of unimaginable qualities of sight, hearing, thought and
    touch:
The two images of the Lord Buddha—if we deign to flaunt
    these, then let us compete.
Precious gold and silver, various kinds of fine silks,
Horses, camels, mules and so on
If we wish to flaunt our dowries, then let us compete.
Our worldly actions, the quality of our handiwork,
The design of our ornaments, our ways of preparing food,
Our crops in the fields, the quality of our spinning and
    weaving, and so on:
If we are to flaunt our craftwork, let us compete!

Thus she replied. Minister Gar, however, still remembered the preju-
diced actions of the Chinese emperor, Princess Kongjo's own heretical words about Tibet and the great tribulations that he underwent in China. He therefore contrived that not a single person attended upon Kongjo and her servants for an entire month.

Then the Chinese princess's retinue spoke out: 'The saying that
Tibet is the realm of the hungry ghosts is true! No food, drink or

entertainments are to be found'. Hearing this and finding the situation intolerable, the Chinese princess summoned Minister Gar: 'Great Minister, I came to Tibet at your behest. Having summoned a dog, surely you do not beat it! Abjure shamelessness and unreasonableness, and bring food and clothing for this mistress and her servants. We have come from a distant land and have suffered great hardships'. Gar said, 'I have no authority to bring food or drink, nor do I have the authority to grant audiences with the king. In all these matters, the Nepalese princess has greater powers than I. You must speak with her'. So saying, he departed. The Chinese princess was stricken by despair, and recalling her family and wealth in her homeland, and being filled with regret and hopelessness, she sang this song to the accompaniment of a guitar:

This girl will not remain here, but will return to her
  homeland.
Bring the Jowo Shakyamuni and send it back.
Bring the discourses on science and divination and send
  them back.
Bring the treasures and fine silks and send them back.

I will return while milk is curdled.
I will return while butter is churned from curd.
I will return while buttermilk is made into cheese.
I will return while dried cheese is grated to powder.
I will return while strips of leather are made into thongs.
I will return while clay is made into pots.
I will return while the water mills are established.
I will return bringing the turnip seeds.

China's good fortune and blessings have declined.
In Tibet virtue and happiness are complete.
A girl has dignity in the land of her mother.
Great are the mental sufferings of an only daughter.
I came to make my home in Tibet;
Yet the dog, once called to the house, is beaten.
In Tibet no face shows shame.

A small knife is sharpest near the handle.
A song is most melodious by the water mill.
A daughter has dignity in her mother's land.

The marriage of Songtsen Gampo and Princess Kongjo

> The king is dominated by his minister.
> Man is dominated by woman.
> The loom is dominated by the yarn.
> The wastelands are dominated by weeds.
> How can this girl remain?
> Minister Gar has acted without shame!

Having sung this lament, she ordered the Jowo Shakyamuni placed upon a carriage, and the horses, mules, camels and other beasts of burden loaded. 'You will recognise the Tibetans' evil deeds as soon as you have seen them!' she cried. As she was preparing for the journey, Minister Gar arrived. 'You cannot return from your new home in Tibet to the land of your family. It would bring great shame. Nor can you travel the road to China alone. When you first came to Tibet, without me, you were delayed on the way and were unable to proceed. Now I will counsel the Nepalese princess, and petition the king'. Having said this, he requested a royal audience.

When the king finally came to the place of the celebratory feast and met the Chinese princess Kongjo, three different perceptions of the event arose. To the Tathagatas of the Ten Directions, it appeared that both king and queen, by the actions of the Twelve Great Deeds, were benefiting sentient beings. To the Bodhisattvas of the Ten Stages, it appeared that the sublime Avalokiteshvara, bodily manifest in King Songtsen Gampo, and the reverend Tara, bodily manifest in the Chinese princess Kongjo,were striving for the benefit of sentient beings. In the perception of the common people, the royal couple were offering drinks to one another while spinning yarn together.

Thereafter, because Songtsen Gampo and Princess Kongjo did not meet for another month, the king's heart was filled with regret, and in order to console the princess, he asked, 'Did you not face difficulties on your journey? Were you not afflicted by hardships? Your unimpeded arrival in Tibet is miraculous! How did you manage to bring the Jowo Shakyamuni? How did you cross the passes, precipices and rivers?' Princess Kongjo replied, 'The Jowo Shakyamuni was placed upon a carriage drawn by the strong men Lhaga and Luga. We crossed by ferry at the bends of a hundred rivers. Even though the distance was great, we managed to proceed by various ways. We detoured around the Nine Sandy Passes. We came holding butter-lamps aloft in the darkness. We came having cast down the Forest of Sengdeng on our right and the Forest of Lawa on our left. In the land of China good fortune and blessings have declined; in Tibet virtue and happiness are complete, but there is no shame'. So saying, she wept.

At that moment, the ministers arrived, and being filled with vituperation and arrogance, Minister Gar said, 'The people of China generally looked down on us. Except for my Chinese hostess, not one considerate person came forward. The Chinese emperor, in particular, displayed great prejudice, and you, Princess Kongjo, how many unfavourable things you said about Tibet!' Once Gar had spoken, the Chinese princess felt ashamed and fell silent.

This chapter,
in which the Chinese princess
is invited to Tibet,
is the thirteenth.

14

The excellent construction of the Shrines for the Subjugation of the Borderlands, the Shrines for Further Subjugation, and Trulnang and Ramoche

Geomantic survey of Tibet

Knowing that the Chinese princess was skilled in astrology, and having sought the intercession of Minister Gar, Princess Tritsun entrusted a gift of one full *dre*-measure of gold dust to a maidservant and sent her to obtain a divination as to the best site for a shrine. Accordingly, the Chinese princess spread out the *Eighty-Chapter Astrological Treatise* and made this divination:

> I perceive that this Land of Snows, the kingdom of Tibet, is in the form of an ogress lying upon her back. I perceive that the lake at Otang, the Plain of Milk, is the ogress's heart-blood and that the three mountains are the bones of her heart.[118] As this lake is directly above the ogress's heart, it will be necessary to

fill it with soil and build a shrine upon it. Here also is a gateway to the lower realms. There is a naga-palace beneath Ramoche, and the nagas will be subdued if the Jowo Shakyamuni is placed there. The cave below Ramoche is the resting place of the black naga-demons; construct a shrine to deprive them of their abode!

In the southwest, at the root of a poison-tree in Dawatsel, the Garden of the Moon, is the meeting place of *teurang* demons and ghosts. Disperse them! Between Dribkyipu and Nyangdrenpu lies a habitual route of *tsen* powers. Build a great stupa at Barchukha. In the east is a malign geomantic influence that resembles a crocodile pursuing a *deu* water creature.[119] This is Lamdrumpari. Place a right-whorled conch facing it. In the southeast, there is a malign geomantic influence that resembles an ogress thrusting forth her vulva. This is Jangto Sengpug. Place an image of Vishnu facing it. In the southwest is a malign geomantic influence that resembles a black scorpion lunging at its prey. This is Sharri, the eastern mountain of Yugmari. Place a *keru* eagle facing it. In the west is a malign geomantic influence that resembles a black fiend keeping watch. This is Shun-gyi Dragtse, the Rocky Peak of Shun. Place a stone stupa facing it. In the north is a malign geomantic influence that resembles an elephant engaged in battle. This is Uri, the central mountain of Nyangdren and Gete. Place a stone lion facing it. Thus all the nearer malign geomantic influences will be subdued.

Following the subjugation of all the malign geomantic influences and the perfection of qualities in the one location, in the east there is a mountain that resembles a stupa. This is Benkho Bangwari. In the south, there is one that resembles a heap of precious jewels. This is Gyabri, the mountain behind Drib. In the west is a mountain that resembles a conch-cup on a tripod. This is the mountain of Drangpu in Tolung. In the north is a mountain that resembles a lotus in bloom. This is the mountain of Gete Lhapu.

Moreover, on the mountain of Penkar in Nyangdren is an umbrella that represents the head of the Buddha. On Gyabri, the mountain behind Meldrong, are the fish that represent his eyes. On the rock of Dangkhar is the lotus representing his tongue. On the glacier at Drib is the conch representing his speech. On the mountain of Dzongtsen is the vase representing his neck. On Yugmari is the endless knot representing his mind. On the mountain of Penkar is the victory banner representing his body. On the marsh of Drangpu at Tolung is the wheel representing his hands and feet. Thus all eight auspicious symbols are complete.

Further, there is an iron mine on the ridge at Garpai Jomo Zeze, a copper mine at Ragadrag, a silver mine at the rock of Ladong and a gold mine at the rock of Chagkhari. In the east there is the lower part of the face of a joyful, grey she-tiger. In the south are the waters of the blue turquoise dragon. In the west on the red rocks at Ja-marpo Shun is the face of a foal. In the north at Pabongkha in Nyangdren is a black turtle.

The so-called Twelve Immutable Nails will restrain the limbs and hands of the supine ogress. The Four Shrines for Subduing the Borderlands are Trandrug in Yoru, Katsel in Puru, the shrine of Tsangtrang in Yeru and the shrine of Drumpa-gyang in Tsang.[120] If these cannot achieve subjugation, then construct the Four Shrines for Further Subjugation: namely the Buchu Shrine in Kongpo, the Khonting Golden Shrine, the Jamtrin Degye Shrine and the Traduntse Shrine. If these cannot achieve subjugation, then construct the Four Shrines for Subjugation of the Districts. These are the Longtang Dronma Shrine in Kham, the Kyerchu Shrine in Bumtang, the Sherab Dronma Shrine of the race of Tsel and the Tsangpa Lung-non Shrine, the Wind-suppressing Brahma Shrine. Build these first. If even these cannot achieve subjugation, place earth-daggers in each of those locations.[121]

Having accomplished all this, you will be able to build a shrine in Lhasa without hindrance. The sky is an eight-spoked wheel, the earth an eight-petalled lotus; on all sides lie the eight auspicious symbols. This location is directly above the heart of the ogress. Carry out each of the relevant symbolic actions described above. Fill the lake with soil borne by a white goat, then duly construct the shrine on top of it. Do not hold incorrect views out of jealousy!

Thus the Chinese princess advised Tritsun's maidservant most thoroughly, but the woman garbled the message in the presence of her mistress. She forgot the detailed descriptions for eliminating hindrances and subduing malign geomantic influences, the existence of qualities and the construction of the Shrines for the Subjugation of the Borderlands and for Further Subjugation, and the subsequent methods and relevant symbolic actions mentioned above.

When Tritsun inquired about a favourable site for the construction of a shrine, her maidservant replied, 'It is said that you must first construct the twelve shrines in all the various directions. Then you must fill the lake with soil borne by a goat. Only then may you construct the shrine on the lake'. Tritsun was filled with doubt. Even if the maidservant was right, a load of soil carried by a goat would not fill a ten-millionth part of one one-thousandth part of the lake. Suspecting that the Chinese princess had given her false advice, Tritsun grew jealous and was deeply anguished. Without consulting the king, she followed the instructions of several ministers and inspected a site on the grassy plain at Ladong and found it to be suitable. The foundations of a shrine were laid, but all the work that had been carried out during the day was destroyed without trace by deities and demons in the night. Unhappy and distressed, Tritsun informed Songtsen Gampo, who said, 'Do not distress yourself: there is one from whom I can ask advice'. That night, the king made supplications to his tutelary deity, and a ray of light shone forth from the heart of the image and was absorbed into the lake.

The king then thought, 'It would be good to construct the shrine on the reclaimed lake,' and he said to Tritsun, 'Saddle your horse. Tomorrow, we two will ride out for pleasure.' The next day, the royal couple rode to the grassy plain beside the lake. 'Remove your ring and throw it into the air. We shall build the shrine wherever it falls,' said the king. Tritsun offered prayers to her tutelary deity and threw her ring into the air. The ring became wrapped in a veil of light and fell into the lake. Tritsun thought to herself, 'If we have to build a shrine on the lake, it will be impossible to complete it in this lifetime!' She dismounted, and as she was distressed, the king said to her, 'Do not weep. Look into the lake. It has many qualities!' Tritsun wiped away her tears and looked. She beheld in the water a nine-terraced stupa composed of various rays of light. Everything in the lake was connected by a web of light radiating out from it. As the design formed by the light resembled a shrine, her faith grew, and the king promised to assist her with the task of construction.

Commencement of Trulnang

The next day, the king and the assembled ministers, accompanied by music and bearing the self-created sandalwood image, came to the water's edge.[122] An earth-dagger was positioned on each of the four sides of the lake, a great prayer flag was erected and prayers were offered. Tritsun made supplications to the lapis lazuli begging-bowl, whereupon unlimited food and drink appeared and all the Tibetan people were set to work. First, a causeway was made by placing layers of sod in the water. Rocks were then carried to the four sides of the lake in order to make it square. On each side, great boulders were submerged in the water in groups of four.

The king proceeded onto the rocks, and turning his attention to the stupa of light in the centre of the lake, he offered prayers, while the ministers cast rocks into the water to the sound of the Six-Syllable Mantra. By the power of the king's prayers, a stone stupa with a square base, resembling the axle of a water-wheel, appeared miraculously in the centre of the lake. The king and queen, together with the assembled ministers, examined the stupa closely and found it to be solid, stable and unchanging. As a result, their faith and devotion waxed stronger.

Sixteen long, thick trunks were cut from juniper trees. The lower end of each was placed upon the great rocks on the four sides, while the upper ends rested on the self-created stone stupa in the centre of the lake, just like the spokes of an umbrella. Next, many long, thick trunks cut from *lawa*-trees were laid in a crisscross pattern upon the juniper logs.

The manifestation-monk by the name of Akaramatishila then travelled by magic to the realm of the nagas, whence he acquired diamond plaster, which was applied to the wood. Thus, even though the timbers might remain submerged in water for an aeon,

The construction of Trulnang Shrine on the Otang Lake

they would not rot; fires would not burn them; nor could they be cut. On top of this framework, planks and bricks were laid and sealed with molten bronze. Having created an even surface with soil, the reclamation of the lake of Otang was duly completed in the Earth-male-dog Year [638], when the Dharma-king was twenty-three years of age. The foundations of the walls of Lhasa were then laid, and in the Earth-female-pig Year [639] the foundations for the shrine were laid.

The self-created eleven-faced image of Avalokiteshvara

When the walls of the shrine had been built to about waist height, everyone was filled with joy, but the following day the walls were destroyed by deities and demons. Again, Tritsun was distressed, and she came before the king and said, 'Great King, it is impossible to construct a shrine on the reclaimed lake. Look at it!' The king replied, 'Do not distress yourself. There is one from whom I can ask advice,' and he supplicated his tutelary deity, whereupon a disembodied voice resounded from the sky: 'If an eleven-faced Jowo is made in the likeness of you, the king, the construction of your shrine will proceed without hindrance'. Having said this, the voice disappeared. The king said to the Nepalese craftsman, 'Can you construct an eleven-faced image of the Sublime One, which will be known as my own likeness?' 'I can', the craftsman replied.

The many miraculous substances that had been brought from India were assembled as raw materials for this image: the 'snake-heart' sandalwood, the 'cow-head' sandalwood, the branch of the Bodhi Tree, fragrant grass from the island in the ocean, sand from the Nairajnana River, earth from the Eight Great Hermitages and so on. Having been thoroughly pulverised, they were mixed with the milk of a red cow and a white goat and were formed into a great mound of plaster, which was placed on a pillow upon the king's precious throne. Songtsen Gampo made supplications to his tutelary deity and thought to himself, 'My tutelary deity Avalokiteshvara manifests in many forms. Which one shall I make? As the eleven-faced Wish-fulfilling Jewel is unique among them, I should construct an image in this form'. As he was contemplating this, all the buddhas and bodhisattvas assembled on a single point the size of a mote of dust in a sunbeam, and were absorbed into the mound of clay. The king beheld this and thought to himself, 'The Blessed Ones appear to have entered my tutelary image'. With these thoughts, he fell asleep on the precious throne. The next morning, the Self-created Eleven-faced Image of the Wish-fulfilling Jewel had appeared, without the agency of the craftsman.

The image's three primary faces were white and smiling, fulfilling the activity of peace. The three faces above these were golden, with furious and wrathful expressions, and fulfilled the activity of increase. The two faces above these were the colour of coral, with laughing and wrathful expressions, and fulfilled the activity of power. The two faces above these were black and wrathful, with furious expressions, and fulfilled the activity of force. Above them was a vermilion Amitabha the same size as the king himself.

As to the implements of the ten primary hands of the Dharmakaya form, the palms of the first two were joined in prayer at the breast. The second hand on the right held a rosary, the third a wheel, the fourth exhibited the gesture of supreme giving and the fifth held an image of Amitabha. The second hand on the left held a white lotus, the third a gourd, the fourth a jewel and the fifth a bow and arrow. [As to the hands of the Nirmanakaya form, they were made by a sculptor. When the self-created image first appeared, it had only the ten primary hands.]

As to the thirty-eight arms of the Sambhogakaya form, taking each of the nineteen hands on the right in turn, the first held a jewel, the second a noose, the third a begging-bowl, the fourth a sword, the fifth a diamond sceptre, the sixth a fire-crystal, the seventh a water-crystal, the eighth a bow, the ninth a rod, the tenth a fly-whisk, the eleventh a shield, the twelfth a vase, the thirteenth a battle-axe, the fourteenth a rosary, the fifteenth a blue lotus, the sixteenth a gourd, the seventeenth a sun, the eighteenth a white lotus and the nineteenth an ear of corn.

Taking the nineteen arms on the left in turn, the first held a white cloud, the second a gourd, the third a lotus, the fourth a sword, the fifth a conch, the sixth a skull, the seventh a rosary, the eighth a bell, the ninth a diamond sceptre, the tenth an iron hook, the eleventh a mendicant's staff, the twelfth an image of the Buddha in the

Nirmanakaya form, the thirteenth a shrine, the fourteenth a book, the fifteenth a wheel, the sixteenth a buddha, the seventeenth a fruit, the eighteenth a lotus corolla and the nineteenth a jewel.

The one thousand arms of the Nirmanakaya form were of utmost beauty, and in the palm of each hand was the eye of wisdom. The hands and feet of the image were ornamented with circlets and golden snakes. As to the wrathful heads, each possessed three eyes, and their brown hair stood on end. The body was decorated with many jewels and radiated rays of light in all directions. A deerskin was draped across the torso, covering the left breast, and the image was graced with the major and minor signs of greatness. The king saw this statue appear in a blaze of light and rejoiced greatly.

Songtsen Gampo said to the Nepalese sculptor, 'Even though this image of yours has been completed miraculously and with great speed, the self-created sandalwood image from India and the relics of the seven previous buddhas are to be placed within its breast'. To this the sculptor replied, 'This is not my image; it was self-created!' Just as he spoke, the statue began to tremble, the hem of the gown that covered the left leg rose above the knee, and a ray of light shone forth from the breast. The relics of the buddhas and self-created sandalwood image were invoked and were placed in the breast in the manner of a wisdom-being.[123] The slight inclination of Amitabha towards the left and the gathering of the gown above the knee remained like this for later generations to behold.

The 'snake-heart' sandalwood became the supporting pillar for the image's head, and the branch of the Bodhi Tree became the supporting pillars for the two legs. The other precious substances formed the body, and flowers were strewn around. The Nepalese sculptor made images of Avalokiteshvara, Khasarpani, Bhrikuti, Tara, Marici, Sarasvati, Amritakundali and the Glorious Hayagriva as a retinue. Auspicious omens appeared in every direction, and the earth shook in six different ways. The royal couple, accompanied by the assembled ministers, brought many offerings and recited prayers.

Because the king had supplicated the image for the aversion of opposing factors and for the accomplishment of favourable factors in the construction of the shrine, at that very moment in the west, at the foot of a poison-tree in Dawatsel, the Garden of the Moon, many demons, ogres and ghosts assembled. 'This duplicitous man called Songtsen Gampo has destroyed our meeting place and covered our habitual routes. Let us prevent the construction of his shrine, stem his virtuous actions and bring down frosts, hail and pestilence!' they cried.

The king realised this, and as a result of his earnest supplications to the Sublime One, a ray of light arose from the smiling countenance of the image and became fire. A ray of light from the wrathful countenance became Hayagriva and Amritakundali. These two furious deities then burned the poison-trees of Dawatsel with the fire of wisdom. Like a thunderbolt striking amidst a pile of peas, demons fell down senseless; some became demented, and others wailed piteously. The two wrathful deities then pursued the demons with the fire of wisdom, and having chased them across the Great Outer Ocean, prevented the demons' return. Where the fire of wisdom struck a rock at Dawatsel, a self-created image of Khasarpani arose. The next day the king, accompanied by the assembly of ministers, came before this self-created image, and having given offerings and prayers, he recited the following eulogy:

> Avalokiteshvara, the Almighty, the Protector of the World:
> The King of Sages ornaments your crown.
> Your body is as white and pure as a snowy mountain,
> Like a lotus, unstained by afflictions.
> Your compassion is great; you are endowed with powers.
> You assuage the diseases and sufferings
> Of all pitiful and destitute sentient beings.
> You have become my protector; I bow down to you!

Thus he spoke. Even though the self-created image appeared clearly upon the rock, for the purpose of accumulation of merit by sentient beings in the future, the Nepalese sculptor carved the image clearly in relief.

Completion of Trulnang

Thinking that there would be no further obstructions to the building of the shrine, the king and all the ministers proceeded onto the reclaimed lake. Once the land had been blessed, the building was marked out. At this time, there came a naga-king, an emanation of the Lord Buddha, white in colour with a hood of snakes and three eyes. Having presented a white, lasso-forming snake to Songtsen Gampo, he said, 'Erect an image of me, and I shall protect this royal shrine from any future damage up to the magnitude of the Lesser Thousand-fold World!' Then the naga-king Nanda came and said, 'Erect an image of me, and I shall protect this royal shrine from any future damage up to the magnitude of the Intermediate Thousand-fold World!' Then the naga-king Upananda came and said, 'Erect an image of me, and I shall protect this royal shrine from any future damage up to the magnitude of the Three Thousand-fold Worlds!' Then the ogre-king Langka Drinchu, the Ten-necked One, came, and having presented a basin full of gold to the king, said, 'Erect an image of me, and I shall protect this royal shrine from any future damage by fire!' The demon Nagakubera came, and having presented a golden *tagzang*,[124] said, 'Erect an image of me, and I shall protect this royal shrine from any future damage by the four elements!' Mahakala came and said, 'Erect an image of me, and I shall protect this royal shrine from any future damage by foreign armies and spirits!' Then Pelden Lhamo came, and having presented an iron cup, said, 'Erect an image of me, and I shall protect this royal shrine from any future damage by humans and *mamo* demons!'

Then the lamas came and said, 'Let the shrine of the king be built in the style of the lamas'. The *ngagpa* came and said, 'Let the shrine of the king be built in the style of the *ngagpa*'.[125] The adherents of Bon came and said, 'Let the shrine of the king be built in the style of the Bonpo'. The Tibetan people came and said, 'Let the shrine of the king be built in the style of the Tibetan people'. The king was greatly pleased and promised to fulfil all their requests.

Songtsen Gampo satisfied the Tibetan people with food and drink and ordered them to begin work. Some made bricks, some constructed the walls, while others applied the plaster; thus the walls of the lower storey were completed. [According to Togden Ngo-nyelma, 745 years elapsed between the laying of the foundations of the walls of Lhasa and the ordination of Tselpa Kunga Dorje.[126]]

Many trunks of the juniper tree were cut, and the king created one hundred and eight manifestations of himself to guard the doors, and another one hundred and eight manifestations bearing chisels to undertake the carpentry within. Food was brought by none other than the Nepalese princess. On one occasion, the king's mealtime coincided with the time at which Tritsun made offerings to her tutelary deity. She therefore sent his food with a maidservant. The maidservant opened the door and entered, but instead of the king, she beheld one hundred and eight carpenters of identical appearance, each holding a chisel. As they were all engaged in carving the noses of one hundred and eight lions, and she did not know to whom to give the food, she left the shrine and returned the food to the Nepalese princess. The maidservant thought to herself, 'It is said that the king knows how to create manifestations. Can it be true?' After Tritsun had taken the food to the king, the maidservant peered through a crack in the door and saw that all the craftsmen were indeed manifestations. She let forth a peal of laughter, whereupon the king's eyes were distracted and the blade of his chisel slipped, with the result that all the manifestation-carpenters made the same mistake, and the nose of every lion was severed![127]

Some workers shaped the pillars, while others trimmed the beams and worked the rafters to make them square. Some then erected the pillars, some hoisted the beams, some arranged the rafters and others laid the planks. Once the roof was completed, the building was decorated. [Atisha's great revealed writings[128] state that the lower storey of the shrine of Lhasa was completed in two days, and then the roof was added.] Once the king had created manifestations of himself in this manner, the walls were completed in four days, the carpentry in six, and the roof in two. The lower storey of Rasa was thus completely finished in a total of twelve days.[129]

Further, as the four gates formed a mandala, the lamas were satisfied; as the pillars were like daggers, the *ngagpa* were satisfied; as the corners formed a swastika, the adherents of Bon were satisfied; and as the shrine formed a chequerboard pattern, the Tibetan people were satisfied. Because the king had created all the images as he had been instructed, the Dharma-protectors, nagas, devils, ogres and so forth were all satisfied.

The main gate of this miraculous shrine of four happinesses faced west towards the land of Nepal. Subsequently, Tritsun summoned many Nepalese craftsmen skilled in Vedas to construct the upper storey. [The upper storey of the shrines of Lhasa and Ramoche each took twelve months to construct and were completed simultaneously.] At the same time, the Chinese princess summoned many carpenters and sculptors from China to build the Gyatag Ramoche Shrine. Its main gate faced east.

Regional shrines

At this time, the king created manifestations of himself to construct the Shrines for the Subjugation of the Borderlands, the Shrines for Further Subjugation and the Shrines for the Subjugation of the Regions. In order to suppress the right shoulder of the ogress, the Immutable Katsel Shrine was built in Uru. As a subsidiary, the Sershang Giti Shrine was built. These were consecrated in the cave of Tsenodong. In order to suppress the left shoulder, the Trandrug Trashi Jamnyom Shrine was built in Yoru. As a subsidiary, the Tsentang Shrine was built. The consecration of these took place at Pugmoche, the Great Cave. In order to suppress the right hip, the Tsangdrang Jangchub Gene Shrine was built in Yeru.[130] As a subsidiary, the Gendrung Shrine was built. The consecration of these took place in the Cave of Tse. In order to suppress the left hip, Drubpa Gyel Drime Namtag,[131] the Shrine of Pure Immaculate Victory Accomplishment, was built. As a subsidiary, the Dre Shrine was built. The consecration of these took place in the Cave of Gyang.

Further, as to the construction of the Four Shrines for Further Subjugation, in order to suppress the right elbow, the Buchu Shrine was built in Kongpo upon the head of the Eastern Tiger. In order to suppress the left elbow, the Khonting Shrine was built in Lhodrag upon the hump of the Southern Dragon. In order to suppress the right knee, the Jamchen Gegye Shrine[132] was built upon the back of the Red Bird of the West. In order to suppress the left knee, the Tra-ngentse Shrine[133] was built upon the forehead of the Tortoise of the North.

Lest this not achieve complete subjugation, the Four Shrines for the Subjugation of the Regions were built. In order to suppress the palm of the ogress's right hand, a shrine was built at Langtang

Dronma in Kham,[134] under the supervision of the Minyag. In order to suppress the palm of the left hand, the Kyerchu Shrine was built at Bumtang in the south, under the supervision of the Tokar. In order to suppress the sole of the right foot, in the glorious land of Kashmir in the west, the Sherab Dronma Shrine of the race of Tsel was built, under the supervision of the Nepalese. In order to suppress the sole of the left foot, Tsangpa Lung-non, the Brahma Wind-suppressing Shrine, was built in the north, under the supervision of the Pelyang of Hor.[135]

Furthermore, the three shrines at Kachu, Kangchu and Lingchu were built in the east to regulate the sun, moon, planets and stars. In the south, the Nyelnangdro Shrine and Lingtang were built to suppress fire, the fire deity Agni having been propitiated. In the west, Gulang and Shingkun were built to suppress water, once the border between Nepal and Tibet was secured.[136] In the north, Geri and Pelri were built to suppress the winds, once the deities, nagas and ogres had been bound by oath.

By the blessings conferred by the construction of these shrines, the Kingdom under the Sun was subdued by brilliance. The construction of the Rasa Trulnang Shrine was miraculously accomplished in the absence of opposing factors and hindrances. The final completion of every detail of the design of this shrine and of Gyatag Ramoche Shrine was achieved simultaneously by Tritsun and Kongjo, each having taken twelve months.

Songtsen Gampo and the miraculous mendicant monk

The king completed the Shrines for the Subjugation of the Borderlands and for Further Subjugation, and then returned to Trandrug. He said, 'Having paid honour and respect to the precious teachings of the Buddha, as I respectfully and reverently make obeisance to any who have the signs of ordination, my ministers and subjects shall therefore do likewise'. Having spoken, he went outside, and before the five-peaked stupa that had been built in atonement for the killing of a snake, the king saw an old beggar who had spread out his ragged gown and was picking lice off it.

Realising that this beggar bore the signs of ordination, Songtsen Gampo made obeisance and said, 'Although I am a king who has won power over a domain, namely this uncivilised region of the

Land of Snows, because I wanted to make the teachings of the Buddha shine like the sun, I built many shrines and I filled them with manifold symbols of the Buddha's body, speech and mind, and made offerings. I have also vowed to make obeisance to anyone who bears the signs of ordination. Is this not miraculous?'

After the king had spoken, the beggar stood up and draped the tattered gown over his shoulder, 'Thinking of the Buddha's teachings, you, the king, have shown reverence to someone with the signs of ordination, and made obeisance to me, a beggar. That is indeed a miracle.' But the monk then lifted up the five-peaked stupa on the five fingers of his right hand and performed a circumambulation of it. 'Is my feat not also miraculous?' he exclaimed. The king then grew somewhat abashed. 'Your deed is certainly a miracle', he said. Songtsen Gampo then removed his headgear to expose the image of Amitabha upon his head and exclaimed, 'But is this not more miraculous?' The beggar-monk then bared his chest and split it open with a sword to reveal all the omniscient Vairochana deities seated inside him. 'You, the king, have but one deity, yet I have many. Is this not an even greater miracle?' The king then rejoiced greatly, his faith burgeoned and he appointed the beggar as his personal chaplain. 'Abjure heretical thoughts and act reverently towards those who bear the signs of ordination, in spite of their ragged gowns, their appearance or actions. Let this be an example.' Thus he counselled.

*This chapter,
concerning the excellent
construction of the Shrines for the Subjugation of the Borderlands, the Shrines for
Further Subjugation,
and Trulnang and Ramoche,
is the fourteenth.*

15

The consecration of
the two shrines in Lhasa,
the Shrines for the Subjugation of
the Borderlands and the Shrines
for Further Subjugation

Songtsen Gampo inspects the shrines

After the shrines that were duly constructed by Tritsun and Kongjo were completed in every detail, the princesses invited Songtsen Gampo to the highest point of the Potala to view them. The next day, Tritsun led the king and his retinue into Trulnang to offer an inspection of the shrine to the accompaniment of incense and music.

When Tritsun opened the door of the shrine to allow the king to enter, he saw that the floor resembled water and that everything above it was reflected upon it. Thinking that the former lake had burst forth, he dared not proceed. Tritsun therefore removed the ring from her finger and threw it to the floor, whereupon it skidded across the surface like a pebble upon the ice. Seeing this, the king resolved to enter and said to Tritsun, 'This shrine of yours is indeed miraculous!'

Because the lake had originally been filled with earth carried by a goat, and because the king had declared that the shrine was miraculous, it became known universally as Rasa Trulnang Lhakhang, or the 'Earth-Goat Miraculous Shrine'.

These were the wonders that the king beheld:

> The Victorious Ones' celestial mansion of peerless wonder,
> Possessing infinite qualities and utmost beauty,
> Rested upon a spontaneously created square foundation.
> Its four great sides formed a swastika,
> The surrounds of the entrances were decorated with
>   mandalas,
> And the floor was the colour of lapis lazuli.
> In the murals above, fish and crocodiles
> Were as true to life as reflections in a mirror.
> All the pillars of the upper and lower storeys
> Were of utmost beauty and resembled diamond-sceptre
>   daggers,
> The beams, pillar-arches and beam-covers were like stupas,
> And the appearance of the craftsmanship was of unsur-
>   passed wonder.
> Historical fables of former times were clearly illustrated in
>   relief
> On all the inner and outer beam-covers and pillar-arches.
> One hundred and eight white snow-lions with turquoise
>   manes
> Were seen in the attitude of leaping
> On the ends of the rafters of the upper and lower light wells.
> Above them hung webs of pearls
> And blue turquoise lotuses of sapphire hue.
> The upper walls, borders, latticework,
> Balconies and parapets were all beautified with ornaments.
> A golden *ganjira*[137] with one thousand rays of light
> Was accompanied by ornaments of manifold crowns,
> Silk ribbons of all descriptions,
> Fly-whisks and bells, both great and small.

The entire perimeter was encircled by chains of iron.

In the central celestial mansion of the lower shrine,
Abounding with ornaments of limitless wonder,
Stood Avalokiteshvara in the gesture of granting refuge,
Excellently adorned with the major and minor signs of
    greatness
And illuminated by the glory of the twofold accumulation of
    merit.
[At that time the primary image was Buddha Mindro
    Sungjon, the one who said, 'I shall not go!']

Buddha Dipankara, the Nirmanakaya form,
Was surrounded by a retinue of the Eight Near Spiritual
    Sons,
And two Wrathful Ones were seen guarding the doors.
On the right of the shrine was the Buddha Amitabha,
Vermilion in colour with hands in the meditative position,
Beautified by the major and minor signs of limitless wonder,
Surrounded by an eightfold retinue of Avalokiteshvara,
    Vajrapani
And the other Near Spiritual Sons,
Seated in the half-lotus posture on a lotus-and-moon
    pedestal.
The image of Guhyapati on the right of the entrance
Was the colour of the sky and thrust a diamond sceptre at the
    heavens.
The image of Krodharaja on the left
Was the colour of coral and displayed the attitude of
    removing defilements.
The Lord Maitreya to the left of the shrine,
In the gesture of turning the Wheel of Dharma,
Was the colour of saffron and also shone with the glory of
    the major and minor signs of greatness.
The circle of outer and inner offering goddesses in the
    attitude of playfulness
Were of boundless wonder and utmost beauty,
And were seated in the half-lotus position upon lotus-and-
    moon pedestals.
The image of Akshobhya-vajra to the south of the shrine,

Excellently adorned with the major and minor signs,
Exhibiting the twin gestures of earth-touching and
    meditative equipoise,
Was a blaze of a thousand lights that resembled a mountain
    of gold.
The retinue of exceeding brilliance that surrounded it
    included:
Tongchen Rabjom with one face and four arms;
Pratisara with one face and six arms;
A blue-black Yamantaka with six legs in the extended-
    retracted posture,
Six extremely wrathful faces and six hands grasping many
    weapons;
A white Prajnataka
With four faces and eight arms in the extended-retracted
    posture;
One ruby-coloured Padmataka
With one face and four arms, in an attitude of extreme wrath;
And a blue-black Vighnantaka with a furious aspect,
One face and four arms, annihilating troops of obstructions.

On either side of the door
Were gold-coloured images of Vaishravana Jambhala
With a jewel in his right hand and a mongoose in his left
For the purposes of relieving poverty.
In the naga-shrine beside the outer gate,
Were three great nagas, each with one face, two arms
And hoods of snakes, in the cross-legged bodhisattva
    position,
White, red and orange in colour.

In the yaksha shrine on the right of the gate
The ten-necked, nine-headed ogre Langka, with a body of
    blue,
Stood on a horse-head platform.
The yaksha and the gandharva spirits were both red in
    colour,
With three faces and four arms.
They too were seated in the cross-legged bodhisattva
    position.

The seven previous buddhas above the gate-shrine,[138]
Excellently ornamented with the major and minor signs,
Were the Nirmanakaya form.
As to the images of the Victorious Ones on the walls of the
    lower storey,
In the murals on the south side, the king beheld the All-
    subduing Continent,
The Great Compassionate One who protects against the eight
    fears,
Manjushri as a primary image with retinue, five in all,
And a design of the Sukhavati Paradise.
In the southwest corner of the swastika, the threefold
    bodhisattvas were depicted,
And on the western pillar-joints were the five Buddha-
    families
And the acts of the King of Infinite Beneficence.
The Buddhas of the Past, Present and Future, surrounded by
    retinues,
Were depicted in the northwest corner of the swastika.
The Twelve Deeds of the Sage were shown
In the murals at the junction of the north and northeast
    walls.
On the eastern side were Tara, Avalokiteshvara and
Muni Marajit, together with an assembly of bodhisattvas.

In the murals in the southeastern corner of the swastika
Were the assembly of the Blessed One and the Menlha or
    Medicine Buddha.
As to the majority of the murals of Tara,
The white Hayagriva and the like inside the central shrine,
They were executed precisely in accordance with the one
    hundred and eight treatises.
Having seen these elegant murals and the rest
In all their many hues, the king was elated.

On the pinnacle in the southeast was a ladder resembling a
    snow-lion.
In the corner of the swastika in that direction was the shrine
    of Pelden Lhamo.
Because the northern shrine, a place of utmost beauty,
Was not occupied by any deity,

This manifested king thought,
'The Self-created Eleven-faced Image
Should be brought from Mt. Potala on a carriage, to the
    accompaniment of music,
To be placed in this location'.
That evening, the self-created image with its retinue
Travelled through the air by magic,
To the welcome of celestial music provided by the gods,
And came to rest, without a throne, in the northern shrine.
Avalokiteshvara, beautified by ornaments,
Lady Bhrikuti, Sarasvati
And Amritakundali stood to the right of the door,
While Khasarpani, Nilagriva,
Reverend Tara, the goddess Marici
And King Hayagriva stood to the left.

At that moment, the mountains and the land shook in six
    ways,
All the gods caused flowers to fall like rain,
And by the power of their faith,
The eyes of the king, queens and the assembled ministers
    were filled with tears.
Each held aloft gifts with deepest reverence and love,
Made obeisance and offerings,
And were able to achieve both common and excellent
    attainments.

As for the protection of the Teachings by the local deities of
    that place,
The naga-kings Nanda and Upananda,
The ten-necked ogre-king Langka,
The assembly of yaksha and gandharva demons,
Kubera, Mahakala, Pelgyi Lhamo and so on
Were appointed lord-protectors of the shrine and doctrine.

Thus it was. The Chinese princess also invited the king to Ramoche
and offered him an inspection of the shrine, and he rejoiced most
heartily.

Consecration of the shrines

The king then wished to consecrate both Trulnang and Ramoche,
and prepared and arrayed the items necessary for a great celebra-

tion, including an unimaginable quantity of offerings. With umbrellas, victory banners and music of every kind, the king proceeded onto the mandala, and holding flowers in his hands, which
were joined in prayer, he spoke these words of truth:

> Son of Shakya, King of Sages, foremost among humans,
> Who benefits beings by your countless manifestations;
> Buddha Sugata and the other buddhas of the ten directions:
> Bestow your blessings of happiness and peace!
>
> By the current of skilful means and compassion,
> Ripening and liberating whomever is suited,
> The reverend Avalokiteshvara and the other bodhisattvas:
> Bestow your blessings of happiness and peace!
>
> Son of the Victorious Ones, Sthavira Subhuti,
> And sublime chief disciples who cause the increase of the
>   sacred religion,
> Which is itself the pure, unblemished instructions of the
>   Victorious One,
> By the four expedient methods of gathering disciples:
> Bestow your blessings of happiness and peace!
>
> Moreover, in all the pure realms of the ten directions,
> May all the past, present and future buddhas and
>   bodhisattvas
> Empower this place and bestow their blessings!

After the king had made these supplications, all the buddhas and
bodhisattvas, heroes and heroines, and all the protectors of the
sacred religion instantly assembled upon a point the size of a mote
of dust in a sunbeam, just as clouds and storms gather in the heavens. All the buddhas then scattered flowers and gave their blessings. The bodhisattvas made auspicious pronouncements and consecrated the shrines. Brahma, Indra and the other gods caused flowers to fall in a great shower. The sons and daughters of the gods,
bearing umbrellas, victory banners, ensigns, ribbons, precious garlands and other ornaments, played great celestial drums, flutes,
gongs, tambourines and many other musical instruments. Sweet
celestial incense pervaded the ten directions as if carried by a gentle
breeze and filled everything with fragrance. The sons and daughters of the gods then spoke as one:

Lord Avalokiteshvara, the Compassionate One himself,
Who is the embodiment of the thoughts of all the buddhas:
For the purpose of increasing the Teachings in this barbaric
    land,
You, the Sublime One, were born as the lord of the people.

Excelling in race, physique, qualities and glory,
Songtsen Gampo, manifestation of the Buddha:
These two shrines which belong to you, the Dharma-king,
Were consecrated by the buddhas,
And the bodhisattvas made auspicious pronouncements.
All the gods gave extensive offerings,
Flowers fell from the sky like rain,
Excellent incense gathered like clouds in the air,
And jewels were strewn upon the ground.

The victory banner of the Buddha's teaching was firmly
    established,
And the sacred drum of the Holy Teaching sounded forth.
Today, the sun of the Dharma shines in the sky.
Today, the lamp of the Dharma's glory illuminates all.
Today, the king has achieved empowerment and blessings.

Like a lotus brought forth by the light of the sun,
Today, the darkness of the mind is totally dispelled.
Like a poor man finding a mine filled with jewels,
You, the Bodhisattva Dharma-king,
Have satisfied the faculties of your mind with joy and
    happiness.

Having spoken thus, the deities withdrew from sight. In this way, the consecration of both Trulnang and Ramoche were accomplished miraculously at one and the same time. These events were clear yet intangible, like reflections in a mirror or the image of the moon upon the water, and the king, the ministers and all their subjects, having witnessed them distinctly, rejoiced and were satisfied, and their hearts were filled with gladness.

Having held a great celebration, all of the people of Tibet harmoniously gave an unimaginable performance of singing, dancing and the like. The king then rose from his precious throne, and expressing words to the melody of Brahma, sang this joyous song:

To the Three Jewels that are the nature of compassion;
And to Avalokiteshvara, guide on the path of liberation;
With a reverential mind, I make supplications.
Heed my auspicious song!

Today, in the sky before us
The buddhas and bodhisattvas
Appeared like gathered clouds,
And the auspicious consecration was miraculously achieved.

Brahma and the other gods
Played cymbals and other musical instruments,
Lotuses fell like rain,
And the auspicious consecration was miraculously achieved.

The victory banner of the Buddha's teaching was
    established,
Thereby vanquishing the forces of darkness,
And by the power and glory of the defeat of accumulated
    evils,
The auspicious consecration was miraculously achieved.

The great drum of the sacred Dharma sounded,
The ignorance of the five poisons[139] was spontaneously
    dispelled,
The great drum of the Three Jewels rang out,
And the auspicious consecration was miraculously achieved.

Today, the sun of happiness shone forth,
Uncontrollable joy arose,
Entertainments for all the desires fell like rain,
And the auspicious consecration was miraculously achieved.

By the good fortune of the tutelary deities,
And of myself, Songtsen Gampo,
I sing this auspicious song
To bring blessings to our Tibetan people.

Thus he sang. The queens, together with the ministers and people of Tibet, rejoiced, were satisfied, and their hearts were filled with gladness. Each made obeisance and offerings to the king.

Draglha Lubug

The king also constructed a shrine at Draglha Lubug, the primary image being Tubpa Draglha Gonpo, or Shakyamuni the Rock-Deity Protector.[140] To the right of this image was Shariputra and to the left Maudgalyanaputra. To the right of these was Maitreya and to the left Avalokiteshvara. Even though the images, the primary one with retinue, five in all, appeared clearly in the rock, the images were carved in relief by Nepalese craftsmen to facilitate the accumulation of merit by future beings. The excavation of the circumambulatory tunnel through the rock was duly undertaken by the Tibetan people. At that time salt was sixty times the price of grain. To each person who excavated a *dre*-measure of rock, the king gave a gift of a *dre* of salt. When about half a *dre* had been excavated and the rubble had been exchanged for salt, the images of the deities and so on inside the shrine were thoroughly completed, and the shrine was consecrated.

This chapter,
concerning the thorough
completion and consecration of
the two shrines in Lhasa, the Shrines for
the Subjugation of the Borderlands,
the Shrines for Further Subjugation
and so on, is the
fifteenth.

16

Treasures are concealed, and all the Tibetan people are led to Dharma in order to bring benefits and happiness

As neither the Chinese princess Kongjo nor the Nepalese princess Tritsun bore a son, Songtsen Gampo married Zhangzhungza, Princess of Zhangzhung. She bore no son, but built the Timbu Kogpa Shrine at Chagkhakhong. He then married Ruyongza, Princess of Ruyong, who bore no son, but built the Migmangtsel Shrine at Khoshaling. He then married Minyagza, Princess of Minyag, who bore no son, but built the Khadrag Golden Shrine at Kharnadong. From among the Mang of Tolung, he married Mangza Tricham, Princess of Mang. It was prophesied that she would bear a son, and indeed in the Iron-female-snake Year [681] at the end of the ninth month and at the beginning of the tenth month of her pregnancy, the prince named Gungri Gungtsen, an incomparable royal scion, was born in the auspicious celestial mansion of Draglha. A great celebration was held to mark his birth, and everyone rejoiced. A shrine and a stupa dedicated to the tutelary deity of mother and son were built upon the lap of a rocky mountain that resembled a seated image of the Holy Tara in the region of Yerpa. After the structures were consecrated, the infant's father, Songtsen Gampo, prayed that they might become life-roots of the Teaching, like the Rasa Trulnang shrine.

The king then issued this command: 'In order to ensure that the Tibetan people abide by the Laws of the Ten Virtuous Actions, a court of fearful terror will be established. Punishment will be meted out to those who harm the teachings of the Buddha and to those who break the laws of Tibet'. Having given these orders, the king created manifestations of himself, and ghosts were bound and beaten, their eyes put out and their hamstrings cut. Although this did not take place in reality, he carried out these acts to instil fear, and everyone obeyed the Laws of the Ten Virtuous Actions.

Songtsen Gampo and the Khotanese monks

At that time, in Changra Mugpo in the land of Khotan, two novice monks had propitiated Manjushri unsuccessfully for eight years, when a voice came from the sky, saying: 'You two novices lack a karmic connection with Manjushri; it will therefore be difficult for you to obtain accomplishment. As your deity is the sublime Avalokiteshvara, and as this Sublime One is at present manifested as the king of the snowy kingdom of Tibet, go there and behold his actual face'.[141]

Having spoken, the voice abated, but the words caused the hairs upon the two novices' bodies to stand on end! They set out for Tibet with regard for neither life nor limb, bringing with them only provisions for their journey. When they reached the precipice that transects the lower Tolung valley, they beheld beside the river birds and dogs devouring a multitude of headless and eyeless corpses. The novices were filled with doubt and asked some Tibetans where the king resided and what had befallen the corpses. The Tibetans replied that the king dwelled in Lhasa and that the corpses belonged to those whom he had punished for breaking the law. Hearing these words, the two novices lost faith and exclaimed, 'Avalokiteshvara is a fiend! So many people have been killed! Let us return to Khotan!' So saying, they turned back.

When their thoughts became apparent to the king, he said to his minister Dri Seru Gongton: 'Go swiftly on horseback to the lower Tolung valley, where you will find two people with shaven heads who wear square saffron robes, the signs of ordination. They were intending to come before me, but now heretical thoughts have arisen in their minds, and they have turned back. Bring them to me by peaceful means'. When the minister apprehended the novices, they were terrified, but he reassured them and brought them before the king. Songtsen Gampo made obeisance to the monks and asked with a smile, 'What brings you to Tibet?' They replied,

> We hail from the land of Khotan, where we had propitiated the sublime Manjushri for eight years without success. A voice came from the sky, saying, 'As your deity is the sublime Avalokiteshvara, and as this Sublime One is at present manifested as the king of the snowy kingdom of Tibet, go there and behold his actual face'. Because the voice had spoken thus, we came to Tibet with regard for neither life nor limb, but we beheld many human corpses upon the road, so we questioned the Tibetan people about them. They informed us that the corpses belonged to those whom the king had punished for breaking the law. We therefore grew afraid and turned back.

Thus they replied. Having satisfied them with food and drink, the king then removed his headdress to reveal the image of Amitabha and said,

> I am the Great Compassionate King of Tibet. From the time I began to rule this realm up until the present I have benefited sentient beings. Not only have I led them to the path of liberation and enlightenment, I have done them no harm, even as small as the point of a needle. As these Tibetans are descended from a monkey and a rock-ogress, I created these terrifying manifestations to instruct them.

Having spoken thus, he snapped his fingers, the corpses vanished like a rainbow and the two novices were filled with devotion and reverence. 'Great King, we two have journeyed far and experienced great difficulties in order to understand the Dharma more fully. We humbly request instruction on the Three Meanings'. The king replied,

O novice monks, heed well! In short, the root of all Dharma is contained in the Three Meanings. Having renounced the taking of life, theft, sexual misconduct and other misdeeds committed through the faculty of the body, perform obeisance and circumambulation before the Three Jewels and sincerely embrace the treasure of moral behaviour, on the basis of which a higher rebirth is achieved. Never relinquish the ornament of precious moral discipline.

Having renounced lies, slander, coarse speech and other misdeeds committed through the faculty of speech, recite the excellent words, the Six-Syllable Mantra. It is the essence of the accumulated thoughts of all the buddhas, the quintessence of the collection of the fundamentals of all Dharma, the treasure-house of all virtue, goodness and qualities, and the root of the accomplishment of all benefits and happiness.

Having renounced covetous, injurious and heretical thoughts and other misdeeds committed through the faculty of the mind, adopt these worthy attitudes: while taking refuge in the Three Jewels, as there is not a single sentient being in the three realms or of the six rebirths who has not been your mother or father, fervently desire to take their unbearable suffering upon yourselves, transfer to them any benefits or happinesses that you acquire, and meditate on holding others dearer than yourselves.

In short, never for a single moment be divorced from loving-kindness, compassion and the precious enlightenment-thought. Excellent thoughts are more special than excellent religion.

If you grasp these Three Meanings, you will achieve Buddhahood in a single lifetime and in a single body. If you fail to integrate them into your own stream of consciousness, even though you have all the teachings, Sutras, Tantras, transmissions and pith instructions in your mind, it is mere lip service to religion, devoid of essence.

He instructed the two novices on the *Three Works on the Great Compassion of Dharma*, the *White Lotus Sutra* and the *Benefits of the Six-Syllable Mantra* and led them onto the liberating path to enlightenment. They rejoiced, their hearts were gladdened, they performed obeisance at the feet of the king and made this supplication:

Alas! Dharma-king, O manifestation!
Compassionate sublime being!
Grant us safe conduct to our own country.

The king replied, 'Do you wish to return to your homeland instantaneously and without obstruction?' The novices said, 'By all means, this is our desire'. The king poured a *dre*-measure of sand into the hem of the robes of each, and blessed it that it would turn to gold. He then placed his hands on their heads and said, 'Use whatever luggage you may have as your pillows, and thinking of your country, sleep'. The two did as the king instructed and fell asleep. When they awoke, they found themselves in their homeland, and the sand in the hems of their robes had turned to gold. In their next lives, these two novices attained the stage of arhat.

Prince Gungri Gungtsen acceded to the throne and took a wife at the age of thirteen. A son, known as Mangsong Mangtsen, was born in the Fire-male-dog Year [686]. Gungri Gungtsen ruled the kingdom for five years, but when he was eighteen years old, his body departed for Mt. Potala.[142]

Gungri Gungtsen predeceased his father,
And his tomb was built at Donkhorda.
It lay to the left of Namri Songtsen's,
And was called Gungchen Gungri.

Concealment of treasures

King Songtsen Gampo returned to the throne, bringing happiness and joy, and thought to himself,

My two shrines, Rasa Trulnang and Gyatag Ramoche, should possess boundless qualities for as long as the teachings of the Buddha persist. As all the buddhas, bodhisattvas, heroes, heroines and dakinis of wisdom manifested themselves in their ordinary forms at the time of consecration, like precious continents, the shrines will endure forever. They will excel all others in the land of Tibet and will possess infinite qualities. Dharma adherents will enjoy wealth equal to the sky, and riches will appear to whomever desires them. All the treasures of the borderlands will be assembled here, and Tibet will conquer nations everywhere. Matchless in this land, rays of light will cover the ten directions. The shrines' renown will spread over all the earth. Their blessings will be like the radiance of the sun and moon. Wealth in the form of treasures, jewels, grain, gold, silver, *yig*-stones,[143] ornaments, clothing and material possessions will fall like rain. After examining the attributes of the land, treasures must be concealed to endow these shrines with manifold qualities. Just as on the shores of the Ocean of the Wish-fulfilling Jewel that satisfies all desires, every village and town possesses great wealth on account of the ocean's power, similarly, in this place where precious treasures are concealed, riches and wealth will arise spontaneously.

As to the treasures concealed for the future benefit of the Tibetan people, the treasure of the sacred Dharma was concealed near the pillar ornamented with vases. By its qualities, the teachings of the Buddha shine like the sun in this land of Tibet and the people enjoy the sacred Dharma. A treasure trove of precious gold and silver was concealed near the pillar ornamented with leaves. By its qualities, all the treasures of the borderlands are assembled at the centre, and gold and silver are enjoyed. The treasure of the Wrathful Mantra of Power was concealed near the pillar ornamented with serpents' heads. By its qualities, all foreign armies, obstructions and adversaries are prevented. Prescriptions for the well-being of livestock were concealed near the pillar ornamented with snow-lions' heads. By the qualities of these, horses and cattle flourish, and dairy products are abundant.

Precious *ratna dewa*[144] herbs were placed in a small box made of *zi*-stone, wrapped in five kinds of fine silk, and were concealed beneath the image of Jambhala. By their qualities, every desirable ornament, item of clothing, jewelry, grain and the like appear.

Precious *tagsha dewa*,[145] wrapped in snakeskin, was concealed in the naga-shrine. By its qualities, there are always good harvests, healthy cattle and timely showers of rain, and harm by geomantic forces and nagas is averted.

The lapis lazuli begging-bowl filled with infinite quantities of foods of various kinds was also concealed in the shrine. By its qualities, all desirable enjoyment in the form of food and drink arise, and crops are abundant.

A great cauldron of gold, silver and jewels of various kinds was concealed beneath the great mandala to provide for repairs in case of damage or cracks that might appear and to provide for offerings over long periods in the Rasa Shrine. Prayers were offered to ensure that individuals might possess good karma and good fortune.

Gold, silver and other valuables were placed in precious vessels, wrapped in various kinds of fine silk, and concealed in the *tsen*-shrine,[146] the naga-shrine and the inner circle of the shrine to ensure that the land remains lush, that rain falls in season, that the various grains ripen, that drought, frosts, hail, blight, famine, disease, pestilence and damage by foreign armies are averted, to render all times and places auspicious and to spread virtue and happiness over everything.

As this is merely a summary, readers who wish to know more about the nature of the concealed treasures should consult the *Record of Royal Commands*. Songtsen Gampo then proclaimed:

> By the qualities of these concealed treasures, the fame and renown of this, my shrine, will spread to all places lit by the sun and moon. It will have no rival in this world, and prospective Dharma adherents and sponsors from the borderlands will increase. Once all the peoples of the borderlands have been brought under my aegis, its glory will be equal to the sky. In future, whenever my descendants, queens, ministers or any of my Tibetan subjects wish to construct a shrine, samples of earth and rock may be brought to my shrine of Rasa Trulnang, and the consecration of their shrines will be achieved miraculously. In the absence of the obstructive activities of fiends and adversaries, being auspicious, their shrines will come to possess many qualities.

Thus he spoke.

Teachings and pronouncements

Then, in Lhasa, on the Plain of Neutang, the king placed his hands upon the head of his grandson Mangsong Mangtsen and thoroughly instructed him on the following: *Pangkong Chaggyapa*; the *White Lotus Sutra*; the *Moon Lamp of the Sacred Dharma*; the *Explana-*

tory Tantra on Accomplishing Avalokiteshvara; the *Future Revelation of Secrets; Service, Obeisance, Offerings and Circumambulation Offered in Lhasa; Revelations on the Qualities of Seeing, Hearing, Thinking and Touching; Restoration of External Boundaries* and the *Benefits Attached to Undertaking Service to Inner Deities.* The prince recorded his grandfather's instructions in a letter, and concealed them like a treasure in the *tsen* shrine. King Songtsen Gampo then prophesied:

> In the fifth generation of my descendants, there will appear a king with the names Tri and De.[147] At that time, many pandits will come from India to translate the complete sacred Dharma. They will properly establish the foundation for the teaching and construct many shrines. In spreading the teaching of the Buddha, they will bring about its increase. There will arise many ordained persons, beautified by the ornament of the three higher teachings, who will wear the victory banner of saffron robes. They will become the central foci of my descendants' veneration. They will be provided with all necessities, and all glory, benefits, happiness, virtue and joy will arise.

After the king had spoken thus, Minister Gar immediately inscribed his words upon a copper scroll and concealed it in the treasury at Chimpu.

The king then gave limitless advice necessary for the conduct of worldly affairs to the ministers of external and internal affairs, to his Tibetan subjects both male and female, and to every adult in turn. By the power of the generation stage of great compassion, he set them upon the path of the Dharma of the Six-Syllable Mantra. [These instructions were also recorded in a letter by Minister Dri Seru Gongton for the benefit of future generations of Tibetans.]

Moreover, the king himself wrote detailed, intermediate and abbreviated versions of his autobiography, rolled them into three scrolls and concealed them beneath the pillar that was ornamented with vases.[148] He then prayed that individuals might possess good karma and good fortune.

The king and consorts had now completed all their deeds, and in the eyes of the inhabitants of the Land of Snows, they were like father and mother, like the leaders of faith for the salvation of sentient beings, like jewels that satisfy needs and desires, like lamps that dispel darkness, and seemed as impartial as the sun and moon. By skilful means, they had no enemies abroad, and by beauteous kindness they protected their subjects at home. All the Tibetan people under their authority came to possess wealth and enjoyed happiness.

*This chapter,
in which treasures are
concealed, and all the Tibetan people are
led to the Dharma in order to bring all
benefits and happiness,
is the sixteenth.*

17

The deeds
of the king and queens
are completed, and they are absorbed
into the heart of the Self-created
Eleven-faced Image

Songtsen Gampo's final teaching

OM MANI PADME HUM! Homage to the deities of great compassion! As soon as the sun had risen the following day, Prince Gungri Gungtsen placed his own clothes upon the palace roof as a seat for his father, Songtsen Gampo, the manifestation of great compassion and great Dharma-protecting king, and offered him many varieties of food. The prince performed manifold prostrations and circumambulations, and made the following request:

> E MA HO!
> Activity of all the buddhas,
> Compassion of Amitabha,

Messenger of Paradise,
Refuge of all Tibetan people:
By viewing us with your compassion,
The common people behold the body of the Victorious One.
Although profound thoughts are indeed appearances—
The compassion of ultimate reality,
Not concealed in the mind of the Victorious One—
Show us the self-appearances that lack object
By clearly revealing those things that are concealed.
Show us the inactivity that is beyond thought.
Having shown the uncontrived nature,
While dwelling in the nature of inactivity,
Yet manifesting through the power of the three forms,
May you instil vigour in our minds.

Thus he prostrated and made his request. Then his father, the king, commanded:

Great celestial son, heed well!
I am the activity of all buddhas.
Having vowed in the presence of Amitabha
I came with enlightenment-thought for the benefit of the
    Tibetan people.
I am inseparable from the Victorious Ones.
All beings are my potential Dharma adherents.
You are the blessings of the Sublime Ones.
Although the profound thoughts of the Victorious Ones
Are the foundation of the sublime path,
The compassion of ultimate reality,
They are not suitable for revelation to inferior minds.
Nevertheless, those things which are concealed will be
    revealed by a mind of compassion.
As fabrication due to misunderstanding is the basis of
    disparagement,
I will disclose the primordial secret to those who have no
    refuge.
Hold it at the very centre of your heart!
The ultimate truth in entirety
I will show you well. Heed!

All the various phenomena are self-appearances.
That which lacks an object is beyond thought.

Beyond thought is inactivity.
It is abiding in its natural state.
Non-abiding nature is the most excellent repose.
Severing of activities on account of freedom from extremities
By individuals who comprehend this
Is labelled 'view'.
The emptiness of grasping and self-luminosity
Is labelled 'meditation'.
That which is devoid of freedom from meaning
Is labelled 'action'.
The destruction of clinging to rejection and acceptance
Is labelled 'result'.
Effortless endeavour for the benefit of sentient beings
Is labelled 'compassion'.
The absence of grief and fatigue in this
Is labelled 'great'.
Striving for the benefit of beings, but being undefiled by
     faults
Is labelled 'sublime'.
One who has accomplished control over compassion
Is labelled 'king'.
One who guides all sentient beings equally
Is labelled '*songtsen*', 'honest and firm'.[149]
Discourse on whatever is beneficial to the mind
Is labelled 'pith instruction'.
Records left posthumously
Are labelled 'lineage of transmissions'.
Evocation of lucid faith of sentient beings
Is labelled 'extraordinary knowledge'.
Self-release from conceptualisation
Is labelled 'Buddha'.
Leading beings onto the path
Is labelled 'Holy Dharma'.
Integrating mind into inactivity
Is labelled 'sangha'.
Effortless dwelling in one's own sphere
Is labelled 'inactivity'.
The transformation of ordinary conceptualisations
Is labelled 'generation stage'.
The various ways of instructing the mind
Are labelled 'Dharma activity'.

Internal knowledge of its freedom of origins
Is labelled 'comprehension'.
The sole understanding of its meaning
Is labelled 'the sole meaning'.
Many which are intrinsically one
Are labelled 'Dharmakaya'.
Pure appearance manifesting as deities
Is labelled 'Sambhogakaya'.
Bringing forth by various means
Is labelled 'Nirmanakaya'.
Maintaining non-thought
Is labelled 'direct realisation'.

Because all of these labels are names,
Let there be no attachment to names!
As all thoughts are intellect,
Renounce and abandon all intellectual activity.
Because this so-called 'renounce' is a word,
Abandon and release your grasp upon words.
Because this so-called 'release' is intellect,
Conceal actions of intellect in the sphere.
This so-called concealment is a worthy concept,
An uncontrived state beyond good and bad,
A vivid state beyond concealment,
A clear state beyond coming and going,
A state of repose beyond rejection and acceptance,
A state of calm beyond partialities,
A state of centredness beyond grasping and detachment,
A state of brilliance beyond clarity or obstruction,
A distinct state beyond forgetfulness or distraction,
A state of clarity beyond activity and inactivity.

Look at objects beyond thought.
Look at the meaning beyond words.
Look at the place beyond good and evil.
Look at the mind which is beyond within and without.
Look at the mind beyond male and female.
Look at the meaning devoid of grasping for duality.
The actual meaning is beyond thought.

While not pursuing the 'beyond',
Look while in the state of freedom from intellect and words.

Since there is no object to be seen through looking,
Through not looking, the ultimate Dharma will be seen.
Through not pursuing, mind itself is accomplished.
Not seizing, not releasing, one will be self-liberated.
In those who see things this way,
I do not perceive the duality of Samsara and Nirvana.
I do not perceive the duality of virtue and non-virtue.
I do not perceive the duality of good and evil.
I do not perceive the duality of permanent and nihilistic.
I do not perceive the duality of male and female.
I do not perceive the duality of pleasure and pain.
I do not perceive the duality of 'is' and 'is not'.
I do not perceive the duality of near and far.
I do not perceive the duality of high and low.
I do not perceive the duality of clear and obstructed.
Through the self-nature of non-seeing
It is self-nature to manifest multifariously.
May multifarious nature be unceasing!
May multifarious nature be free from grasping!
May multifarious nature be free from rejections and
    acceptances!
Multifarious nature free from grasping is the Dharmakaya.
Unobstructed clarity is the Sambhogakaya.
Freedom from multifarious nature is the Nirmanakaya.
Ordinary non-thought is the Dharmakaya.
Desiring the ultimate Dharma is ordinary.
That itself is beyond thought.
If there is freedom from desire, there is freedom from
    meaning.
If there is liberation from grasping at dualities, then
    realisation has occurred.
If there is no acceptance and rejection, one will obtain great
    achievements.
If there is endeavour for the benefit of beings, one will
    accomplish these activities.
If the mind is decisive, it arrives at its destination.
If there is no arriving, one is an outcast.
To individuals of this class,
All awareness is self-awareness,
All knowing is self-knowing,

All liberation is self-liberation,
All clarity is self-clarity,
All emptiness is self-emptiness,
All existence is self-existence,
All abiding is self-abiding,
All joy is self-joy,
All suffering is self-suffering.
Everything is self-awareness and self-projection.
Owing to lack of meditation, there is nothing to think about.
Owing to inactivity in one's continuum, there is no
    distraction.
As there is nothing to leave, there is nothing to send.
If there is nothing to forget, there is no erring.
Wisdom of this nature is incessant.
In deep meditation, there is neither session nor non-session.
Nor in visualisation is there grasping or detachment.
In conceptualisation, there is no good or bad.
With regard to the object of the mind, there is no within or
    without.
In immaterial things, there is no within or without.
If hopes and doubts are abandoned, there is freedom from
    faults.
Without desire, there is no obtaining.
Without striving, faults are purified.

If there are none who pursue the result, the thoughts of the
Buddha will perish. As thinking and speech are beyond
thought, speech is void. Once independence has been achieved
in this way, the lineage will be held by oneself. Releasing will
take place within. The symbols of grasping and holding will
perish. Appearance and existence will be the lineage of instructions. All action will become Dharma action. All seeing and
hearing will manifest in the three *kayas*. Wisdom will burst forth
from within. All defilements will be self-purifying. Oneself will
be instilled with faith and reverence. The origin of Samsara
and Nirvana will be recognised as self-awareness. One will
know how to understand clearly happiness and suffering. The
grasping of self will be liberated into the Dharmakaya.

   Having seen the base, there is no view. Having found it, there
is nothing to meditate upon. By controlling self, there is

nothing to be acquired. By recognising one's own mind, there is no awakening. Since wisdom bursts forth by itself, it is resting unforgetfully. The multifarious nature is unceasingly liberating, having purified the feeling without trace, since awareness is attached to stupidity. Liberation from seeing the unadorned Dharmakaya, since it continues to pursue awareness alone, is the *kaya* of non-duality. It remains in the nature of the great self-awareness. As it is self-arising, miraculous accomplishment arises. As it is self-illuminating, the depth appears clearly. As it is self-appearance, it will appear in clear light. As it is self-awareness, it arises in Dharmakaya. As it is self-liberating, unobstructed passage arises.

Further, in not acting oneself, will others act? Having nothing for oneself to think about, can one find in others an example? Without seeing oneself, would beings be subdued? Would one find through seeking? Without meeting and separation? Staying without departing? Without objects, can one obtain anything in one's hand? Can one's eyes see that which cannot be shown?

Would one seek more than one can possess? In addition to clarity does one look for more? In addition to liberation does one dismantle it? Does one bathe for more than cleanliness? Does one drink after one's thirst has been quenched? Eat after one is replete? Burn oneself after one is warm? Realise after knowing?

Thus, once thought is free from causes, there will be freedom from a mind obsessed with acquisition and accomplishment. Is there any use for antidotes for immaterial things? By not heeding appearances through lack of time, appearances of eternalism and nihilism will be purified by themselves. By self-liberating from grasping, the extremes of hope and fear are abandoned. By liberation from grasping from within oneself, freedom from rebirth is maintained. Having seen freedom from conceptualisation from within oneself, enemies and obstructions will be self-subduing.

Oh! This wandering of the mind without antidote is called the activity of self-appearance of wisdom. Abiding in the mode of selflessness is called freedom from rejection and acceptance. Wisdom arising from within is called self-liberating

conceptualisation. Inconceivable 'is' and 'is not' are called freedom from refutation and assertion. Grasping at identification
of endeavour is called the bursting forth of the profundity of
the ultimate Dharma. Spontaneous accomplishment free from
rebirth is called the self-arising result.

Oh! Thus, understanding and realising are simultaneous.
Knowing and liberating are simultaneous. Clarifying and see-
ing are simultaneous. Adhering and touching are simultaneous.
Moistening and fluidity are simultaneous.

Oh! To individuals who know this, by impartiality in their
views, they may wear the sky. By freedom from clarity or obstruction in meditation, they may carry the sun. By freedom
from obstruction, they may ride the wind. By freedom from
acceptance or rejection in the result, they may behold a continent of gold. Among yogins with this realisation, there is an
object for their view. There is an object for their meditation.
There is an object for their activity. There is something to be
accomplished in the result. Therefore dismantle awareness of
predispositions. Let the signs be self-liberating. Destroy the
grasping of within and without. Abandon acceptance of good
and rejection of evil. Let go of attachment and grasping. Release the pride of desiring good. Release the envy of competitiveness. Extinguish the great fire of anger. Enlighten the ignorance of non-understanding. Remain undistracted in a state
of inactivity. Seal the mind that grasps at duality in the sphere
of the sky. In reality, by freedom from objects of meditation, let
it be.

Oh! Individuals of this kind:
If one meditates in the generation stage, one becomes the
    tutelary deity.
If one remembers the completion stage, the signs of grasping
    are destroyed.
If you desire unity, look at the rainbow in the sky.
If you wish to see ultimate meaning, do not adhere to
    ordinary Dharmas.
Until you see, adhere to the gurus of the lineages of
    instruction.
If you wish to carry out Dharma activity, abandon the
    grasping of selfishness.

If you desire the armour of fearlessness, transform the three
doors into deities.
If you strive for the benefit of others, generate beneficial
thoughts for beings.
If you wish to accomplish for their benefit, abandon the
distractions of mundane activities.
If one subdues enemies and obstructions, one will generate
unconditional compassion.
If you desire the result of happiness in subsequent lives,
practice patience now.
If you wish to subdue beings, cherish others above oneself.
If you wish to overcome laziness, then meditate on death
and impermanence.
If attachment or grasping arise, meditate on dream and
illusion.
If you are alarmed by the evil of hindrance, stabilise your
own mind.
If you wish to act in accordance with the Dharma, abandon
all that is non-Dharma.
Even if one were to accompany me, there is nothing more
than this.
Even if one met another Buddha, there is nothing more than
this.

Thus, at the very moment when the Dharma-protecting king made
clear his thoughts, the celestial prince and all his subjects were effortlessly liberated into the great realm of self-arising, self-liberating ultimate Dharma. At that very moment, free from acceptance
or rejection of pleasure and suffering, free from the concepts of
good or evil, of Samsara and Nirvana, there being no distinction
between this life and future lives, the faces of the sublime ones
were seen, just as mortals may look upon one another. Thus all the
people, in their thoughts of self-arising self-liberating awareness,
were freed from the distinction between subject and object.

Then the celestial prince and all the subjects rejoiced, and having gladdened their father, the king, with extensive inner and outer
offerings, they showed their profound gratitude. After the king
had sat in thoughtful silence for a moment, he looked up and spoke
these words:

AGSAM! Great royal prince, heed well!
At some time at the end of the era,
This, my domain of Lhasa,
Which is like a fish, a frog, a tadpole and a monkey,
Will gradually be destroyed by water.[150]
Its resemblance to a fish is the self-nature of the mother of
    the Victorious Ones.
The *reri* pattern of cloth is like the actual Buddhas of the Ten
    Directions.
The Victorious Ones perform service for the Victorious Ones.
For whoever is in the mouth of this fishlike city,
It is no different from touching the mother of the Victorious
    One.
That is because purifications have already been
    accomplished
And the cessation of the Samsaric sufferings has been
    attained.
This is an endeavour of great significance. The people of
    Tibet
Who collect stone, slate, pebbles or mud, as little as an egg,
Will thereby be paying obeisance to the buddhas
And will thus embark upon the path of happiness.
When members of my race pay respect to the city,
When it resembles a fish, it is like giving it fins.
When it resembles a frog, it is like placing a hat upon it.
When it resembles a tadpole, it is like spreading out a
    mattress.
When it resembles a monkey, and when it assumes a form,
Having displayed great offerings,
It is best to make fervent supplications with faith and
    devotion.
Having done this, Lhasa may endure for a little while longer.
If the inner deities are propitiated, it benefits the outer
    boundaries of the city.
If the outer boundaries are restored, the inner deities will be
    pleased.
If supplications are made while offerings are prepared,
All the wishes of the Tibetan people will be fulfilled.
In degenerate times, even though one has committed many
    wicked acts,

By seeing, hearing or touching Lhasa, city of mine,
Most sentient beings may be liberated from Samsara,
Due to the compassion of the sublime ones.
This is the merit of my Tibetan subjects.
For this reason, those who seek refuge, men and women
    alike:
Generate great courage and redouble your efforts
To see, hear and touch Lhasa, city of mine.
This will establish you upon the path of liberation.
By fervently making offerings in Lhasa, city of mine,
Those who desire to dispel all faults,
And those who desire to accomplish all qualities:
All wishes will be fulfilled.
Whatever you desire, request it of the Victorious Ones.

Thus the father, the great king, commanded the celestial prince: 'Great prince, conceal treasure troves of gold, silver and other riches as a means to guarantee the restoration of Lhasa, should the city be damaged by floods and it becomes necessary to undertake such work'. At that very time, therefore, a treasure trove of gold, silver, jewels and many other riches was concealed under the gown of the left leg of the image of the *yaksha* Nagakubera to assist the celestial prince in making offerings in Lhasa. The prince then prayed and entrusted the treasures to individuals possessing good karma and good fortune. By this means, the benefit of beings in the south and west was also accomplished. Thus King Songtsen Gampo revealed the instructions relating to concealments.

The royal valediction

The Dharma-king then ruled for seventy years, bringing other countries under his power. He caused the teachings of the Buddha to shine like the sun, and sensual enjoyments and material wealth to fall like rain. He led all Tibetan people to happiness. When the manifestation-king Songtsen Gampo was eighty-two years of age, on the tenth day of the month of Kartika in the Iron-male-dog Year [710],[151] he came before the image of Avalokiteshvara in the northern shrine of the Trulnang Shrine, with the Nepalese princess Tritsun on his right, the Chinese princess Kongjo on his left, Mangza Tricham behind him, his grandson Mangsong Mangtsen at his feet, the two ministers Tonmi and Gar before him, while the ministers Zhanglon Nachenpo and Be Chang Pelgyi Pagzang stood guard at the door of the shrine. Holding many gifts, the king made offerings before the tutelary deity and prayed. He then instructed his grandson:

> Son of my race: I transformed the royal law into Dharma law, promoted the propagation of the teachings of the Buddha, and led the Tibetan people to happiness. You shall also protect this kingdom of mine in accordance with the Dharma without decline! Maintain these two shrines of mine and cause them to flourish! Hold and protect my palace, which resembles the abode of the gods. Be like a parent in whom my queens, ministers and all the people of Tibet can invest their hopes and trust. Cause benefits and happiness to spread in every direction!

> In the fifth generation descended from me,
> A manifestation of Manjushri,
> A king with the name De will appear.[152]
> He will also cause the sacred Dharma to increase.
> In the second generation descended from him,
> A manifestation of Vajrapani,
> A king with the name Tri will appear.[153]
> He too will cause the sacred Dharma to increase.
> Then a manifestation of the Evil One,
> A king known by the name of an animal, will appear.[154]
> His mind possessed by demons,
> He will cast down shrines and destroy the sacred Dharma.
> The lives of those who embrace the doctrine will be
>   extinguished.
> All those who practice Dharma will be killed and
>   vanquished.
> All the scriptures will be consumed in flames.
> He who destabilises the teachings of the Buddha
> Will enslave the lamas and the teachers.
> The noble ordained ones will be deprived of the Dharma.
> The doctors of divinity will be made to work as butchers.
> The raiments of the Buddha will be cast into the river.
> The three symbols of the body, speech and mind
> And offerings will be struck with rocks.
> He will cause even the name of the Dharma to be no more.

Then, in a rocky cavern at Yerpa
The manifestation of Vajrapani,
A monk known as Pel,
Will destroy the evil king.[155]
For a period of ninety-six years,
The teachings of the Buddha will vanish.
Alas! How pitiful each sentient being!
These, my tutelary deities,
Will also be concealed like treasures in this shrine.
During the last five hundred years of the doctrine
An ember of the teachings of the Buddha
Will rise up from Dokham Gang,[156]
Flaming up again like a guttering lamp
For the sentient beings of the Land of Snows.
The teachings will spread and flourish,
Leading the faithful to make offerings,
And perform prostrations and circumambulations.
The noble ordained ones will become many,
And the teachings of the Buddha will spread.

Having spoken thus, he sat in profound meditation upon loving-kindness. This is merely a summary of these prophetic pronouncements, but they are given in great detail in the *Testament of the Pillar* revealed by Atisha. A little later, the king continued:

> When ministers of internal and external affairs and my Tibetan subjects come, saying, 'I desire an audience with King Songtsen Gampo', if they wish to meet me, they should make supplications to the sublime Avalokiteshvara. This will be no different.

Then the Nepalese princess Tritsun turned and said:

> Whenever the people of Tibet who are dear to my heart come, saying, 'I desire an audience with the Nepalese princess Tritsun', if they wish to meet me, they should make supplications to the reverend Bhrikuti. This will be no different.

Then the Chinese princess Kongjo turned and said:

> Whenever the people of Tibet who are close to me and cherish me come, saying, 'I desire an audience with the Chinese princess Kongjo', if they wish to meet me, they should make supplications to the reverend Tara. This will be no different.

Minister Gar then inquired, 'The great king has given these instructions, but whither will the king, our father, and the consorts, our mothers, go?' The king replied, 'We three will not go far'. The king then rose and touched the Nepalese princess Tritsun with his right hand, whereupon she became a white *utpala*-lotus flower and was absorbed into his right shoulder. He touched the Chinese princess Kongjo with his left hand, and she became a blue *utpala*-lotus flower and was absorbed into his left shoulder. Then Songtsen Gampo came before the Self-created Eleven-faced Image and eulogised the Sublime One:

> From the state of emptiness of the Dharmakaya,
> An image created for the benefit of beings
> With four peaceful faces and seven wrathful ones:
> I pay homage to the Eleven-faced One!
>
> Three white, peaceful primary faces,
> Beautified by exquisite smiles,
> Pacifying karma and afflictions:
> I pay homage to the faces of the Dharmakaya.
>
> Above these are the golden ones,
> The three furious faces representing the glory of laughter,
> Causing increase of life, merit and wealth.
> To these I pay homage.
>
> Above these, as red as coral,
> Are two faces fulfilling the activity of power:
> Bhrikuti in grimacing attitude.
> To these faces of the Sambhogakaya I pay homage.
>
> Above these, fulfilling the activity of wrath,
> Are the two faces, the colour of smoke and cloud,
> With three furious glaring eyes.
> To the faces of the Nirmanakaya I pay homage.
>
> Above this, the guru Nirmanakaya,
> The embodiment of all buddhas, vermilion in colour,
> A crown adorned with Amitabha, the protecting victorious
>   one.
> To you I pay homage.

Resembling the petals of a lotus,
The first pair of hands are folded in prayer on the heart,
Exhorting the compassion of all the buddhas.
To you I pay homage.

The four hands on the right, properly exhibiting in turn
A rosary, a wheel, the gesture of supreme giving
And the Buddha of the Three Ages, Amitabha.
To you I pay homage.

The four hands on the left, properly holding in turn
A white lotus, a precious gourd,
And a bow and arrow representing the non-duality of
    method and wisdom:
To you I pay homage.

The nineteen lesser arms on the right,
Holding a jewel, a noose, a begging-bowl, a sword,
A diamond-sceptre, a lens, a water-crystal, a bow,
A rod, a fly-whisk, a shield, an excellent vase,
A battle-axe, a rosary, a blue lotus,
A gourd, a sun, a white lotus
And an ear of corn:
To you I pay homage.

The nineteen lesser arms on the left,
Holding a white cloud, a gourd, a lotus, a sword,
A conch, a skull, a rosary, a bell
And a diamond-sceptre:
To you I pay homage.

Those holding an iron hook, a mendicant's staff, a
    Nirmanakaya image,
A mansion, a book, a wheel,
An image of the Buddha, a fruit, a lotus corolla
And a jewel:
To you I pay homage.

Possessing the ten root hands of the Dharmakaya,
The thirty-eight limbs of the Sambhogakaya,
And the thousand minor limbs of the Nirmanakaya:
To you, the King of the Sky, I pay homage.

On the lotuslike palms of your hands,
The eyes that resemble utpala flowers
As bright as the stars:
To you, King of the Sky, I pay homage.

The crown of the Victorious Ones upon your head,
Your arms and legs encircled with bangles of gold,
Your body possessing a sweet fragrance:
To you, King of the Sky, I pay homage.

Wearing garments of fine silks of various kinds,
Bedecked with ornaments of many jewels,
A body of such beauty that one never tires of beholding it:
To you, King of the Sky, I pay homage.

Your breast covered by the skin of a deer,
Your limbs adorned by snakes of four kinds,
Your body shining with the brilliance of the major and minor
    signs of greatness:
To you, King of the Sky, I pay homage.

Possessing a complexion of great beauty
Like the flanks of a snowy mountain tinged with red,
From your breast radiates the light of compassion:
To you, King of the Sky, I pay homage.

The jewel which is the crown of the king of deities,
Two legs standing beautifully,
Your body reposing upon the lotus and moon:
To you, King of the Sky, I pay homage.

Precious manifestation of the minds
Of all the Buddhas of the Three Ages,
You, possessor of skilful means and compassion,
I beseech you to gaze upon all sentient beings.

You, refuge of all beings,
I beseech you to gaze with eyes of compassion
Upon sentient beings afflicted by all sufferings
And stricken by troubles.

Ignorant and bewildered beings,
Who, due to accumulation of negative karma, obtain
    undesirable rebirths,
Those who have fallen to the Three Lower Realms,

> I beseech you to rescue them with the iron hook of your
> compassion.

Thus he besought. Having removed his headdress, he touched the breast of his tutelary deity and prayed, 'Sublime One! Look upon sentient beings wandering in the three realms of Samsara and those stricken by troubles!' By the power of his faith, the king began to weep, and while in the state of devout supplication, he dissolved into light and vanished into the breast of the image. [The gap between the two hands held in prayer at the breast of the Sublime One arose at this time.] Thus, although everyone saw these things clearly, having no course of action they simply stared at one another.

Then Mangza Tricham spoke: 'If the king and two queens, our father and mothers, have disappeared and abide no longer among us, what are we to do? In whom shall we invest our hopes and from whom shall we seek compassion?' Thus she inquired. The king's face then reappeared from the breast of the self-created image and uttered these words:

> All heed me! First, having been born, death is certain. Secondly, the essence of composite things is impermanence. Third, human life is as fleeting as that of dewdrops upon a blade of grass. Act as if your present behaviour is a dream or an illusion!

The face of the Nepalese princess Tritsun also appeared at the right breast of the image and spoke these words:

> First, the illusory nature of life is like a rainbow in the sky. Secondly, the illusory nature of speech is like a rolling clap of thunder in the air. Thirdly, the illusory narure of the body is like a flower in summer. Act as if you know that your present actions are but reflections in a mirror.

The face of the Chinese princess Kongjo then appeared at the left breast and spoke these words:

> First, the impermanence of the body is like an old tree with rotten roots. Secondly, the impermanence of life is like lightning or clouds in the sky. Thirdly, the impermanence of wealth is like the honey of the bee. Carry out actions at the present time knowing that they are like bubbles on the water.

Having spoken, she vanished from sight. Then the two great ministers said, 'If the great king has vanished and abides no longer among us, what are we ministers of internal and external affairs and the Tibetan subjects to do? We beseech you to show us your compassion'. Having requested thus, the king showed his face again and spoke these words:

> Heed well, my retinue and subjects:
> This life is as impermanent as dewdrops upon a blade of
>   grass.
> Do not procrastinate or be lazy.
> The Lord of Death is as unstoppable as a mountain cataract.
> Do not grasp at things as if they are durable and permanent.
> The illusory human body is like a summer flower;
> It is uncertain when it will be killed by frost.
> Reject mundane actions and practice the holy Dharma.
> Ponder impermanence and death, and generate diligence.
> You and I are inseparable and will always be together.

Having spoken, he vanished from sight. Looking at one another, some said, 'The king and two queens were indeed manifestations!' and 'While they were among us, we showed them but little reverence!'

Zhanglon Nachenpo and Be Chang Pelgyi Pagzang entered the shrine and three times they asked, 'Where are the king and queens, our father and mothers?' Thinking that the two ministers would not believe them if they described the actions of the king and queens and the manner in which they had been absorbed into the tutelary deity, Tonmi and Gar stood staring mutely at one another, not knowing how to explain the situation. The two ministers grew angry, and as they had asked three times where the king and queens had gone, but received no explanation, they cried, 'You two evil ones will die!' and drew their swords. The Princess of Mang then intervened: 'The king and queens, our father and mothers, being manifestations, were absorbed into the breast of the Self-created Elevenfaced Image and have left us!' So saying, she wept. Still incredulous, they asked the king's grandson, who related carefully how the king had given a detailed testament, how the two queens were absorbed into the king's body, how his grandfather the king was then absorbed into the breast of the tutelary image, and so on. Finally, the two ministers were convinced.

Minister Tonmi then described how the king was a manifestation, how he had revealed the face of Amitabha to the mendicant monk at Trandrug and the two novice monks from Khotan, how, when Lhasa was consecrated and the king made supplications, all the buddhas and bodhisattvas had instantly become clearly visible in the sky and so on. After Tonmi had described these events, everyone was convinced and all declared, 'The king appears to have been the true Avalokiteshvara. While the king and queens, our father and mothers, were among us, we showed them but little respect!' Saying, 'The Dharma-king was indeed a manifestation!' all fell to the ground in sorrow.

Just then, however, the deities caused flowers to fall like rain, and the earth shook in six ways. From the breast of the Self-created Eleven-faced Image, there arose eight rays of light of various colours. One was absorbed into the breast of the bronze image of Lord Akshobhya-vajra; one into the breast of the bronze image of the 'Wheel of Dharma' Maitreya; one into the breast of the Buddha Amitabha; one into the breast of the Buddha Achala; one into the breast of the Krodharaja; one into the breast of the Bhaishajyaguru [a painted image in the southeastern corner of the swastika in the lower storey]; one into the breast of the white Hayagriva [a painted image in the intermediate storey]; one into the breast of the reverend Tara [a painted image in the intermediate storey]. These then became known as the Eight Light-emanating Deities. From the breasts of these deities, rays of light then shone forth and fell upon all the deities within the shrine, linking them with a web of light. This was the miraculous accomplishment of the secret consecration of Trulnang. The suffering experienced by the king's grandson, the queens, ministers and all those who were present was eased and they came to abide in happiness, free from misery.

All the ministers then counselled that since Songtsen Gampo's son, Gungri Gungtsen, had predeceased his father, and as his grandson, Mangsong Mangtsen, was still a minor, they themselves should build a tomb for the king. Because the absorption of the king and his consorts into the breast of the Self-created Eleven-faced Image was a secret, it was announced in all parts that they had passed away at Zelmogang in Penpo. The peerless tomb of the father and two mothers was therefore built at Chongpo in Yarlung.

This chapter,
in which the deeds of the
king and queens are completed,
and they are absorbed into the
breast of the Self-created
Eleven-faced Image,
is the seventeenth.

* * *

The great manifestation Dharma-king
Held the throne for exactly seventy years.
By building shrines, he caused the holy Dharma to increase.
He made offerings to the Three Jewels and aligned the laws
    to the Dharma.
At the age of eighty-two,
In order to generate diligence among the lazy,
To lead procrastinators to the Dharma,
And to bring about renunciation among those who grasp at
    permanence,
In the northern shrine of the Trulnang Shrine
The king and consorts dissolved into light
And were absorbed into the breast of the tutelary deity.
The one who was dedicated to the benefit of beings,
The human manifestation of the Buddha,
The inseparable son of Avalokiteshvara,
The Compassionate One who leads evildoers to the Dharma,
Sole protector of infinite sentient beings,
In the manifestation-body of the Dharma-king, I seek refuge!

By the blessings of the Great Compassionate One,
Songtsen Gampo's tomb was built at Chongpo.
As to its size, it was about one mile square.
In the centre of the square tomb, cells were made.
Having created an image of the great king
From a mixture of the ashes of fine silks and paper,
It was brought on a wooden carriage to the accompaniment
    of music
And was interred within the tomb.
All the cells were filled with jewels,
And the tomb became known as Nang-gyenchen,
    'Ornamented Within'.
It is said that five shrines were also built inside it.
The tradition of constructing square tombs arose from this.
It was styled 'Kuri Mugpo'.[157]
The Buddhas of the Ten Directions and the Sixteen
    Shravakas,
The bodhisattvas and the holy Dharma-protectors,
Having arrived at that place,
Performed services to consecrate the tomb.
The king's grandson, Mangsong Mangtsen,
And the ministers, together with a retinue of Tibetan
    subjects,
Brought unimaginable quantities of items as gifts
To this place, and made prostrations and offerings.
Having thus propitiated the deity-protectors of that region
For the protection of the tomb of the peerless king,
They made supplications and returned to their own districts,
Causing the light of benefits and happiness to spread in all
    directions.[158]

Thus it was.

PART III
THE LATER KINGS

18

Mangsong Mangtsen

Songtsen Gampo's grandson, Mangsong Mangtsen, ascended the throne when he attained the age of thirteen. He took as his wife Queen Droza Trimalo, Princess of Dro, and reigned over his kingdom. At that time, it was rumoured that the emperor of China had learned of King Songtsen Gampo's demise. Recalling the various deeds of Minister Gar, the emperor dispatched an army of five hundred thousand to invade Tibet and to retake the Jowo Shakyamuni. Fearing an invasion, the image was moved from Ramoche to Lhasa[159] and was placed behind the Mirrored Southern Door. The door was plastered over, and an image of Manjushri was constructed in front of it. Mangsong Mangtsen ruled over the kingdom for fifteen years and died at Barnang-gang in Tsang at the age of twenty-seven.

> The tomb of Mangsong was to the left of Songtsen Gampo's.
> It was also filled with precious jewels,
> And its name was Ngozhe Hrelpo.

19

Dulsong Mangpo
Je Lungnamtrul

The son of Mangsong Mangtsen was Dulsong Mangpo Je Lungnamtrul. He was born seven days after the death of his father, at Dragpu in the Water-male-mouse Year [712]. With Nyatsen Dembu, who was the son of Minister Gar, and Tagra Khonglo as his ministers, he ruled over the kingdom. He took Chimza Tsunmotog, Princess of Chim, as his wife.

During the reign of this king, the Seven Powerful Ministers appeared. Ngogring La Nagpo could carry an elephant. Ngogling Kham could lift a yak. Non Gyaltsen could cut a vulture in half with the hatchetlike blades of his arrows. Tabdonggong could shoot an arrow three times further than the eye can see. Go Yagchung was able to carry and brandish upon his head the skin of a deer filled with sand. Choro Drongsher could restrain a wild yak that was charging down a hill. Non Tridun Gyujin could lift into the air a horse that was leaping into an abyss. Their strength and glory were equal to the gods', and they conquered the borderlands in all four directions with their magical powers.

Dulsong Mangpo Je established offerings in Lhasa in commemoration of his forefather Songtsen Gampo, and was able to subdue the kings of neighbouring countries. This king, more powerful than any of the preceding kings of Tibet, having ruled over his kingdom, died in the region of Jang at the age of twenty-nine.

His tomb, which lay to the left of Mangsong's,
Became known as Lharichen.
Built by the people of Hor,[160]
It is said that it was called Sengge Tsigpa, 'Snow-lion Walls'.

20

Tride Tsugten
Me Agtsom

The son of King Dulsong Mangpo Je was known as Tride Tsugten Me Agtsom. He was born in the Iron-male-dragon Year [740] at Podrang Denkar and took the throne at the age of ten. With Kyizang Tongtsen, Chimgyel Shugteng and Drochu Zangor as his three ministers, he ruled over his realm. Me Agtsom took as his wife the queen known as Jangmo Tritsun. He discovered the testament of his forefather Songtsen Gampo embossed upon a copper scroll at Chimpu, wherein he read, 'In the time of a king known as *Tri* and *De* in the fifth generation descended from me, the holy Dharma will spread, many pandits will come, and the teachings of the Buddha will increase'. Thinking that he himself was the king to whom the testament referred, Me Agtsom sent Drenkha Mule Shoka and Nyag Nyanam Kumara as messengers to the snowy mountain of Kailash to invite two pandits, Buddhaguhya and Buddhashanti, to visit Tibet. On reaching the holy mountain, however, the messengers were unable to persuade the pandits to go with them. Instead, they memorised the five Mahayana Sutras, and on their return, transcribed them in five volumes. They accordingly built five shrines as repositories for the scriptures: Karu in Dragmar, Drinzang in Kashmir, Khadrag in Lhasa, Namrel in Chimpu and the shrine of Manggong. In addition, they translated the *Holy Golden Light Sutra* and the *Classification of Various Actions of Vinaya Vibhanga* from Kemashi in China. Petsi Chandrashri also translated many medical texts at that time.

By virtue of these actions, Queen Jangmo Tritsun bore a son known as Jangtsa Lhaon, who had the body of a god and was exceedingly handsome. As no suitable spouse could be found for him in Tibet, some said that the precedent of his forefather Songtsen Gampo should be followed. Accordingly, precious gifts for Zhongzong, the Emperor of China, and for the princess Kyimshing Kongjo were prepared and dispatched.[161] Tibetan ministers presented the gifts to the emperor, who then asked his daughter if she wished to go to Tibet. Kyimshing Kongjo duly consulted a magical looking-glass that showed good and evil. Having wiped it carefully, the princess peered into it and perceived that a perfect spouse would be found in Tibet. When she saw that he was also handsome and agreeable, she resolved to go.

The emperor gave his daughter boundless gifts, and thinking of her constantly, he accompanied her with a great retinue as far as the mighty fortress known as Shipingxian. There he pitched a great tent and provided lavish entertainment for the Tibetan ambassadors. The emperor wept profusely and gave his daughter copious advice. He then liberated all the prisoners held in that jurisdiction, disbanded the army, dispensed with his retinue and all luxuries for the period of one year, and renamed the fortress Jinchengxian in her honour.

Two great ministers, accompanied by a military escort, were dispatched to Tibet, and when they arrived at the border, the Tibetan ambassadors sent an invitation to the prince to join them. That night, the royal retinue urged their horses onwards through the moonlight in order to meet the princess. The Tibetan prince also pressed on his steed, but the horse threw its rider and the prince was killed. Before the princess had even reached the border, they were all engulfed with grief at the news of his death.

The tomb of Jangtsa Lhaon, which lay before his forefather's,
Was built in the shape of a circle,
And it is said that treasures were concealed within it.

Having reached the border with her servants, Kyimshing Kongjo
was suddenly stricken by suffering as if an arrow had pierced her
heart. She immediately wiped her magical mirror and peered into
it. Instead of the handsome prince whom she had seen before, she
beheld the image of an ugly old man whose face was covered with
whiskers.[162] The heartbroken princess then uttered this lament:

Seeing this image in the mirror,
Sorrow now presses upon this girl's heart.
If I return to my own land, the road is long,
But my family is kindhearted.
The hopes I held in going to Tibet are shattered.
The Tibetan ministers are wicked
And I wander inexperienced in a foreign land.
The mirror of karma has deceived me!

With these words, Kyimshing Kongjo struck the looking-glass and
wept. The king of Tibet then sent a messenger with a letter to the
Chinese princess and her retinue, in which he wrote, 'My godlike
son, who was a suitable partner for you, has died in a tragic acci-
dent. Will you now return to your own land, or having laid eyes
upon me, will you come to Tibet?' The Chinese princess replied,
'This girl has but one intention: whatever happiness or suffering
should be in store, I shall go to Tibet'. So saying, she proceeded
hither.

On her arrival, Kyimshing Kongjo declared, 'I must visit the
shrine of my aunt',[163] but when she reached Ramoche and found
that the Jowo was no longer there, she proceeded to Trulnang where
the image had been concealed behind the Southern Mirrored Door.
The princess opened the door, extracted the Jowo and placed it in
the central shrine. Because the image had been kept in a darkened
chamber for three generations, she established the 'Offering for
Beholding the Visage of the Deity'. When she finally reached
Chimpu she was invested as King Me's consort.

One year later, Kyimshing Kongjo learned she was pregnant with
an infant prince, but a senior consort named Nanam Zang Zhiteng

grew jealous and falsely declared, 'I also carry the king's succes-
sor'. When Trisong Detsen was born to the Chinese princess in the
Iron-male-horse Year [790] at Dragmar, Nanam Zang came to her,
and although she showed her great affection, she stole the princess's
infant and announced deceitfully, 'This baby was born to me!'

Kyimshing Kongjo exposed her breasts, uttered lamentations and
wept, but Nanam Zang refused to yeild the child. The Chinese
princess therefore informed the ministers and petitioned the king,
but Nanam Zang rubbed upon her own breasts an ointment that
cause the milk to flow, and having done so, she too showed the
ministers. They became filled with doubt, not knowing who was
the true mother. As Kyimshing Kongjo's baby had been stolen by
the senior consort, and as she could not withstand the older
woman's aggression, she had no further course of action.

Kyimshing Kongjo then thought to herself, 'It is difficult for the
baby to benefit me at this juncture. I shall therefore destroy this
land of Tibet!' She studied the geomancy of the mountains, and in
order to sever the royal line of descent, she drew a wheel with her
own menstrual blood on the summit of the king's life-force mountain, which resembled a snow-lion leaping into the sky. The princess then concealed the cipher beneath a stupa. Next, in order to
prevent the advent of intelligent ministers, she blocked the 'nose'
of the ministers' life-force mountain with molten bronze, and severed the conjoined 'tails' of Tagri, 'Tiger Mountain', and Sengri,
'Snow-lion Mountain'. In order to cause famine, she cut the 'roots'
of Mena Mountain at Yarlung, which resembled tender shoots of
rice, and in order to bring leprosy to Tibet, she removed the 'bill'
of Mangkhar Mountain, which resembled a great eagle soaring in
the sky.

When she had accomplished all this, as it was her son's first
birthday, the families of the two consorts were invited from China
and Nanam to attend a festivity to celebrate the boy's first steps.
They duly reached Tibet from their respective lands, and the people
of Nanam brought gifts, ornaments, clothing and garlands of flowers for the little boy's amusement.

The king sat upon his golden throne in the centre of the royal
palace with the family of Nanam on his right and the family of the

Chinese princess on his left. His father, the king, adorned the boy with many ornaments, placed a golden cup filled with rice-beer in his son's hands, and said,

> My only son, born of two mothers,
> Although small, your body is the manifestation of a deity.
> Place this vessel, a golden cup filled with rice-beer,
> Into the hands of your uncle.
> By this we will determine who is your true mother.

So saying, he offered prayers and sent his son, who was just able to walk, on his way. Taking the cup, the boy set off. Although the people of Nanam enticed him with clothes, ornaments and garlands of flowers and beckoned to him, the child ignored their exhortations and went instead to the Chinese, to whom he gave the golden cup and addressed these words:

> I, Trisong Detsen, am a nephew of the Chinese.
> I do not understand my uncles from Nanam.

With that, he sat down in the lap of his Chinese uncle. His mother was overjoyed and said:

> By the virtue of good karma accrued in former lives,
> To me, a girl who came from China,
> The son of a matchless king was born.
> But on account of my adverse karma,
> This boy who was born to me was stolen by another.
> Ignoring my honest pleas,
> Although I showed my breasts, the infant was not returned.
> The body and mind of this Chinese princess were seared
>   with pain,
> And being unable to bear the suffering of mental fury,
> I undermined the beneficial geomantic influence of the
>   mountains of Tibet.
> Today, the sun of the deity has arisen:
> Son, you recognised your uncle.
> You mother's body and mind repose in happiness.
> The decline of the geomantic influence of the mountains of
>   Tibet
> Will be reversed without harm.

Thus she spoke. Knowing that the boy was indeed the son of the Chinese princess Kyimshing Kongjo, a great celebration was held. When the prince was five years old, however, his mother died. His father, King Me Agtsom, passed away at the age of sixty-three at Batselkhar in Yamdrog.

> Me Agtsom's tomb was built on Murari
> To the left of the tomb of the manifestation-king.
> It was styled 'Lhari Tsugnam'.

Thus it was.

21

The Dharma-king
Trisong Detsen

he Dharma-king Trisong Detsen took the throne at the age of eight and ruled over his kingdom. Before the king attained his majority, Mazhang Tronpakye and some other ministers who were hostile towards the Dharma promulgated laws forbidding its practice and prepared to return to China the precious Jowo of Lhasa. Despite the efforts of one thousand people, however, the image could not be moved, and was therefore buried below the earth at Khardrag. Some of the ministers who opposed the Dharma then became delirious and died. The backs of others split asunder, and they also perished. [At Kharnadong] famine and epidemics broke out, and many inauspicious omens appeared, whereupon the soothsayers unanimously proclaimed, 'These events are caused by the burial of the Chinese deity!' The Jowo was therefore disinterred, and was loaded upon two mules with the intention of sending it to India. When the image reached Mangyul, word was sent that the road was impassable, and there it remained for fourteen years. [This event is also described in the history of the Lords of Yarlung and other sources.]

The ministers also planned to send the Jowo Akshobhya-vajra to China, but when this image reached the plain of Domo in the east, it could not be moved for seven days.[164] [The Chinese then realised that it was not their own Jowo and left it there.] [Cholungda] became known as Ogyeltang, the 'Plain of Exhaustion'. This image was later reinstated in Ramoche.[165]

Although King Trisong Detsen was favourably disposed towards the Dharma, the ministers Mazhang Tronpakye, Tagra Lugong and the like were more powerful than he, and none could oppose them. When the king came of age, the sovereign and his ministers reached agreement on the practice of the Dharma. Mazhang was deceived by various means and was buried alive in a tomb at Drangpu in Tolung, and Tagra Lugong was banished to the north. The king then decreed that everyone must practice the Dharma, and he retrieved the Jowo Shakyamuni from Mangyul by carriage. It was welcomed to the accompaniment of music that defied the imagination and returned to the central shrine at Rasa.[166]

At that time, Ananda, son of Kyezang the Kashmiri, was engaged in trade at the Dartsag Gangseb market between Rasa and Ramoche. Having summoned him to act as their interpreter, the Buddhists held a debate with the Bonpos, and as the latter were defeated, all their teachings were concealed at Dragmar and elsewhere, or were thrown into the river. With the exception of practices for averting temporary adverse conditions, Bon was forbidden.[167]

The king then consulted all his ministers, and by the power of the prayers offered by the three youths at the stupa of Bodhnath in a previous existence, Be Selnang was dispatched to India to invite Shantarakshita, the Bodhisattva-abbot, to Tibet.[168] When Trisong Detsen received the abbot upon his arrival at the palace, the king's sash was loose, and he held a *dre*-measure of gold dust in his hands. The abbot said, 'O King! As you wear a turban upon your head, there will be a law relating to the size of hats in Ngari in the upper region of Tibet. As you wear shoes upon your feet, there will be a law relating to the size of boots in Amdo and Kham in the lower part of Tibet. As the sash around your waist is loose, there is a danger that the royal laws will deteriorate rapidly in Central

Tibet. However, as you are bearing a precious gift, it will be possible to practice the Dharma'.

With Ananda the Kashmiri as his interpreter, the abbot instructed the king and his ministers in the Dharma. This evoked the displeasure of malicious demons and ogres from the side of evil, who caused lightning strikes, crop failures and epidemics. The Master of Instruction, Padmasambhava, was therefore invited from the land of Ugyen to bind the malefactors under an oath of submission.[169] He duly accomplished this and thereby freed the religious practices of the king and ministers from adverse conditions.

The Master offered Water of Longevity and Intelligence to the king, but those ministers who were hostile towards the Dharma petitioned the sovereign: 'Do not drink this madness-inducing water from Mon; it is poisonous!'[170] The king vacillated and declined the offer.

Padmasambhava wielded his diamond sceptre, and Meldro Zichen, the king of the nagas, was bound under oath to prevent the outbreak of leprosy. Manifesting himself in the form of a boy, the naga-king befriended Trisong Detsen and promised to bestow upon him whatever attainments he should desire. The king showed favour to the nagas thereafter and swore an oath of friendship with them.

When the Master was considering the transformation of the entire desert of Ngamsho into a meadow, the evil ministers petitioned the king, saying that this would be an act of mere conjury on Padmasambhava's part. The meadow would therefore not endure and the deed would be unworthy. So saying, they requested the king to reject the proposal. [The Master had also accepted Trisong Detsen's consort Kharchenza Tsogyel, Princess of Kharchen, as an offering for the king's initiation, and had taken her as his wife. This displeased the ministers, who slandered the king, saying that in disregarding their advice regarding the Master, he had committed three grave mistakes and so on.] Moreover, the ministers were convinced that the Master would bring harm to the realm as he was more powerful than they. They therefore petitioned the king to send him back to his own country. [The *Great Samye Record of*

Edicts states that the Master first returned to Ugyen, but having conferred with the king, dwelt thereafter in Tsari and elsewhere. It records that he returned to Samye after the death of Mazhang Tronpakye.]

The king then assembled his subjects, and as there had been no precedent for the ordination of Tibetans in earlier times, seven gifted sons of both ministers and commoners took their vows before the Bodhisattva-abbot in order to determine the suitability of such a practice. They were Ratna, son of Ba Sangshi; Shakya Drawa, son of Chim Anu; Vairochana, son of Pagor Ratna; Ngenlam Gyelwa Chogyang; Ma Acharya Rinchen Chog; Khon Luiwangpo Sungpa[171] and Tsang Legdrub. [In one account, however, it is said that Khon Luiwangpo was not one of the Seven Chosen Ones.] These seven, having been ordained, became known as the Seven Chosen Ones.[172] Similarly, three hundred sons of the royal consorts, ministers and commoners were also ordained, and the most talented among them were sent to India to study Sanskrit and the art of translation.

Establishment of Samye

Trisong Detsen desired to build the Glorious Immutable Miraculously Accomplished Shrine of Samye, and having conferred with Minister Go and the other Dharma-ministers, the king declared:

> If difficult tasks are not undertaken,
> Even simple tasks will not be accomplished!

He then gathered together his ministers and his Tibetan subjects and said:

> I am mightier than any preceding king of Tibet, and I intend to create a great monument. Shall I construct a crystal stupa as high as Sharri, the Eastern Mountain? Or a fortress from which one can see China, the land of my uncles? Shall I cover Mt. Hepori with copper? Or sink a well on the Plain of Kachutang to a depth of nine hundred and ninety fathoms? Or fill the Walung Ravine with gold dust? Or dam the Tsangpo River? Or shall I build a shrine the size of a *dre*-measure to house the Three Jewels? Choose one!

While the king was speaking, his words weighed upon the minds of the assembled ministers as heavily as a boulder of gold, and they stood staring mutely at one another, not knowing how to respond. Then Go, Zhang Nyangzang, Nyertag Tsendongzig and the other Dharma-ministers arose and said:

> Only sovereign! It would be impossible to complete a crystal stupa the height of Mt. Sharri in a single lifetime. Although one might imagine a fortress from which China could be seen, it could never be accomplished. One might collect all the copper in the possession of your Tibetan subjects, but it would be insufficient to cover Mt. Hepori. One could not fill the Walung ravine with sand, let alone with gold dust. It is not possible to sink a well one hundred fathoms deep, let alone nine hundred. One might dam the Tsangpo River in the winter, but never in the summer. Instead of these, pray construct a shrine the size of a *dre*-measure for your tutelary deity, as the object of refuge for your subjects and as the foundation from which all benefits and happiness may arise.

After they had made this petition, all who were present said in agreement, 'This is best'. The king then inquired of Padmasambhava: 'Great Master, where are my mother and father now?' The Master replied, 'O King! Your father has been reborn as a great pandit in the land of India, and will return to Tibet during the reign of your grandson. [This prophesy refers to the pandit Danashila.] Your mother was reborn as the daughter of a poor couple in Zangkhar. Such are their names and parentage'. Thus he responded.

Trisong Detsen took five consorts: Tsepangza Metogdron, Princess of Tsepang; Kharchenza Tsogyel, Princess of Kharchen [who was given to Padmasambhava as an offering for the king's initiation], Droza Jangchubdron, Princess of Dro; Chimza Lhamotsen, Princess of Chim. In order to repay his mother's kindness, he married the daughter of the poor family mentioned above, who became known as Poyongza Gyelmotsun, Princess of Poyong. [In one account, the girl who was the reincarnation of the king's mother was said to have been found at Zurchu in the land of Penyul. Whichever is the case, both accounts agree that she became the Princess of Poyong.] The Master then examined the geomantic prognosis for the construction of a shrine:

> Sharri, the Eastern Mountain, resembles a king seated upon a divan and is beneficial. Richung, the Lesser Mountain, resembles a mother bird sheltering her young and is beneficial. Menri, the Medicine Mountain, resembles a pile of precious stones and is beneficial. Mt. Hepori resembles a queen clad in fine white silks and is beneficial. Rinag, the Black Mountain, resembles an iron dagger thrust into the earth and is beneficial. Meyar resembles a mule drinking water and is beneficial. The Plain of Deltang resembles a curtain of fine white silk and is beneficial. The site itself resembles a golden basin filled with saffron and is beneficial. Establish a shrine for the sovereign's tutelary deity here!

After he had spoken, the Master transcribed the prognostication, and having bound the malevolent demons and ogres under oath, removed all adverse conditions. Fifty sons and daughters of genteel and noble families, whose parents, grandparents and great-grandparents were still among the living, were adorned with many ornaments. Bearing precious vases filled with the Water of Good Fortune, they thrust daggers into the earth, and thus the site was sanctified.

The king then set the ministers and all the people of Tibet to work, but just as they were about to lay the foundations of the great, central Utse Shrine, modelled on Mt. Sumeru, the King of Mountains, the reverend Tara instructed them to build first the Aryapalo Ling Continent Shrine. In this shrine, to the right of the primary image of Lord Avalokiteshvara, stood Tara, and to the left, Marici. Further to the right was Yige Drugpa, the Six-Syllable Mantra Bodhisattva, and further to the left was the Glorious Hayagriva and so on. Thus, five images, the primary one and retinue, were created. Above these were added five images, consisting of Amitabha with retinue.

Padmasambhava then bestowed upon Trisong Detsen the transmission of the accomplishment of Hayagriva. When the king had accomplished Hayagriva, the neighing of a horse was thrice heard throughout two-thirds of the world, and the Master therefore prophesied that the king's realm would reach this extent.[173]

The lower storey of the great Utse Shrine was built in the Year of the Hare. A self-created stone statue of Shakyamuni was brought from Mt. Hepori as the primary image and was covered with a plaster made from precious stones. Possessing the major and minor signs of greatness, it was placed in the shrine. To its right stood Maitreya, Avalokiteshvara, Ksitigarbha, Nandashri, the wrathful Tridhatuvijaya and so on. To its left were Samantabhadra, Vajrapani, Manjushri, Sarvanivaranivishkambini, Upasaka Vimala and the wrathful Achala. The thirteen images, the primary one with retinue, were all created in the Tibetan style.

Around the central core were celestial murals depicting the Twelve Deeds of the Buddha, inside it was a mural of the lineage of Tog, and in the fore-shrine were murals of the sovereign's tutelary deity. The lower storey was entrusted to the dakini Senggei Gochen, the Lion-headed One.

Next, the middle storey was constructed. The primary image was Vairochana, with Dipankara to the right, Maitreya to the left, and Shakyamuni, Bhaishajyaguru and Amitabha, these three, in front of it. Further to the left and right stood the eight Bodhisattva Near Spiritual Sons, Upasaka Vimala, the bodhisattva Nandashri and the wrathful Kang and King. All were created in the Chinese style. The murals depicted the introductory chapter of the *Extensive Perfection of Wisdom Sutra*, in front of which stood images of the Four Great Kings. On the exterior of the circumambulatory hall were eight stupas and murals of the *Passing into Nirvana Sutra*, and inside were murals of the *Great Cloud Sutra*. The mantra hall held the Buddhas of the Ten Directions, the assembled deities of Yamantaka and images of the Dharma-protectors of Samye. The entire middle storey was entrusted to the Dharma-protector king Shingchachen.

In the upper storey was Buddha Vairochana – the primary image, each face provided with a retinue of two: the eight Bodhisattva Near Spiritual Sons, the inner deity Bodhisattva Vajradvaja, the other bodhisattvas and Buddhas of the Ten Directions, the wrathful Achala and Vajrapani. All were made in the Indian style. The murals illustrated the *Sutra of the Ten Stages,* and the whole upper storey was entrusted to the Dharma-protector king Zangmai Belogchen.

The upper pagoda-style roof was decorated with a pattern of fine silks. On the four sides were images of Buddha Nandashri surrounded by retinues of bodhisattvas. The roof was entrusted to the four Dharma-protectors Vajrapani Go-ngonchen, the Blue-clad Ones.

The intermediate circumambulatory route was then constructed. On its southern side was the naga-treasury, filled with musical instruments. This was entrusted to the three yaksha brothers, Lagna Yugto Togpa, the Holders of the Staves. On the western side were three hundred Dharma-treasuries filled with volumes of Sutras and Tantras from Tibet and India, and three images of hermits holding razors in their hands. On the northern side, the three treasuries of precious treasures were filled with gold, silver, copper and the like. These were entrusted to Yamantaka Dandapani, the Club-wielding One. The murals depicted the *Lalitavistara Sutra,* in the midst of which were eleven thousand images of the Buddha and so on. The glorious mandala of Vairochana Durgatiparishodhani was constructed around the great circumambulatory route. On three sides of the balcony were the images of the five buddha families facing outwards. Inside were Dugpo Gyanpa and Jambhala. The entire structure was entrusted to the Dharma-protector naga-king Nanda. A stele, entrusted to the Dharma-protector Singhamukha, the Lion-headed One, was erected behind it.[174]

> The three gates of the Utse Shrine represent the doors of liberation.[175]
>
> The six flights of stairs represent the Six Perfections.[176]
>
> The lower storey was built of stone, the middle one of bricks.
>
> The upper storey was a celestial mansion built of precious timbers.
>
> The styles of each were in accordance with the Vinaya.
>
> The murals were all in accordance with the Sutras.
>
> The images were all in accordance with the secret mantras.

Thus it was.

The Continent Shrines

Three shrines were then constructed in the east on the model of the three semicircular eastern continents of Purvavideha. In the Namdag Trimkhang Ling, the Continent Shrine of Pure Law, were five images consisting of Shakyamuni and retinue, and murals of the *Perfect Renunciation Sutra*. It was entrusted to the Dharma-protector Tsangpa Dunggi Tortsugchen, the Spiral-coiffed One. In Khenrab Jampel Ling, the Continent Shrine of the Wise Manjushri, were seven images consisting of the sublime Manjushri with retinue and two Yamantaka door-guardians. The murals showed the *Manjushrimula Tantra* and the *Durgatiparishodhani Tantra*. It was entrusted to the Dharma-protector Shinje Khorlochen, the Holder of the Wheel. In the Continent Shrine of Dajor Brahma Ling were seven images consisting of Shakyamuni and retinue, and murals of the *Passing into Nirvana Sutra*. It was entrusted to the Dharma-protector Druggi Logwachen, the Wearer of the Dragon Robe.

Three shrines, shaped like shoulderblades, were constructed in the south on the model of the three southern continents of Jambudvipa. In Dundul Ngagpa Ling, the Continent Shrine of the Mara-subduing Mystic, were five images, consisting of a primary one with retinue in the Buddha Marajit tradition. In the centre were murals of the *Sutra of the Ten Stages*, and in the circumambulatory hall were murals of Akashagarbha. It was entrusted to the twenty-eight Dharma-protectresses. In the Continent Shrine of Aryapalo Ling were five images consisting of Khasarpani with retinue. In addition, there were five images consisting of Amitabha with retinue. To one side were an image of the king made from sandalwood and covered in silver, a stupa and murals of the *Zamatog Sutra* and the One Thousand and Two Goddesses. It was entrusted to the Dharma-protector Rishi Dharmaraja. In Dra-gyur Gyagar Ling, the Indian Continent Shrine of the Translators, were five images consisting of the Buddha in the Indian style with retinue, and murals of Amitayus and translators and pandits engaged in translation. This was entrusted to the Dharma-protector yaksha Rahula.

Three shrines were constructed in the west on the model of the three circular western continents of Godaniya. In the Continent Shrine of Pawo Betsa Ling was an image of Vairochana made of copper with a retinue of the Four Secret Consorts, and murals of the *Vairochana-abhisambodhi Tantra*. It was entrusted to the Dharma-protector yaksha Langgi Gochen, the Bullock-headed One. In Ganden Jampa Ling, the Maitreya Paradise Continent Shrine, were seven images consisting of the Lord Maitreya with retinue and two door-guardian images of Yamantaka. The murals showed the Sixteen Arhats, the manner of the construction of Samye and the evolution of the Universe. It was entrusted to the Dharma-protector Trowo Go-ngonchen, the Wrathful Blue-clad One. In Miyo Samten Ling, the Continent Shrine of Unmoving Deep Meditation, were the five classes of Vairochana Buddhas and the Sixteen Shravakas. The murals depicted the rain-causing boy from the *Holy Golden Light Sutra*. This shrine was entrusted to the Dharma-protector king Ngulgochen, the Silver-headed One.

Three shrines were constructed in the north on the model of the three square northern continents of Uttarakuru. In Rinchen Natsog Ling, the Continent Shrine of Varied Treasures, were five images consisting of Shakyamuni with retinue and murals depicting the Lord Buddha giving teachings in the Dharma to his mother in Paradise in repayment of her kindness. It was entrusted to the Dharma-protector king Chaggi Dermochen, the Iron-clawed One. In Semkye Jangchub Ling, the Continent Shrine of Enlightenment-Thought, were Buddha Padmapani, Sarvanivaranivishkambini, Vajrapani and Amritakundali. The murals showed the *Sutra of the Clouds of Three Precious Ones*, and Sadaprarudita seeking the *Sutra of the Perfection of Wisdom*. It was entrusted to the Dharma-protector dakini Senggei Gochen, the Lion-headed One. In Pekar Kordzo Ling, the Pekar Treasury Continent, were nine images consisting of Shakyamuni with retinue and murals depicting the *Sutra of Buddha's Meeting with His Father*. The treasures left over from the construction of Samye were held in repositories there, along with a register of the locations of each shrine's contents. This shrine was entrusted to the guardian, the King of the Tramkhang.

To guard the doctrine in all the shrines, the Master brought from the land of Zahor the Great Celestial *Genyen* Devotee[177] and the Great General of the Army of Fiends, who subdued the eight classes of gods, demigods and ogres of the Illuminated Realm, and could steal away the breath of all living beings. The entire shrine-complex of Samye was entrusted to the Great Lord of Life, Pehara, and images of the two guardians were installed in the Continent Shrine of Pekar.

In the Shrine of the Sun, the shrine of the great yaksha Purnabhadra, were five images consisting of Shakyamuni with retinue, and murals of one thousand and two buddhas. In the Shrine of the Moon, the shrine of the lesser yaksha Manibhadra, the images and the murals were the same as those in the Shrine of the Sun.

On the upper storey of the Continent Shrine of Tsangmangkeu Ling was the Baso Lhakhang, the Ivory Shrine. In the Dagche Trukhang Ling, the Continent Bathhouse of the Holy River, was a well filled with sandalwood fragrance. In the Tute Lukhang Ling, the Bestowal of Power Naga Continent Shrine, were eight great nagas on an eight-branched rose-tree, with Vajrapani in the centre, and murals of *shantidamara*,[178] turtles, fish, crocodiles and so on.

The White Stupa, the Stupa of Great Enlightenment, ornamented with snow-lions in the style of the Shravaka school, was constructed under the supervision of Shupu Pelgyi Sengge, and was entrusted to the Dharma-protector devil Kardachen, the Meteorlike One. [After the central pillar of the stupa was put in place by the Four Great Kings, a Magadha *dre*-measure of relics of the Buddha, the ancestral tutelary deities known as the Secret Antidotes,[179] and the five classes of Sutras were placed within it. Thus it received great blessing.] The Red Stupa, ornamented with lotuses in the style of the turning Dharma-wheel, was constructed under the supervision of Nanam Gyeltsa Lhanang, and was entrusted to the Dharma-protector Zamigmar, God of Mars. The Black Stupa was constructed under the supervision of Ngam Tagdra Lugong in the style of the Pratyeka Buddhas, and was entrusted to the Dharma-protector yaksha Chagkyi Chuchen, the Iron-beaked One. The Blue Stupa was constructed after the tradition of the Tathagata, who descended from the Glorious Realm of the Gods, and its shrine was ornamented with sixteen doors. It was built under the supervision of Chim Dorje Trelchung, and was entrusted to the Dharma-protector devil Nyimaidong, the Sun-faced One.

At that time, Ochenma, the Demoness of Light, was causing harm and mischief among all the people. The Master Padmasambhava therefore built a radiant stupa in the Maitreya Continent Shrine which subdued the demoness and brought the troubles to an end.

One hundred and eight stupas were erected upon the polygonal surrounding wall, which resembled a diamond sceptre, and a relic of the Buddha was placed inside each.

As to the three continent shrines of the consorts, Jangchubdron, Princess of Dro, built Gegye Jema Ling, the Continent Shrine of Virtue Increasing Like Sand. Inside it were seven images consisting of Amitabha with retinue, all made from gilded bronze. On the right were the Three Bodhisattvas, and on the left were Bhaishajyaguru, Samantabhadra and Achala. As the princess had no sons and her family lived far away, she feared that no one would come to carry out repairs to the shrine should they be required in the future. She therefore made bricks for the walls from lead, covered the roof with copper, installed a *jang* wind chime to provide music,[180] fitted a light-emitting jewel to a beam in place of a lamp, and sunk a well for offering-water.

Tsepangza Metogdron bore three sons, Mune Tsepo, Murug Tsepo and Mimug Tsenpo Senaleg. She constructed the Khamsum Zangkhang Ling, the Continent Shrine of the Copper Mansion of the Three Realms, modelled on the Utse Rigsum Shrine built by the boys' father, King Trisong Detsen.

Gyelmotsun, Princess of Poyong, constructed the Butsel Serkhang Ling, the Continent Shrine of the Golden Mansion of the Children's Garden, in the form of the mandala of Vajradhatu. Whenever a meal was served to any of the sculptors or other craftsmen, thirteen varieties of food were offered. In order to repay this kindness, thirteen special designs were incorporated. The shrine resembled a diamond sceptre, it had no external walls, and the strength of the design was unique. It also resembled a tent, it had no internal pillars, and the beauty of the design was unique. The site was covered with brass. A golden horse galloped upon a turquoise beam. A turquoise dragon was set upon a golden beam. The shrine had a pagoda-style roof that could be seen from within and without. Each of the deities inside it had its own canopy and parasol. A golden coral emitted a sound when the gate was opened. The Twelve Deeds of the Buddha were carved in relief. Such were the thirteen especially miraculous designs that were incorporated.

As to samples of building materials from the excellent construction of the Glorious Immutable Miraculously Accomplished Shrine of Samye and its peripheral structures, samples of the woodwork were used in Lhasa to construct the great gate, adorned with a pediment, at the front of the central shrine. Samples of earth were used to make Four Great Kings who guarded it.

Consecration of Samye

The foundations of Samye were laid in the Year of the Hare, and the entire complex was finally completed in the following Year of the Hare after one twelve-year cycle had elapsed. Unlimited amounts of food and drink were assembled for the consecration of the shrine, and once all the people under the king's dominion were gathered together, a great celebration was held. The king made presentations of gold to Padmasambhava and to the Bodhisattva-abbot. Then, wearing robes ornamented with many precious stones, he performed seven times the wondrous consecration ceremony of the Shrine of Samye and its surrounding buildings, and revealed himself to be a manifestation-being. Murals depicting these events may be found behind the gates of the Utse Shrine and on either side of the door of the circumambulatory hall [according to the *Record of Royal Commands*].

> During the festivities
> To mark the consecration of Glorious Samye,
> In the centre of a sea of tents,
> Like a lotus,
> The king sat upon a golden throne.
> His five beautiful consorts
> Were there in all their finery.
> All the venerable ones, the translators and pandits,
> Expounded upon the Dharma while rejoicing,
> And all the chief Dharma-ministers
> Surrounded the enthroned sovereign.
> The subjects under his dominion

Celebrations to mark the completion of the great monastery of Samye

From every town and clan in U and Tsang
Were gathered there without exception.
All sated themselves upon every kind of food and drink,
According to their own desires.
Joyous dancing and songs of happiness
Continued uninterrupted every day.
Parasols, victory banners, pennants and the like
Obscured the midday sun
And left no space for birds to fly!
The black-headed throng covered the ground,
Cymbals roared like thunder,
And there was no room to ride a *gyiling* horse![181]
All the boys and girls, beautifully adorned,
Held fly-whisks in their hands,
And beat drums while singing and dancing.
Those who danced 'The Yak and the Snow-lion',
'The Youth and the Snow-lion',
'The Tiger and the Snow-lion',
And 'The Dragon' and 'The Young Snow-lion'
And the glorious, beautiful ceremonial dancers holding
    drums and so on
Made offerings to the king.
The sovereign and all his subjects
Felt that their rejoicing bodies
Were beyond their own control.
Like rain from the heavens,
The dancing caused their elated minds to swoon,
And all sang songs of their own choosing.
The deity who ruled as sovereign over the people,
The Dharma-king Trisong Detsen,
Rose from his precious throne
And sang 'The Song of the Rejoicing King':

My Utse Rigsum
Is made from five precious materials.
It does not look like it was built;
It looks like it simply grew!
My shrine is miraculous:
The mere sight of it gladdens the heart
And the thought of it eases the mind.

The three eastern shrines,
Modelled on Purvavideha,
Are made from five precious materials.
They do not look like they were built;
They look like they simply grew!
My shrines are miraculous:
The mere sight of them gladdens the heart
And the thought of them eases the mind.

The three southern shrines,
Modelled on Jambudvipa,
Are made from five precious materials.
They do not look like they were built;
They look like they simply grew!
My shrines are miraculous:
The mere sight of them gladdens the heart
And the thought of them eases the mind.

The three western shrines,
Modelled on Godaniya,
Are made from five precious materials.
They do not look like they were built;
They look like they simply grew!
My shrines are miraculous:
The mere sight of them gladdens the heart
And the thought of them eases the mind.

The three northern shrines,
Modelled on Uttarakuru,
Are made from five precious materials.
They do not look like they were built;
They look like they simply grew!
My shrines are miraculous:
The mere sight of them gladdens the heart
And the thought of them eases the mind.

The upper and lower yaksha shrines
Shine like the sun and moon in the heavens.
The three continent shrines of my consorts
Are laid out like a turquoise mandala.
This, my White Stupa, is like a right-whorled white conch.
This, my Red Stupa, is like a tongue of flame licking the sky.

This, my Blue Stupa, is like a pillar of turquoise.
This, my Black Stupa, is like an iron dagger thrust into the
    earth.
My stupas are miraculous:
The mere sight of them gladdens the heart
And the thought of them eases the mind.

Trisong Detsen sang this and other songs of rejoicing,
After the style of the celestial songs of the king of gods
Of the Thirty-three Realms.
The king also sang 'The Turquoise Mansion and Golden
    Throne'.
The celestial prince, Mune Tsenpo, sang 'Lantern of the
    World'.
The celestial prince, Mutig Tsenpo, sang 'The Proud
    Snow-lion'.
The consorts sang 'The Swirling Turquoise Ocean'
And 'A Branch with Turquoise Leaves'.
As to the songs sung by the venerable ones,
The Bodhisattva-abbot sang 'The White Meditation Garland',
The Master Padmasambhava sang 'Suppressing Deities and
    Demons'.
The savant Vairochana sang 'The Crooked Vowel'.
Nubwen Namkhai Nyingpo sang 'The Eagle Soaring in the
    Sky'.
Ngenlam Tsunpa Gyelchog sang 'The Song of the Dignified
    Hayagriva'.
The savant Chogro Pelzang sang 'The Nine Glories of
    Happiness'.

As to the songs sung by the ministers,
The great Dharma-minister Go the Elder sang 'The Straight
    White Tree'.
His son Yablhag Tribzang sang 'Magic Key to Learned
    Writings'.
Shupu Pelgyi Sengge sang 'Little Grunts and Long
    Turquoise'.
The general Lhabzang Lupel sang 'Saddle Rugs, Large and
    Small'.
Nyang Zang Zhangpo Trigyel sang 'The Great Snow-lion
    Commentary'.

Be Tenzang Pelleg sang 'The Eight Desires and Hopes'.
Gar Khyungpo Dumtsug sang 'The Soaring Vulture'.
Chim Dorje Trelchung sang 'The Forgotten Song of Chim'.
Nanam Gyeltsa Lhanang sang 'The Deity of Superior
    Strength'.
Tridring Lhao Khugcho sang 'Excellent, Mediocre and
    Inferior Chanting of the Sutra'.
Nyag Trizang Yangbon sang 'The Pervasive Moonlight'.
Li Ngam Tagdra Lugong sang 'The Iron Monkey with Six
    Faces'.

The older men sang 'The Miraculous Golden Flower'.
The young men sang 'The Nine Storeys of Tiger Mountain'.
The women sang 'A Garland of Flowers'.
The young girls sang 'Endless Village Gossip'
And other songs too numerous to mention.
For the duration of one year,
Every person sang one song.

At this time of rejoicing, the span of glory was extended, and everyone revelled in merriment, happiness and pleasure. For an entire year, benefits and bliss radiated in all directions like the light of the sun and the moon.

The king then proclaimed: 'I now desire to strive for liberation and enlightenment in this life. The joy and happiness of the present have in truth seduced us'. While spreading the teachings of the Buddha and causing their increase, the king invited many savants, including the pandit Vimalamitra, from the land of India. The translators Vairochana, Ananda the Kashmiri, Denma Tsemang, Nyag Kumara, Ma Acharya Rinchen Chog, Khon Luiwangpo, Kawa Peltseg, Chogro Luigyaltsen, Zhang Nanam Bande Yeshe De and others established themselves in the Indian Continent Shrine of the Translators and rendered the Tripitaka into Tibetan.[182] [These Three Early, Three Middle and Three Late Translators are universally known as the Nine Translators.]

Monastic communities were established, and the teachings of the Buddha spread like the rising sun and were caused to flourish. All the Tibetan people abided by the Laws of the Ten Virtues and were happy.

The Samye Debate

The Bodhisattva-abbot then said, 'The Master Padmasambhava bound the twelve *tenma* earth goddesses under solemn oath to prevent the entry of heretics into Tibet.[183] In the future, however, there will be a time when views contrary to those of the Buddhists will arise. At such a time, my disciple by the name of Kamalashila should be invited to Tibet. He will restore the views to harmony'. Having given these final instructions, the abbot passed from this world of misery. The king then appointed Yeshe Wangpo as holder of the doctrine of the Dharma.

Just as the abbot had foretold, a person by the name of Hashang Mahayana arrived in Tibet from the land of China, and there arose views known as *Tonminpa*, the 'Doctrine of Absolute Inaction', and *Tsenminpa*, the 'Doctrine of Non-meditation', which diverged from those of the Middle Way.[184] As these were contrary to the views of the Buddhists, a doctrinal dispute erupted. At that juncture, in accordance with the abbot's testament, the savant Kamalashila came to Tibet at the invitation of Yeshe Wangpo. When Kamalashila arrived at the far side of the river opposite Samye, Hashang said, 'I shall go to welcome this pandit on his arrival'. So saying, he proceeded to the riverbank nearer the shrine. When Kamalashila saw that Hashang had come to meet him, he thought to himself, 'If this Hashang is astute, I will certainly be compelled to subdue him. Otherwise, there will be no need'.

In order to test Hashang's abilities, Kamalashila thrice brandished his staff above his head to indicate the question 'What causes wandering through the three realms of Samsara?' Seeing this, Hashang gripped the hem of his robe and twice cast himself upon the ground to indicate the reply 'Wandering in Samsara arises from grasping and holding'. Kamalashila thought to himself, 'As Hashang is indeed astute, I must indeed subdue him', and he rejoiced greatly. When they arrived at Samye, the king said,

> I have been deeply reverent towards the teachings of the Buddha and have constructed this shrine and its peripheral shrines. I have brought pandits from India, I have had the Dharma of the Tripitaka translated, thus setting it upon a firm foundation, and I have established monastic communities. Although

everyone was in agreement on the Dharma, Hashang came
from China and caused the divergence of differing views. I
therefore invited the savant Kamalashila from India. As it is
inappropriate for one teaching to have two sages, let there be a
debate of harmonious exposition upon the thoughts of the Lord
Buddha. Abjuring arrogance, let the loser shower flowers upon
the victor!

A great throne was erected in the Continent Shrine of Enlightenment Thought. The king sat in the centre, the master Hashang
and his disciples sat on the right and the master Kamalashila sat
with his disciples on the left. In the course of the debate,
Kamalashila gained the upper hand, Hashang accepted defeat and
duly showered the victor with flowers. Hashang then returned to
the land of China, but leaving one of his boots behind, he declared,
'There may still be some who adhere to my views in Tibet'.[185]

Again, pandits and savants arrived from India. The king acted
as their patron and commanded, 'Practice this Dharma, which the
translators and savants have established through their translations!'
The savants' thoughts were all in harmony, and while propagat-
ing the Dharma, they caused it to flourish.

Trisong Detsen then entrusted his kingdom to his son Mune
Tsenpo, and retired to the Nyugmakhar Palace in Zungkhar. As
this is only a summary, the *Great Samye Record of Edicts* may be
consulted for further details. The Dharma-king Trisong Detsen died
at the age of fifty-six in the Wood-male-ox Year [845] at Zungkhar.

> His tomb was built during his own lifetime at Murari,
> Behind and to the right of his father's.
> Its name was Trulri Tsug-nang,
> And a stele stands before it.
> It became known as Chi-gyenchen, 'The Tomb of External
>   Ornament'.

22

Mune Tsenpo

Mune Tsenpo was born at Dragmar in the Water-male-tiger Year [822], ascended the throne at the age of twenty-eight and ruled over his kingdom. He took Ruyongza Dogyel, Princess of Ruyong, as his consort and upheld the laws based on the Ten Virtues. Mune Tsenpo established the rites of the Vinaya, Abhidharma and the Sutras to fulfil the wishes of his father. He suspended chains between the canopies of the four great stupas and the eaves of the Utse Shrine, hung great flags and pennants from them and made countless offerings.

King Mune Tsenpo decreed, 'People of Tibet! Render unto me all gold, silver, turquoise, pearls and other property in your possession, with the exception of horses, cattle and weapons'. As the sovereign's commands were binding, some of his subjects presented great amounts of gold, silver and jewels. Some gave turquoise, woollen cloth and fine silks. Others offered their own clothing and ornaments, while some gave only ragged garments and skins lined with cotton.

The king said, 'You, my Tibetan subjects, differ greatly in the depth of your devotion. Some have given limitless wealth, but others have given nothing but rags and skins lined with cotton'. The

Tibetan people replied, 'None is more devoted than others, but the rich have the capacity to give while the poor do not'. As this was their reply, the king said, 'It is inappropriate that such distinctions between rich and poor exist among people under my dominion'. Thrice the king equalised rich and poor, but on each occasion, after a year had passed, the rich were as rich as before and the poor were as poor. The king then said, 'Although I have thrice equalised rich and poor, why is there still such a disparity in happiness and suffering? What is its cause?' The venerable ones replied, 'This disparity is the result of the generosity that they exercised in their former lives'. Thus the king came to have faith in the causes and effects of karma.

King Mune Tsenpo propagated the teachings of the Buddha and brought about their increase. He valued the venerable ones and the ordained monks as highly as his own crown and provided their livelihood. The realm was thus nourished with benefits and happiness.

Queen Poyongza Gyelmotsun, Princess of Poyong, was the reincarnation of her own grandmother, the Chinese princess who had been the mother of Poyongza's father, King Trisong Detsen. As Trisong Detsen had been fond of Poyongza, on retiring to Zungkhar he entrusted her to his son, who duly took her as his own wife. When Trisong Detsen died, Princess Tsepangza[186] heard that Poyongza had not removed her jewelry or mourned his passing and became jealous. Tsepangza engaged an assassin to murder Poyongza, but Poyongza was protected by Tsepangza's own son, King Mune Tsenpo. Heretical thoughts then arose in Tsepangza's mind, and she sent poisoned food to the king. Having ruled the kingdom for one year and nine months, Mune Tsenpo died at the age of twenty-nine in the Palace of Yumbur.

> The tomb of Mune Tsenpo
> Lay to the right and in front of the tomb of Agtsom
> And was known as 'Lhari Dempo'.

Thus it was.

23

Mutig Tsenpo
and Tride Songtsen
Senaleg Jingyon

When Trisong Detsen was still alive, his second son, Mutig Tsenpo, procured the death of the minister Zhang Uring, although the latter had committed no crime. Thus, when the throne was transferred to Mutig Tsenpo, he was murdered by members of the Nanam clan.

> His tomb, built at Donkhorda,
> Was known as Kyari Kyangdem.

The throne then passed to Trisong Detsen's youngest son, Tride Songtsen Senaleg Jingyon. He ruled over the kingdom, established monastic communities and commissioned the translation of Sutras that had not previously been available. The king paid homage to the pandits Vishvakara, Vairochana, Kamalashila and other venerable ones. He also made offerings and presented butter-lamps in the shrines constructed by his late father. When he reached the age of nineteen, he married the queen known as Lhatse, who bore one son. Tride Songtsen Senaleg Jingyon died when this boy was thirteen years old, and his tomb was built at Donkhorda.

24

Dengtri

Dengtri, the son of Tride Songtsen Senaleg Jingyon, took the throne at the age of fourteen. He had five sons: three were born to his senior consort, and two, Lhaje and Lhundrub, were born to one of his junior consorts. He established monastic communities and rendered even greater service to the shrines constructed by his forefathers. King Dengtri died at the age of fifty-five at Dragkyipu in the Fire-female-bird Year [877].

His tomb lay to the left of the manifestation-king's,
And it, too, contained many treasures.
Being filled with the tears of his queens, it was uplifted[187]
And was called Gyelchen Bangso, 'Tomb of the Great King'.

Thus it is said.

25

Lord Relpachen

ᘍ**D** engtri's oldest son, Tsangma, delighted in the Dharma and was ordained. His youngest son revelled in vice and was unfit to rule. The kingdom therefore passed to his middle son, Relpachen, who was born in the Fire-male-dog Year [866]. Relpachen ascended the throne at the age of twelve, on the death of his father, and with Drenkha Pelgyi Yonten as his minister, he ruled over his realm. Relpachen took five queens, senior and junior, including Chogroza Pelgyi Ngangtsul, Princess of Chogro. He upheld the Laws of the Ten Virtues and invited to Tibet Indian pandits such as Jinamitra, Shrinalendra Bodhi and Danashila. Kawa Peltseg, Chogro Luigyaltsen and Bende Yeshe De translated the Dharma into Tibetan, and all the teachings were set down according to their revisions. The Three Edicts were proclaimed,[188] and Relpachen rendered the measures including the *dre*, *sang* and *zho* compatible with their Indian equivalents.

A meditation college was established for hearing, reflecting and meditating upon the Dharma, and a philosophical college was established for explaining, debating and writing about it. Thirty establishments were founded for monastic communities, and a

Vinaya college was set up to promote scholarliness, discipline and excellence. The upkeep for each ordained monk was provided by seventy households of commoners.

Relpachen was accustomed to sit in the centre of his court with silken ribbons tied to locks of his hair, left and right. Two rows of members of the monastic community would then be seated upon the ribbons, as if they were sitting upon the sovereign's own tresses.[189] They became known as the Twin Classes of the Monastic Community of the King's Head.

The king desired to construct the Incomparable Auspicious Ushangdo Shrine of Increasing Virtue for his tutelary deity, and invited many craftsmen skilled in the Vedas from Khotan, and sculptors and stonemasons from Nepal.[190] In creating the nine-storeyed shrine, the doorways and walls[19] of the three lower levels were made of stone, those of the three middle levels were made of brick, and those of the three upper storeys of timber. The shrine was endowed with nine pagoda-style roofs, and images of ordained monks listening to or expounding upon the Dharma were placed on the balconies below each roof. Whenever the wind blew, the uppermost roof, adorned with gold and turquoise dragons, revolved like an umbrella. The intermediate walls were surmounted by precious tiles, parapets and railings, and were beautified with designs of necklaces and half-necklaces. Complete with umbrellas, victory banners, precious garlands, silk pennants, tinkling wind chimes and the golden rooftop dragon, the shrine was as high as the mountains behind it. In the whole of Tibet, it was without equal. The mere sight of Ushangdo inspired clarity of mind.

Iron chains were suspended below the revolving roof to four stone lions, one on each side. Images of the sovereign's tutelary deity were placed in the three upper storeys, the venerable ones and monastic communities dwelled in the three middle storeys and the king with his retinue of ministers occupied the three lower storeys.

As to the samples of construction materials from Ushangdo, specimens of earth were donated for the construction of images of Brahma and Indra in Lhasa. Samples of woodwork were used for the Four Great Jewel-studded Pillars that Exceeded the Sky, and samples of mural work were presented for old works worthy of restoration. Samples of castings of the hundred and eight volumes were donated and so on.[192]

The venerable ones who attended upon the king, and several ministers, including Nyang Shai-chen, built the following shrines: Karu and Meru in the east of Lhasa, Gawa and Gawai-o in the south, and Drenkhang and Drenkhang Tama in the north.

King Tritsug Detsen Relpachen was endowed with magically acquired knowledge, his achievements were comparable with those of the gods, and in his power and wealth, he was equal to the celestial king Indra. His lordliness and strength inspired terror among malevolent fiends. With convincing victories over the borderlands in the four directions, he conquered two-thirds of the world.

Chinese accounts of Tibet[193]

From the earliest times, whenever the successive kings of Tibet and China, like nephew and uncle, were in harmony with one another, they exchanged gifts. Whenever there was enmity, however, each engaged in military contests. There are many examples of this. According to the great Chinese annals known as *Tangshu tufan juan*, the first emperor of the Chinese dynasty known as Tang arose 1566 years after the Lord Buddha passed into Nirvana. This was during the time of the Tibetan king Namri Songtsen. The first Chinese emperor's son Taizong was a contemporary of the Tibetan king Songtsen Gampo, who dispatched messengers to request the hand of the emperor's daughter. The emperor declined the request, but the messengers returned to Tibet and falsely declared to the king, 'The emperor was most favourably disposed towards us, but as he was about to give us the princess, the Tuluhun of Horser slandered us before him'.[194] Such was their response. The king of Tibet was enraged, and leading an army of one hundred thousand soldiers, penetrated as far as a place known as Zung-chiu. The command of the army was then made over to a minister by the name of Yatung. He was dispatched to conquer the land of the Tuluhun, and they fled as far as the shores of Kokonor. All those who remained behind and all their wealth were seized by the Tibetans.

The king of Tibet then entrusted various precious gifts to the minister Sele Tongtsen[195] and sent him to request again the hand of the Chinese emperor's daughter. He returned to Tibet with Wencheng Gongzhu,[196] the Jowo Shakyamuni and many gifts. King Songtsen Gampo died in the Iron-male-dog Year [650], and envoys came from China bringing many treasures as offerings for his tomb.

[The Chinese army also came to Tibet and burned the Potala. Although they sought the precious Jowo, it could not be found, but they held the Akshobhya-vajra[197] for an entire morning. These and other anecdotes may be found in the Chinese annals. Such events all took place at the time of Songtsen Gampo.]

Songtsen Gampo's grandson, Mangsong, took the throne at the age of thirteen, but was young and accomplished little in the kingdom. While Minister Gar was enforcing the law in the borderlands in the four directions, the Chinese army came to conquer Tibet. The Tibetans placed Minister Gar in charge of the army, and leading a force of two hundred thousand, he defeated the Chinese. Having plundered the citizens of China, Minister Gar was killed during the campaign. At the time of the miraculous king Dulsong, son of Mangsong, envoys came from China bringing many treasures as offerings for his father's tomb.

Minister Gar's son Nyentsen Dembu and two renegade ministers of the Tuluhun, leading an army of thirty thousand men, conquered the fortress and the peoples on the banks of the Yellow River. They met the Chinese army of Likying Henachen and defeated him in battle. Likying immediately reinforced his army with three thousand men, and when he came to engage the Tibetans, they retreated. This Tibetan king, Mangpo Je, was mightier than all preceding kings.

Dulsong's son Tride Tsugten Me Agtsom was a contemporary of the Chinese emperor Zhongzong. At that time, the emperor's daughter Jincheng Gongzhu[198] went to Tibet. The girl's dowry included many tens of thousands of bolts of silk, books dealing with all the various arts and crafts, and every kind of insignia that was carried before the emperor. Two civilian ministers, Zayatai Jangkun and Yang Guihen, leading many troops, accompanied her and concluded a treaty with the Tibetans.

As the Tibetans had dominated the regions of Ganzhou and Xiazhou for thirty years, at the time of King Trisong Detsen, son of Me Agtsom, there was disharmony between the nephew and uncle, Tibet and China, and they engaged in many wars. Zhang Gyatsa Lhanang, General Lhabzang Lupel and others led a Tibetan force of about two hundred thousand and conquered the region of Lintao, the fortress of Cheu and Mentse. Thereafter, nephew and uncle exchanged gifts of peace, and although they had pledged to refrain from war, and the Tibetan king had himself said, 'Each must behave harmoniously towards the other', it is said that the most wicked thoughts arose in his mind.

Thus, during the reigns of Mune Tsepo and Senaleg, when there was peace, gifts were exchanged, but when there was strife, each side engaged in warfare. Thus it was. Likewise, as there was friction between nephew and uncle, Lord Relpachen led a Tibetan army of many tens of thousands of soldiers and captured every Chinese fortress. Chinese monks and venerable Tibetan personages acted as intermediaries and caused the warring parties to take an oath before witnesses, and gifts were presented to mollify the nephew. Thereafter, having agreed to refrain from further hostilities, the two kings, like nephew and uncle, each built a shrine at a place in China called Meru, and having carved images of the sun and the moon upon a boulder, the following treaty was concluded:

> Sun and moon complement each other in the sky. The two kings are like nephew and uncle on earth. The Tibetan army shall proceed towards China no further than Meru; the Chinese army shall proceed towards Tibet no further than Meru. Each shall guard its own side of the frontier. No grain of dust, no pebble shall be disturbed. May the Tibetans enjoy happiness in Tibet and may the Chinese enjoy happiness in China. The Three Jewels, the sun, moon, planets, stars and the mighty deities have been called upon to bear witness, and the two kings, as nephew and uncle, swear to abide by the treaty.

The words of the agreement were then carved upon three stele. On the two faces of each stone, the kings inscribed the words of the treaty. On the two edges were inscribed the names and lineages of the ministers and the astrological advisers of Tibet and China. One stele was then erected in Lhasa, one was placed before the Chinese emperor's palace, and the third was erected at Meru on the frontier between the two countries. If Tibet invaded China in disregard of the terms of the treaty, and if the Chinese then intoned three times the words on the stele before the emperor's palace, all of Tibet would be vanquished. Similarly, if China invaded Tibet, and the words of the stele in Lhasa were then intoned three times, the whole of China would be vanquished. The two sovereigns affixed their seals, and the minister-astrologers of Tibet and China confirmed the treaty by oath. As this is merely a summary, those who desire the precise wording of the treaty between Tibet and China should consult the stele in Lhasa.[199]

Relations between Tibet and China were severed sometime thereafter because a Mongol general invaded Tibet and killed the Minister Khyungzhag, it is said.

This history of the relations between China and Tibet was compiled originally by Song Qi, a writer who lived at the time of the Chinese emperor Taizong. It was subsequently expanded in recent times by the Chinese translator U Kyang-dzu, who rendered it into Tibetan at Lintao. Although the chronologies differ in some respects and various historical personal names are inconsistent, when Lama Gushri Rinchen Trag lived in China, he accepted as accurate these accounts of the relations between the two countries. He published a version of this account in Lintao in the Wood-female-bird Year [1285], in which these events are described in detail. As this is merely a summary, that work itself should be consulted by those who desire a thorough description of the relations between Tibet and China and the histories of their respective kings, who were like nephew and uncle to one another.

Murder of Relpachen

The king Lord Relpachen, considering the precious teachings of the Buddha, vested authority in the monastic community, laid the foundations for the Dharma-law and the royal laws and rendered service in the shrines built by his forefathers in Lhasa, Samye, Karchung and elsewhere. He brought all the Tibetan people under the Laws of the Ten Virtues. Once theft, robbery and deceit and the like had been eliminated, all the ministers and subjects who were hostile towards the Dharma felt that their behaviour had been severely curtailed. They asked one another, 'Why is our behaviour so restricted? Who is to blame?' Saying 'It is they who are the cause!' they pointed their fingers at the reverend ones and glared at them malevolently. When the king learned of this, he said, 'It is improper to point threateningly or stare malevolently at my ordained ones. I shall therefore put out the eyes and cut off the fingers of anyone who does so hereafter'.

Be Tagnachen, the 'Tiger-eared One', and other evil ministers were greatly displeased by the king's great devotion towards the Dharma and secretly agreed that the Dharma-laws should be abolished. Some said, 'Unless the king is killed, it will be impossible to abolish the Dharma-laws'. Others said, 'Even if we kill the king, because the celestial prince Tsangma and the minister Drenkha Pelgyi Yonten are both devoted to the Dharma, we will still not be rid of these laws'. They decided, therefore, to eliminate the celestial prince Tsangma and the minister Drenkha Pelgyi Yonten, and then the king.

The ministers bribed the soothsayers, who prognosticated with one voice, 'If the celestial prince Tsangma remains here, the king's life will be plagued by untoward occurrences, and the kingdom will perish'. The prince was therefore banished to Peldromon. Be Tagnachen then spoke slanderously to the king and informed him that the great Dharma-minister Drenkha Pelgyi Yonten and Queen Chogroza Pelgyi Ngangtsul were conducting an illicit affair. The great Dharma-minister was thus incriminated, though he was blameless, and was put to death.

Following this, in the Iron-female-bird Year [901], at the age of thirty-six, Relpachen fell asleep after drinking rice-beer, and Be Tagnachen and Chogro Lhalo strangled him to death. These times were known thereafter as the Twelve-and-a-Half Generations of Happiness and the Five Generations of Supreme Happiness.

> The tomb of Lord Relpachen
> Was built in the left-hand corner of Donkhorda.
> It, too, was filled with precious treasures
> And was called Triteng Mangri.

The power of the sovereigns diminished thereafter like winter rain. The Laws of the Ten Virtues disintegrated like a rope of rotten reeds. The merit accrued by the Tibetan people guttered out like a lamp with no oil. The kingdom's benefits and happiness vanished like a rainbow in the sky. Evil actions raged like swirling tempests, while kindly thoughts were forgotten like last night's dreams. As this was the situation, and there was no one to provide for the translators, pandits and venerable ones, each returned to his own land. The unfinished translations of the Dharma were cast aside. The ministers and commoners who had embraced the Dharma were oppressed by misery and had no further recourse.

26

Tri Langdarma
Udumtsen

Suppression of the Dharma

Be Tagnachen and the other evil ministers were very powerful, and King Tri Langdarma Udumtsen, the manifestation of a fiend, was hostile towards the Dharma and had an evil mind. He took the throne and ruled over the kingdom. At that time, the pandit Danashila was in retreat at the Meru Shrine in the east of Lhasa when obstructions arose during his propitiation of Jambhala. He grew angry and struck the stomach of the plaster image of the deity with the end of his mendicant's staff, whereupon many pieces of gold poured forth. [It is also said that he struck it with an iron diamond-sceptre.] With this gold he created an image of Khasarpani as a symbol of the Buddha's body, a golden throne as a symbol of his teachings and a singing silver bird as a symbol of his mind. His disciple Utpala the Kashmiri created a silver image of Maitreya and established offerings to commemorate it.

At that time, frosts, hail, blight and famine occurred, and both people and livestock were smitten by pestilence. The king, whose mind was possessed by demons, used these calamities as a pretext for suppressing the teachings of the Buddha. Some monks were made to work as butchers, some were disrobed, and others were forced to hunt wild animals. Those who refused were put to death. When the king began to destroy the shrines in Lhasa, the Dharma-ministers contrived by various means to conceal two Jowos beneath their respective pedestals, saying that they had been cast into the river. The image of Maitreya was wrapped in cloth and hidden on the banks of Otang Lake. A rope was fastened around the neck of the Vajrapani, with the intention of throwing it and all the other images from the inner chambers into the river, but the person who tied the knot suddenly began to vomit blood and died, whereupon the destruction of the shrine was halted. The doors of the shrines of Lhasa and Samye were bricked up, and all the smaller shrines were destroyed [with the exception of Meru]. Some scriptures were thrown into the river, some were burned, yet others were concealed like treasures.

The ministers who favoured Dharma, realising that the mind of the king was possessed by demons, let forth heartfelt laments and cried with one voice, 'Great King, it is wrong to desecrate the precious teachings of the Buddha. Consider the excellent practices of earlier times and read the collected writings of your forefathers!'

At that time three monks, Yo Gejung, Tsang Rabsel and Mar Shakyamuni, were meditating in the college of contemplation at Chuwori.[200] A monk with his robes hiked up, a bow and arrows in his hands and feathers upon his head, was roaming about, hunting wild animals with a dog. When Yo Gejung saw this, he asked, 'Am I an old man who is insane, or is that monk mad? What is afoot?' When he had pointed out the hunter to Tsang Rabsel and Mar Shakyamuni, they said, 'It is not you but he who is insane!' They then summoned the monk and asked the reason for his behaviour. The monk replied, 'You three who ignore the king's punishment are in great danger!' and he recounted in detail the suppression of the Dharma. They became very afraid, and without a moment's delay, they gathered three mule-loads of Vinaya scriptures and fled by the northern road to Kham, where they dwelt in the cave of Dentigshel. Following this, Kao Chogdragpa and

Lhalung Pelgyi Dorje dressed in black on his way to kill Langdarma

Rongton Sengge Gyaltsen also took many Abhidharma scriptures and fled to Kham, where they lived in the cave of Senchung Namdzong.

Downfall of Langdarma

At this time, Lhalung Pelgyi Dorje was engaged in meditation in a cave at Yerpa. At midnight one night, Pelden Lhamo, the Dharma-protectress of Lhasa, appeared to him and said, 'Apart from you, there are none in Tibet who have gained *siddhi*.[201] King Langdarma has obstructed the teachings of the Buddha, and the time has come to kill this wicked sovereign. I will assist you. Have no fear!' The next day, he asked his disciples about the reason for Pelden Lhamo's visitation, and on learning that she had spoken the truth, without regard for his own life and thinking only of the Buddha's teachings, he summoned up the courage to kill the king.

Lhalung Pelgyi Dorje first took a white horse, and by rubbing it with soot, rendered it black. He donned a black cloak with a white lining and placed a black hat upon his head. Having rubbed a mixture of oil and soot upon his face, he concealed a bow and arrow inside his sleeve. He mounted the black steed, and crying, 'I am Dud Nagpo Tragme, the Swarthy Black Devil!' rode to Lhasa.

Lhalung Pelgyi Dorje came before the king, who was reading the inscription on the stele in the capital. Pretending to prostrate himself, the would-be assassin made a vow to his tutelary deity and withdrew the bow and arrow from his sleeve. At the first prostration, he fitted the arrow to the bowstring. At the second, he drew the string. At the third, he loosed an arrow which struck the king in the forehead. Lhalung Pelgyi Dorje fled, and the king died instantly, clutching the arrow in his hands. [King Langdarma was born in an Ox Year, took the throne in a Bird Year, suppressed the Dharma for five years, and died in a Tiger Year at the age of thirty-eight.]

Search parties were summoned, and hastened in all directions. Those who searched the east reported, 'Just as we were about to capture the assassin at Gamodong, darkness fell, and as we could not see him, he escaped'. Those who searched the south said, 'Night fell when we reached the banks of the Drib River, and as we could not see him, he escaped'. Those who went west said, 'Night fell at Shun-gyi-drang, and as we could not see him, he escaped'. Those who had searched the north said, 'Night fell at Dongkhardong, and as we could not see him, he escaped'. In fact, Lhalung Pelgyi Dorje had caused his horse to lie in Dardong River in Drib, where the waters washed away the black soot, so that the steed appeared white again. He cast aside his black hat, rinsed the oil and soot from his face and reversed his cloak to reveal the white lining. Crying, 'I am Lha Namtel Karpo, the White Sky God!' he made his escape.[202]

As a manifestation of the assassin had appeared before each of the search parties that had hastened in the four directions and caused their accounts to be contradictory, they surmised, 'The assassin must in truth be Lhalung Pelgyi Dorje!' and set off for Yerpa to find him. Inside his cave, Pelgyi Dorje appeared to be in a state of deep meditation. He had earlier caught a pigeon and by the beating of its wings had stirred up the dust in his abode. Pelgyi Dorje had then caused moths, ants and the like to crawl upon the floor. When the search party saw the tracks made by these creatures, they doubted that the monk could have been the assassin, and returned to Lhasa.

One intelligent person among them, however, entered the cave and placed his hand upon Pelgyi Dorje's breast. He felt the monk's heart beating, yet he remarked, 'Why should one man's plough be used in everyone's fields?'[203] So saying, he departed. Pelgyi Dorje then grew very afraid, and without a moment's delay, fled to Kham.[204]

27

Ngadag Osung
and Ngadag Yumten

After the death of the evil king Langdarma, one of his junior consorts discovered that she was pregnant with his son, who was heir to the throne. The senior consort thought to herself, 'This child will truly detract from my own prestige'. She therefore wrapped clothing around her body as if she was growing large with child, and she too announced that she was pregnant. When the junior consort's time had come, she gave birth to a prince, who was the true heir. Being very affectionate towards him, people surrounded him during the day, and at night watched over him by the light of butter-lamps. He was therefore called Ngadag Osung, 'the Lord Guarded by Light'. The senior consort, however, purchased a newborn infant from a beggar-woman, and clasping the baby to her bosom declared, 'I have also given birth to a baby!' Everyone was suspicious, but the infant's alleged mother, the senior consort, was very powerful and none dared contradict her. Because his mother's every word had to be accepted as the truth, the boy was named Ngadag Yumten, 'On his Mother's Word'. Before these two came of age, the Jowo Shakyamuni, the

Jowo Akshobhya-vajra and the image of Lord Maitreya were disinterred at the request of ministers who were favourable towards the Dharma. Each was reinstated upon its respective throne, offerings were made, and those shrines that had been destroyed were rebuilt.

As the two brothers were politically opposed, Osung seized Yoru and declared war. A rebellion erupted in the Earth-female-ox Year [929], and the tombs were ransacked in the Fire-female-bird Year [937]. Lord Osung's son was Je Pal Khortsen. Je Pal Khortsen's son by his senior consort was Kyide Nyima Gon [from whom the kings of Yatse and Ngari are descended.] His son by his junior consort was Trashi Tsegpa [from whom the Latopa and lords of Yarlung are descended.] Such dominions as these two could acquire were seized by Yumten. They therefore fled to Ngari and became the kings of that region.

> The beggar's child cherished with affection became Lord
>   Yumten.
> Because he was raised from lowly birth to nobility,
> The Royal Laws of the Ten Virtues disappeared.
> Turnips were valued more highly than meat.
> The sun of benefits and happiness was obscured.
> As the royal heirs were exiled to the borderlands
> The royal line of descent was severed.

Thus it was.

28

The royal descendants of Yumten

Yumten's son Tride Gon-nyen had two sons: the elder was Rigpa Gon, the younger Nyima Gon. Nyima Gon's son was Nyio Pelgon, whose many descendants dwell in Lungsho, Penyul, Amdo and Kham. Tri Rigpa Gon's elder son was Dewo. The descendants of the younger son, Dorje Bar Depo, are the Bugpa Chenpas and the Tangla Dragpas.

Tri Wangchug Tsen was the son of Dorje Bar. His son was Tsana Yeshe Gyaltsen. His son was Ngadag Tripa. During the time of these two, Tsana Yeshe Gyaltsen and his son Ngadag Tripa, the embers of the Teachings were retrieved from Amdo and Kham. Ngadag Tripa had four sons: Atsara, Gelong, Lama and Lhatsun Bodhi Ratsa. The descendants of Atsara include the Trongpowas, Chang Gyabpas, Lagpa Lampas, Dribpas, Nyetangwas and Lupa Tsangwos, etc. The descendants of Gelong are the Pezhipas and Ondo Mongkharpas. Lama died without issue. The descendants of Bodhi Ratsa include the Lhatsun Ngonmo Nyugrumpas and

Lhamdri Gangwas, etc., who dwell at Samye today. Their descendants, each having multiplied in every direction, are those who bear the title of *jowo*, Lord, throughout Kyiyor. It is said that this lineage is impure in the extreme.

29

The spread of
the Buddha's teachings
from Kham

ing Langdarma launched the suppression of the Dharma in the Iron-female-bird Year [901], and as the embers of the Teaching were also retrieved in an Iron-female-bird Year, it is said that the Dharma disappeared from U and Tsang for nine calendrical cycles. In truth, however, even the name of the Dharma disappeared for eight cycles, or ninety-eight years.

As described above, the three monks Yo Gejung, Tsang Rabsel and Mar Shakyamuni fled from Chuwori to Kham. Thereafter, the three monks Kao Chogdragpa, Rongton Sengge Gyaltsen and Lhalung Pelgyi Dorje also escaped one after the other. As to the first disciples to appear in Kham, Mazasel, the son of a Bonpo, was leading cattle to pasture when he came upon the three monks who had arrived from Chuwori. Faith arose in him by the power of his karma, he requested ordination and the monks complied. Having become their disciple, he was given the name Shakya Gewa Sel, drawing on the names of his three masters, and became well versed in the Tripitaka. Following this, many learned and righteous people from Kham came forward, including Bel Dorje Wangchug, Nub Pelgyi Jangchub, Yanggong Yeshe Yuru, Bar Rinchen, Chang Yeshe Sengge and Choro Sherab Jangchub. There were in addition the lesser-known Sherab Drag, Yenbarwa Jangchub, Drum Yeshe Gyaltsen, Nub Pelgyi Jangchub,[205] Dro Manjushri and so on.

By this time, sixty years had passed since the evil king had suppressed the Dharma. At Zhog in Penyul, a young boy called Muzapen, the son of a Bonpo named Musel Shenbar, entered the Nangsel Shrine and inquired about the murals that depicted ordained monks listening to religious instruction and giving explanations. An old woman told him that they were monks.[206] Faith arose in the boy by the power of his residual karma, and weeping, he asked if any such ordained ones were still in existence. 'There were monks when I was a girl', the old woman replied, 'but when King Langdarma suppressed the Dharma, they were cast down and stripped of the marks of ordination. Some were killed; others died naturally. Now there are no monks in U or Tsang, but the many who fled from Chuwori, Yerpa and so on are certainly still in Kham'. Overjoyed, the boy journeyed thither, with regard for neither life nor limb, and met Lhalung Pelgyi Dorje. His faith grew still stronger and he requested ordination, but Lhalung Pelgyi Dorje said, 'Because I killed the evil king, I have broken my vows. Yet I may still be able to help you'. The boy then met the other learned and righteous ones, and having been ordained, he adopted the name Lachen Gongpa Rabsel.

Eighty years after Langdarma suppressed the Dharma, the teachings of the Buddha were flourishing in Kham, but Central Tibet remained enveloped in darkness without them. The lord of Samye, Tsana Yeshe Gyaltsen, dispatched the first group of individuals to travel to Kham to take vows: Lume Sherab Tsultrim, Dri Yeshe Yonten, Tsongge Sherab Sengge, Loton Dorje Wangchug, Sumpa Yeshe Lodro, Gya Lodro Sherab and Zhonben Chochog. Known as the Seven Men of U and Tsang, they invited Drum Yeshe Gyaltsen to become abbot of Samye and Choro Sherab Jangchub to serve as master of instruction. These favours were granted.

After the Seven Men of U and Tsang, five others went to Kham: Tazhi Gyelpag, Ragshi Tsultrim Jungne, Batsun Lodro Wangchug, Kyeleg Nyangdren Chokyab and Drum Shing Sherab Monlam. The seven who had already made the journey to Kham to receive their vows were returning to Central Tibet when they met upon the road the five who had set out after them. 'Whither are you going?' asked the seven. 'To Kham to take our vows', the five replied. Those who had already made the journey said, 'As we have taken the Three Vows, we can confer the vows of ordination upon you. This long journey is unnecessary!' But the five paid no heed and travelled to Kham regardless, where they met the learned and righteous ones of old and took their vows.

The lord of Samye, Tsana Yeshe Gyaltsen, had died by the time the seven returned to Central Tibet, but his son Tsepo Tripa commissioned Lume and the others to construct a vast number of shrines throughout U and Tsang and to establish monastic communities.

The precious teachings of the Buddha had at last returned, and like a blazing fire in a stack of tinder, they flourished and spread in all directions. The pillar of the teachings was firmly established, and the embers became a flaming beacon in Tibet, once a benighted continent.

Great indeed was the generosity of the successive learned and righteous ones of Kham and U mentioned above, and of Lord Yeshe Gyaltsen and his son!

30

The royal
descendants
of Osung

Following the above account of descendants of the
Tibetan kings who bestowed great favour upon the
precious teachings, Kyide Nyima Gon, who was the son of Je Pal
Khortsen's senior consort, became the king of Ngari, and also
brought Purang under his aegis. The eldest of his three sons, Pelgyi
Gon, seized the land of Mangyul. [Jowo Rechen was the last of his
descendants.] Kyide Nyima Gon's second son, Trashi Gon, seized
Purang. His youngest son, Detsun Gon, took Zhangzhung. These
three are known as the Three Gon of the Upper Regions.

Detsun Gon had two sons, Khorre and Song-nge. When he was
young, Song-nge took a consort who bore him two sons, Nagaratsa
and Devaratna. Later in life, Song-nge was ordained, adopted the
name Lha Lama Yeshe O, and built the Glorious Shrine of Tonting.
Lha Lama Yeshe O dispatched twenty-one gifted men, including
the translator Rinchen Zangpo and Ngog Legpai Sherab, to India
to study the Dharma and invited the two pandits Shraddhakara

and Varmata to Tibet. Through their translations, they brought about the establishment of the Sutrayana and the four classes of Tantra, and promoted the Vinaya school of Upper Tibet. King Khorre constructed the Shrine of Khachar. His son, Lha Depo, invited to Tibet the two pandits Subhashita and Meru.

Lha Depo had three sons: Zhiwa O was the eldest, Lha Lama Jangchub O was the second, and Ode the youngest. During the time of these three, Lha Lama Yeshe O, thinking of the teachings of the Buddha, went to India to invite pandits to Tibet, but was seized on the road by an army of heretics.[207]

His captors cauterised all his bodily channels that generated virtuous qualities, and thereby caused his mind to become clouded. When word of this reached Lha Lama Jangchub O, he gathered vast amounts of treasure and sent it as ransom, but Lha Lama Yeshe O's captors demanded the equivalent of his body-weight in gold. Lha Lama Jangchub O therefore amassed all the gold that could be found, but on weighing it, found that it still fell short of the required amount by the weight of the hostage's head. Lha Lama Yeshe O then declared, 'At such a time as this, even if you could raise the ransom, it would be of no benefit. As my bodily channels have been cauterised, I am no better than an animal. It is best that I should die. Take to India the gold with which you intended to ransom me. In the shrine of Vikramashila, son of King Gewa Pel, there sits one by the name of Jowo Je Dipankara,[208] who shines like a jewel among the five hundred other pandits who are skilled in the five sciences. Offer him the gold and invite him to Tibet to propagate the teachings of the Buddha and bring about their increase!' So saying, he passed away. Lha Lama Yeshe O's remains were returned to Purang, where they were enshrined in a stupa.

The ransom of Lha Lama Yeshe O

31

Lha Lama
Jangchub O's invitation
to Atisha

In accordance with Lha Lama Yeshe O's injunction, the gold was given to Gya Tsonseng and others, and they were dispatched to invite Atisha to Tibet. They entreated him to come by every means, and being mindful of Dharma adherents in Tibet and Ngari, he duly agreed, as prophesied by the reverend Tara. The disciple Nagtso, the trio consisting of Khu, Ngog and Drom, the translator Rinchen Zangpo, the junior translator Legpai Sherab and other learned and righteous personages then arose in succession. Lha Lama Jangchub O thereby showed great kindness in causing the teachings of the Buddha to shine like the rising sun in Tibet, this Land of Snows.

32

The royal
descendants
of Yatse

L ha Lama Jangchub O's younger brother Ode, who invited to Tibet the pandit Danashri the Kashmiri, had a son named Tsen De. His son was Bha De. His descendants, Trashi De, Bhare and Naga De, ruled over the kingdoms of Guge, Purang, Mangyul and so on. Naga De's son Tsenchug De went to Yatse and became king. His son was Trashi De. His son was Dragtsen De. His son was Dragpa De. His son was Arog De. His son was Asog De. His sons were Dzidar Mel and Ananda Mel. Ananda Mel's son Rilu Mel built the golden roof above the precious Jowo in Lhasa. Rilu Mel had two sons, Sangha Mel and Dzitar Mel. The latter had a son called Adze Mel. His son was Kalen Mel. His son was Barti Mel. Thereafter, the line of royal descent in Yatse was broken, and Ngadag Sonam De was invited from Purang to Yatse to take the throne. He adopted the name Puni Mel. His son Triti Mel and the minister Pelden Drag constructed the golden roof above the Eleven-faced Avalokiteshvara in Lhasa.

As this is merely a summary of the history of royal descendants of the Upper Regions based on the writings of Sertogpa Rindor, those who desire detailed descriptions of the deeds and achievements of each successive king may refer to those documents themselves.

33

The royal descendants, the Lords of Yarlung

Following the above account of descendants of the Tibetan kings, Trashi Tsegpa, who was the son of Je Pal Khortsen's junior consort, had three sons: Pelde, Ode and Kyide [from whom sprang the true descendants of the Tibetan kings: the lords of Lato, Tsangto, Tsongkha Dome, Yarlung and so on.] These three are known as the Three De of the Lower Regions. The descendants of Trashi Tsegpa's elder son, Pelde, namely, the Khabgungwas, Lugyalwas, Chipas, Tatses, Langlungs and Tsekhorwas, reached Ngonpo Tsompo below the region of Lato. The younger son, Kyide, settled at Tanag in Shang. Five of Kyide's six sons departed for the north: Droi Tsepo, Yeru, Rulaggi Tsepo Pam, Mupa and Jang-nyangto.

Trashi Tsegpa's middle son, Ode, had four sons: Pawa Dese, Tride, Trichung and Nyagde. The descendants of Pawa Dese are found in the regions of Nub, Rong, Yagde, Nyangto and Tagtsel.

Chen-nga Donchen, the king of Shar Tsongkha and the other kings of Amdo and Kham are the living descendants of Tride. Nyagde's descendants are found at Yeru in Tsang, as far as Kyinkhar Tsepo.

Trichung [also an ancestor of the lords of Yarlung] came to Yarlung and seized the fortress of Ching-nga Tagtse. His son was Okyibar. Okyibar had seven sons, the eldest of whom was Zhangje Tsatribar, King of Zhang. Zhangje Tsatribar's younger brothers were the Six Fraternal Kings. Zhangje Tsatribar's six sons established the lineages of Yutog, Namowa, Ching-ngawa, Donkharwa and Tangkhorwa. As to the Six Fraternal Kings, they were Lhache [no issue], Yuchen [from whom the Lords of Yarlung are descended], Dar [no issue], Lhunpo [no issue], Ode and Gungtsen. The descendants of Ode and Gungtsen are the Trandrugpas, Jingwas and Jarwas of Chumig Gogpo. Yuchen went to Jesa at the invitation of Garmi Yonten Yurung and dwelt there. Yuchen's son was Joga. Joga had three sons, of whom the eldest was Jasa Lhachen [who built the Jasa Shrine]. Joga's youngest son, Tridarma, was ordained. Tridarma had four sons: Tsugde [no issue], Tritsug, Jowo Neljor [who dwelt at Bentsig], and Jowo Monlam [who was ordained, built Pugui Zimkhang Karpo and lived there].

Tritsug seized Je and Do-ngon. Tritsug's son Tritsen, Tritsen's son Shakhatri, Shakhatri's son Lhatri and so on were the Yamdawas. Jowo Neljor had three sons, of whom the eldest was Jabag Jungwa, the second was Lhachenno [who held the seat of Chilpu] and the youngest was Lha-ngam Shopa [who was ordained and had no issue].

Five sons were born to Jobag: Jowo Shakya Gonpo, Lha Drowai Gonpo [who held the seat of Chilpu and who possessed a great following], Depo [who occupied Bentsig], Dechung [who died without sons] and Jogyel [who took the throne]. Depo's son was Jowo Shakya Gyel. Jowo Shakya Gyel's son was Jowo Shakya Pal [who was ordained by Dron-gon Pagpa and had no issue]. Jogyel's son was Jobar. Jobar had two sons; the elder was Lha Zurkhangpa [who held the seat of Chilpu], and the younger was invited by the Trompowas to become their overlord and became known as Lha Trompopa.

Jowo Shakya Gonpo established his younger brothers in Tatang and built his own palace, Nechung. His power and wealth were as great as the heavens. His son, Jowo Shakya Trashi, built the Nyingma Palace. Jowo Shakya Trashi had two sons; the elder was Lha Dragkhapa, and the younger was Ngadag Dragpa Rinchen, who accompanied Dron-gon Pagpa to China as an attendant. Having instructed Emperor Sechen in the spiritual precepts,[209] he built many palaces, including Dragkha, and brought everything under his control. His power and wealth were also as great as the heavens.

Ngadag Dragpa Rinchen had three sons, the elder of whom was Lodro O. The second was Ngadag Shakya Gonpo [who held the seat of Chilpu. Being the last Shakya Gonpo, he was the most glorious]. The youngest was Lhatsun Tsultrim Zangpo [who was ordained at Densatil]. The race, bodies and qualities of the successive lords of Yarlung from that time until the present are especially sublime because they are the direct descendants of the early kings of Tibet.

As these accounts are an abbreviated compilation, those who desire more detailed descriptions of the deeds and achievements of the successive Lords of Yarlung may consult the history compiled by Lhatsun Tsultrim Zangpo.

*   *   *

The history of the spread and growth of the Buddha's teachings in this snowy land of Tibet, the accounts of the kings of India, China, Mongolia and Minyag, and the biographies of the successive Dharma-kings of Tibet in particular, have all been compiled and summarised above. Being free from the oral accounts of others and from the author's own judgments, which may be coloured by personal assumptions and opinions, the following texts were assembled: the teachings of the Buddha, comprising the Sutras and Tantras, the *Gyalpoi kabum* or *One Hundred Thousand Royal Edicts*,[210] the *Great Records of Edicts* of Lhasa and Samye, the major and minor writings revealed by Atisha,[211] the major and minor histories of the Dharma, the *Record of Royal Commands*, the annals of the Mongols, and the manifold historical documents written by

Tselpa[212] and other local potentiaries and individuals versed in the scriptures. Each text was scrutinised, uncertainties were removed, and obtuse, archaic and regional terms were revised and clarified. This volume was compiled without the ornamentation of verse or compositional technique so as to be readily comprehensible to everyone. It was duly composed to inspire fervent devotion and pleasure among the faithful who wish to know the history of the Teachings. Understand that this work represents the truth!

If readers of the present day who are keenly interested in these matters become uncertain as to the veracity of the text, they may scrutinise the ancient documents mentioned above and delve deeply into them. However, let only the ignorant harp and criticise!

> This work describes the spread of the Teachings in the Land
>   of Snows.
> May the propagation of the Sage's doctrines in the ten
>   directions
> By the successive generations of Dharma-kings
> Cause the Teachings to spread, flourish and endure!

> The patrons of the Teachings, the lords and sovereigns,
> Who are as lofty as the twin heaps of accumulated merit and
>   wisdom,
> And who are intent upon protecting the twin royal and
>   religious codes like the Dharma itself:
> May they rule for the glory of benefits and happiness!

> At the behest of Lhatsun Rinchen Pel,
> Sonam Gyaltsen, Holder of the Diamond-Sceptre,
> Duly wrote this summary of the lives of the Dharma-kings,
> Avoiding all contradictions and errors.

> By the virtue of this work,
> May the flourishing teachings of the Buddha,
> Like a thousand rays of sunlight in a cloudless sky,
> Bring forth blooms in the lotus garden of benefits and
>   happiness
> And redouble the enjoyment of the faithful bees.

Although the feet of the Buddha, the fully enlightened teacher, never trod this wild and snowy land of Tibet, it was rendered exceptional by the light of his teachings. While the sublime Lord

Avalokiteshvara led all beings onto the path of liberation and enlightenment, taming each by appropriate means, the unique emanation of his mind, the Dharma-protecting king Songtsen Gampo, and the successive Tibetan Dharma-kings with their retinues of ministers, spread the Dharma in every possible way and caused it to flourish.

This account of their deeds, entitled *The Clear Mirror on the History of the Dharma*, was duly compiled by Sakyapa Sonam Gyaltsen in the Great Shrine of the Glorious Samye monastery in the Earth-male-monkey Year [1368] to provide pleasure for the faithful and for those who desire a history of the propagation of the Teachings.[213]

May
this work
bring auspiciousness
to all times and
places!

Notes

1. Haarh, *Yar-luṅ Dynasty*, p. 41.

2. For example, see Shakabpa, *Political History*, pp. 23-60.

3. Often given as *Phags-pa* in Western texts, on the basis of the Tibetan spelling.

4. The five primary vows taken by lay practitioners: to refrain from taking life, stealing, indulging in sensuality, lying and intoxicants. *Tishri* (Chin. *dishi*) is a title bestowed by the Chinese emperor, meaning 'imperial preceptor' or 'royal chaplain'.

5. Kuznetsov, *Rgyal rabs*, p. ix.

6. Sørensen, *Fourteenth Century*, p. 64.

7. Dowman, *Power-places*, p. 136.

8. An exhaustive study of the sources of *The Clear Mirror* has been undertaken by Sørensen, *Fourteenth Century*, and *Tibetan Buddhist Historiography*.

9. Kuznetsov, *Rgyal rabs*, p. 204.

10. For a complete list of works, see Vogel, *Thon-mi Sambho-ta*, pp. 10-11.

11. Sa skya bsod nams rgyal mtshan, *Rgyal rabs gsal ba'i me long* (Beijing: Mi rigs dpe skrun khang). Chinese: Sajia Suonan Jianzan, *Xizang wang-tongji* (Beijing: Nationalities Publishing House).

12. For a detailed description of the Tibetan calendar, see Shakabpa, *Political History*, p. 15-17.

13. Krang Dbyi Sun (ed.) 1985. *Bod rgya tshig mdzod chen mo*. Beijing: Mi rigs dpe skrun khang. Chinese: Zhang Yisun (ed.) *Zang-han dazidian*. Beijing: Minzu Chubanshe.

14. Aoki, *Study on Early Tibetan Chronicles*.

15. Buddha Shakyamuni, the historical Buddha.

16. Mahasammata, 'Honoured by Many', was the first Indian king.

17. Ikshvaku was the progenitor of the royal line of which Gautama, the Buddha Shakyamuni, was a scion.

18. The ten directions include the four cardinal points, the four intermediate points, the nadir and the zenith. For convenience we have rendered the unit of distance *pagtse* (*dpag tshe*, Sanskrit *yojana*), which is approximately 4000 fathoms or 8 km, as 'mile'.

19. One of the three major sections of the Buddhist canon.

20. Tib. *sa' lu*.

21. For an alternative version, see Rockhill, *The Life of the Buddha*, p. 12.

22. Traditionally a *palaksha* tree.

23 A fine cloth from Varanasi.

24. Later, Prajapati Gautami became the first woman to be ordained as a Buddhist nun.

25. The order in which the Twelve Great Deeds are listed in the text is slightly unorthodox. Traditionally they are as follows: (1) Descent from Tushita Heaven, (2) Entrance into Queen Maya's womb, (3) Birth, (4) Youth and skill in worldly arts, (5) Marriage, (6) Setting forth to homelessness, (7) Arduous discipline of asceticism, (8) Conquest of the maras, (9) Enlightenment, (10) Turning the Wheel of the Dharma, (11) Display of miraculous deeds, and (12) Departure into Nirvana.

26. Lama Tishri Kunga Lodro (1296-1327), son of Dagnyi Zangpo Pal (1262-1325), and the half-brother of the author, was a leading figure in the Khon family of Sakya at that time.

27. I.e. Pagpa (*'phags pa*). The *Illumination of Knowledge* has been translated into English by Hoog (*Prince Jin-Gim's Textbook*).

28. A Buddha exhibits thirty-two major and eighty minor physical marks of greatness, including coppery finger- and toenails, webbed fingers, etc.

29. Tib. *chu mtshan ma med pa*. Magical water that has no physical form.

30. Tib. *indranila, indra go ba, mthon ka, mthon ka chen po, bkod mdzes*. The precise nature of these five celestial substances is unclear.

31. The Three Poisons are greed, hatred and ignorance.

32. This image of the historical Buddha at the age of twelve is referred to as the Jowo ('Lord') Shakyamuni in *The Clear Mirror*. It was given by the Indian king Dharmapala to a Chinese emperor. The image was subsequently brought to Tibet by Songtsen Gampo's Chinese bride, Wenshing Kongjo (see Chapter 13). Tradition holds that this is the very image still venerated today in the Tsuglagkhang or Jokhang ('House of the Jowo') in Lhasa.

33. The mother-figure in this tale was the last surviving person to have beheld the face of the historical Buddha, a fact well known to a Tibetan audience.

34. 'Enlightenment-thought', or *bodhicitta*, is the aspiration of a bodhisattva to attain supreme

enlightenment for the welfare of all beings.

35. Four is the minimum number of monks required to bestow ordination.

36. The Great Vehicle, or Mahayana, comprises the teachings of the 'Northern School' of Buddhism that is followed in Tibet, Mongolia, China, Korea and Japan.

37. The past, present and future buddhas.

38. I.e. the Zhou dynasty.

39. The great-grandfather of the historical Buddha Shakyamuni.

40. Note that there are two images known as the 'sandalwood Jowo', the first, created by Tratasame (see Chapter 2), and this one, created by King Utrayana.

41. Tib. Wenshing Kongjo.

42. Tib. Kyimshing Kongjo.

43. The first emperor of the Song dynasty.

44. A Tibetan-speaking people known as Tangut who founded the Xixia (Hsihsia) kingdom in what is now Gansu and Qinghai in north-west China, 1038-1227.

45. I.e. the Southern Song dynasty.

46. The Tibetan name for the upper reaches of the Yellow River.

47. One Mongol chronicler claimed that Bortechino was the youngest son of Trigum Tsenpo. As the Tibetan kings were said to be descended from the Indian royal family, this then established a 'link' between the Mongolian emperors and the Indians (Shakabpa, *Political History*, p. 24).

48. Chinggis or Genghis Khan.

49. Kubilai Khan.

50. The Khanate of Persia.

51. I.e. the Ming dynasty.

52. The *Red Annals*.

53. I.e. a rebirth in one of the three higher realms of humans, demigods and gods. The lower realms are those of the animals, hungry ghosts and hell beings (see below).

54. I.e. born of the womb, hatched from an egg, sprung up from heat and humidity, delivered miraculously like a deity.

55. The Irreversible Stage is the eighth of the ten stages (*bhumi*) in the career of a bodhisattva.

56. The *dorje* (Sanskrit *vajra*) is the symbolic thunderbolt or diamond-sceptre that represents the power of truth.

57. Mirror-like wisdom, wisdom of equanimity, wisdom of discrimination, wisdom of accomplishment and wisdom of Dharmadhatu.

58. Greed, hatred, ignorance, pride and envy.

59. On the Three Spheres, see p. 31.

60. Consort of the great Tibetan king Songtsen Gampo. See Chapter 12.

61. Also a consort of Songtsen Gampo. See Chapter 13.

62. Tibetan readers equate Singhala with Sri Lanka.

63. Yama is the Lord of Death.

64. The waving or shaking of clothing would be understood by a Tibetan audience to indicate the ogresses' utter contempt for their menfolk.

65. I.e. in India.

66. A Vajra-master is a teacher of tantric practice.

67. Tradition holds that a cave on Zotang Gongpori near Tsetang was the couple's home. The name *Tsetang* means 'Field of Play,' as it was here that the monkey-children came to frolic.

68. Zotang Gongpori, rising 800 m above Tsetang, is one of the four sacred mountains of Central Tibet, and is one of the residences of Yarlha Shampo, the mountain progenitor deity of the Yarlung dynasty.

69. Greed, hatred, ignorance, jealousy and pride.

70. By inference, Lhatotori was the twenty-seventh.

71. The marks of greatness include hooded eyelids and webbed fingers, the signs of a Buddha.

72. Note how these Buddhist historians seek to legitimise the Tibetan kings by tracing their descent from the royal lineage of India.

73. Dowman states that Yarlha Shampo dominates Yarlung from afar, appearing as a snow-walled fortress of the gods, and frequently possessing a cloud-cap that gives it an enigmatic and ethereal look. It is said to be approximately 7000 m high and has traditionally been likened to a crystal stupa (*Power-places*, p. 184).

74. Snellgrove and Richardson note that although this story is very popular, it is 'simply based on a piece of folk etymology which sought to make sense of an unfamiliar name sounding something like *Nya'*. Documents from Dunhuang indicate that his original name was Nyagtri (*nyag khri*) (*Cultural History*, p. 23).

75. The modern form of this name is given as Yumbulagang, Yambu Lhakang, etc. The four-storeyed fastness stands on a low hill 4 km above the confluence of the Yarlung and Chonggye rivers. It was reduced to a single storey during the 1960s, but was subsequently rebuilt.

76. The two spirits that resided on the king's shoulders belong to the sphere of aboriginal, pre-Buddhist Tibetan spirituality, and are of great antiquity.

77. Progenitor mountain of the Tibetan royal dynasty, upon which Nyatri Tsenpo came to rest. Note that despite the queen's insemination by the mountain-spirit in the form of a yak, Trigum Tsenpo is still considered to be Rulakye's father. When Padmasambhava arrived in Tibet, Yarlha Shampo, described by Dowman as an important Bonpo deity, again manifested as a white yak to obstruct the guru and caused snow to fall upon him (Dowman, *Power-places*, pp. 184-185).

78. For an authoritative study of this subject, see Snellgrove, *Nine Ways of Bon*.

79. Other histories include here Senol Namde's son, Senolpo De. Denolnam was the latter's son. See Haarh, *Yar-luṅ Dynasty*, p. 40.

80. 'Secret', as their significance was unknown; 'antidote', as the Dharma is the cure for the sufferings of Samsara. This event is traditionally ascribed to the year 233. So important was the arrival of the objects that pre-1950 Tibetan currency was dated so many years since that date (Shakabpa, *Political History*, p. 25).

81. For a detailed study of the tombs of the Tibetan kings from Lhatotori onwards, see Tucci, *Tombs*.

82. Nep. Bhrikuti Devi.

83. The text actually reads 'the Palace of Zimshing Trigo'. *Zimshing* is Tibetan for Chang-an.

84. Dragla is probably the same as Draglha.

85. I.e. *Om mani padme hum.*

86. Not taking life, not taking anything that is not given, behaving chastely, speaking truthfully, speaking gently, keeping promises, refraining from slander, refraining from covetous behaviour, shunning evil thoughts about others and maintaining the perfect view of the Dharma.

87. The desire for beauty, music, sweet scents, touch and fine foods.

88. A scholarly examination of this chapter has been undertaken by Vogel (*Thon-mi Sambho-ta's Mission*).

89. 'Sambhota' means 'clever Tibetan' in Sanskrit.

90. The 'relative truth' is that things are as they appear. The 'absolute truth' is that nothing possesses any inherent existence.

91. Lantsa and Vartula are decorative scripts used for prayers, inscriptions, etc.

92. A 'son' may take a surmounted consonant above it, and a 'mother' may take a subjoined consonant below it.

93. Each syllable in the first four lines of the eulogy contains the vowel *a*. The syllables in the last four contain the vowels *e, i, o* and *u* respectively.

94. I.e. Hinduism.

95. A location in the south of India.

96. Presumably to subdue the cobra that was guarding the tree.

97. I.e. Kyirong; see Wylie, *Geography*, p. 64.

98. Tib. *stag sha de, ratna de.*

99. The Indus, Sutlej, Ganges and Brahmaputra, all of which rise near Mt. Kailash in Western Tibet.

100. Barley, wheat, peas, buckwheat and rice.

101. A *dzomo* is the female offspring of a yak bull and a domestic cow.

102. The twelve deeds of a buddha's life. See Chapter 1.

103. A precursor of the Potala Palace on Marpori in Lhasa.

104. 1 *gyangdrag* = 500 *dom*. A *dom* is the distance between the fingertips of a person's outstretched arms, i.e. one fathom.

105. This palace is said to be the precursor of the Potala Palace on Marpori, the 'Red Hill', in Lhasa.

106. *Zimshing* is the Tibetan name for Chang'an.

107. Gesar of Ling is the hero of the great Tibetan epic that bears his name.

108. *Bha ta hor*. Possibly the Bedehor people against whom Trisong Detsen campaigned (Shakabpa, *Political History*, p. 43).

109. Tib. *gsam*.

110. During a traditional Tibetan wedding, the groom's representative still plants an arrow with ribbons of five colours on the bride's collar (Shakabpa, *Political History*, p. 18).

111. The Four Lakes are Tso Mapam (Manasarowar) near Mt. Kailash in Western Tibet, Namtso Chukmo (Tengri Nor) in the northwest, Yamdrog Yumtso in Central Tibet and Tso Ngonpo (Kokonor) in the far northeast.

112. Tib. *rdo srin zan, rtsa dred ma*.

113. Tib. *byis pa'i gdon, bgegs rigs, 'byung po'i gdon*.

114. The meaning of the princess's explanation is unclear.

115. The bend in the Great River (Tibetan: Machu; Chinese: Huanghe or Yellow River) in Amdo formed the border between China and Tibet.

116. Minister Gar wished to convey the impression that his archers could hit an arrow in full flight.

117. Hoffmann (*Religions of Tibet*, p. 18) lists 'burial mounds formed in the shape of a *black boar's snout*' among sites favoured by potentially malevolent nagas.

118. Marpori, Chagpori and Bongpori, the three main hills in Lhasa. Elsewhere, they are said to be the ogress's two breasts and *mons veneris*, respectively (Dowman, *Power-places*, p. 284). On the question of Tibet as an ogress, see Gyatso, 'Down with the Demoness.'

119. The meaning of *deu* and *keru* below are obscure.

120. Puru probably should be Uru, 'Central region'.

121. Ritual daggers thrust into the earth to subdue adverse geomantic influences were also employed at the consecration of Trulnang and Samye (see below).

122. This appears to be the 'snake-heart' sandalwood image of Avalokiteshvara found under the herd of sleeping elephants (see Chapter 11).

123. This refers to a Jnanasattva, or the transcendental wisdom of the deity, which is invoked and absorbed into the image.

124. The meaning of *tagzang* is unknown.

125. A *ngagpa* is a lay tantric practitioner or exorcist.

126. Author of the *Red Annals*. Lived 1309-1353.

127. The one hundred and eight snow-lion capitals still adorn the pillars that surround the central courtyard in the Jokhang.

128. I.e. the *Testament of the Pillar*.

129. Rasa, meaning 'Place of the Goat' or 'Goat Earth', is a reference to the legend of the goat which carried earth to reclaim the lake of Otang. This and Trulnang both refer to the Jokhang, or, more correctly, the Tsuglagkhang, which is still the pre-eminent place of worship in Lhasa.

130. Equivalent of 'Tsangtrang' above.

131. Equivalent of 'Drumpa-gyang' above.

132. Equivalent of 'Jamtrin Degye' above.

133. Equivalent of 'Traduntse' above.

134. Equivalent of 'Longtang Dronma' above.

135. The identity of the twelve shrines varies slightly from one historical source to another. For an overview, see Dowman, *Power-places*, pp. 284-287.

136. These may be the shrines known as Gulang Wangchug and Swayambunath (Tib. Pagpa Shingkun) in the Kathmandu Valley, Nepal.

137. Tib. *gan dzi ra*. A multi-lobed ornamental spire.

138. The seven buddhas who have appeared on earth in times past are Vipashiyan, Shikhin, Vishvabhu, Krakucchanda, Kanakamuni, Kashyapa and Shakyamuni.

139. Greed, hatred, ignorance, pride and jealousy.

140. This shrine, known as Draglha Lupuk or Palha Lupuk, occupies a series of grottoes on the eastern side of Chagpori, or 'Iron Hill', opposite the Potala Palace.

141. Snellgrove (*Buddhist Himalaya*, p. 147) suggests that this episode is a folk-memory of the flight of Buddhist monks from the west in the face of Muslim persecution.

142. In this sense, the mountain home of Avalokiteshvara.

143. Tib. *dbyig*.

144. Tib. *ratna de ba*.

145. Tib. *stag sha de ba*.

146. *Tsen* are spirits inhabiting rocks, buildings and trees. Shrines for their propitiation are built on rooftops. Naga-shrines are constructed on low-lying sites.

147. Tib. *khri* and *lde*.

148. This was to become known as the *Testament of the Pillar*, a text which was duly 'revealed' by Atisha.

149. This is also the king's personal name.

150. The significance of these four allusions is rather obscure. There are parallels with the stages of gestation of conceived consciousness. Perhaps the four creatures are an analogy for the various stages of growth of the city of Lhasa. Other references such

as *reri* (*ras ris*), translated as 'pattern of cloth', are obscure.

151. All early indigenous histories of Tibet agree that Songtsen Gampo was born in a Fire-ox Year (557 or 617). The Dunhuang Chronicles, the Chinese dynastic histories and some Tibetan works, such as Buton's *History of the Dharma*, state that the king died at the age of thirty-three in the Iron-dog Year (650). Pawo Tsuglag Trengwa records that Songtsen Gampo died at the age of eighty-two in the Earth-dog Year (638 or 698). The present work appears to have confounded these two accounts and states on the one hand that Songtsen Gampo died at the age of eighty-two, yet on the other that the Iron-male-dog Year (650 or 710) was the year of his demise.

152. Tride Tsugden Me Agtsom (see Chapter 20).

153. Trisong Detsen (see Chapter 21).

154. Langdarma: *lang* (*glang*) means 'ox' (see Chapter 25).

155. Lhalung Pelgyi Dorje (see Chapter 26).

156. Eastern Tibet.

157. Like many of the dynastic tombs, this one apparently has two names, possibly one formal and one popular.

158. For a discussion and description of the tombs of the later Tibetan kings, see Tucci, *Tombs*.

159. I.e. Trulnang.

160. Probably Uighurs.

161. Chinese: Jincheng Gongzhu.

162. The king's name, Me Agtsom, means 'bearded forefather'.

163. Her 'aunt' was Onshing Kongjo, the Chinese princess who married Songtsen Gampo and built Ramoche to house the Jowo Shakyamuni.

164. This is the image brought to Tibet by the Nepalese princess Tritsun when she married Songtsen Gampo.

165. Ramoche was gutted in the 1960s, and the image disappeared. It is said that in 1983, the lower half was discovered on a Lhasa rubbish heap, and the upper half was found unmarked in Beijing. The two were united, and the image was reconsecrated in 1986 (Dowman, *Powerplaces*, p. 59). It is likely, however, that the original seventh-century image was lost during the Mongol invasions.

166. I.e. Trulnang.

167. For example, preventing hail and frost, rainmaking, etc.

168. Tradition holds that the three brothers who built this famous stupa in Nepal vowed that they would be reborn in the future to strive for the Dharma in Tibet. They were respectively reincarnated as Trisong Detsen, Be Selnang and the Indian pandit Shantarakshita, referred to as the Bodhisattva-abbot in this text. Some sources include Padmasambhava. See Dowman, *Legend of the Great Stupa*.

169. Padmasambhava, 'The Lotus-born', was a great tantric master

from the land of Swat, which lies between Kashmir and Afghanistan. His role in the early establishment of Buddhism in Tibet is usually accorded great importance, but in the *Clear Mirror*, he seems a rather shadowy figure. On Padmasambhava, see Hoffmann, *Religions of Tibet*, pp. 50-65.

170. Mon, in modern Bhutan, was said to be one of the abodes of Padmasambhava.

171. Like Pagpa, the present head of the Sakya lineage is a descendant of the Khon family.

172. There is some variation in historical sources on the identities of the seven.

173. Hayagriva, 'The Horse-headed One', is a wrathful emanation of Avalokiteshvara, and is usually depicted with a horse head protruding from his crown.

174. A stele, said to be this one, still stands near the Utse Shrine. For a critical examination see Richardson, *Corpus*, pp. 26-31.

175. Emptiness, signlessness and wishlessness.

176. Generosity, morality, patience, diligence, meditation and wisdom.

177. Tib. *dge bsnyen*, 'lay devotee'.

178. A mural designed to bring about subjugation through peaceful means.

179. See Chapter 8.

180. The meaning of *jang* is obscure. As it is an instrument that provides

music without human agency, a wind chime is a reasonable guess.

181. Tib. *gyi ling*. A particularly fine breed of horse from Amdo.

182. The 'Three Baskets' are the Sutras, the Vinaya and the Abhidharma, which comprise the Buddhist canon.

183. According to Wylie, *Geography*, p. 65, these *tenma* (Tib. *brtan ma*) lived on a mountain called Gungtangla near Mt. Everest.

184. Tib. *ston min pa* and *tsen min pa*. The Chinese school of Buddhism favoured a Zen-style enlightenment through absolute inaction. The Indian/Tibetan school held that enlightenment was only possible through the accumulation of merit throughout countless rebirths. On this famous debate, see Demiéville, *Le Concile de Lhasa*.

185. This incident may have been included to explain the following anecdote: adherents of the unreformed Nyingma tradition were said to use the phrase 'the shoe left behind by Mahayana Hashang' to denigrate followers of the more recent traditions (Roerich, *Blue Annals*, p. 41).

186. Trisong Detsen's former senior consort.

187. *Yum gyi chab gang bskang pas mtho ba yin*. The translation of this line is uncertain.

188. The Three Edicts of Relpachen are unknown. Perhaps this refers to the Three Edicts of Trisong Detsen, which effectively established Bud-

dhism as the state religion of Tibet. See Tucci, *Tombs*, pp. 44-55.

189. The king's personal name, Relpachen, means 'The Maned One'.

190. The ruins of Ushangdo, or Onchang Doi Lhakhang, are located about 50 km southwest of Lhasa near the banks of the Kyichu River opposite Netang (Shakabpa, *Political History*, p. 50; Tucci, *Tombs*, p. 15; Dowman, *Power-places*, p. 142).

191. The word *pe* (*dpe*) is unknown, but the context suggests that 'wall' is intended.

192. Literally 'were presented for/ as *jong* (*ljong*) and so on'. As we have been unable to identify *jong*, we have omitted it.

193. The following paragraphs are a Tibetan paraphrasing of the Chinese source, the Tufan (Tibet) section of the *Tangshu*, the History of the Tang, mentioned below.

194. 'Tuluhun' is usually given as Tu-yu-hun in Chinese sources.

195. This is the Chinese form of Seru Gongton.

196. Tib. Onshing Kongjo.

197. The image brought from Nepal by Princess Tritsun.

198. Tib. Kyimshing Kongjo.

199. This stele still stands in the forecourt of the Jokhang. See Richardson, *Corpus*, pp. 106-143, for a critical translation and discussion.

200. 'The mountain that towers behind the Tsangpo bridge [at Chaksam, 65 km southwest of Lhasa] is known as Chuwo Ri, and it is magically related to Tibet's prosperity. One hundred and eight springs are said to rise on its flanks, 108 hermitages were built here, and 108 yogins achieved the Buddha's enlightenment here…. The original hermitage on Chuwo Ri, the location of which is uncertain, was founded by the Emperor Trisong Detsen'. Dowman, *Power-places*, p. 137.

201. Spiritual powers.

202. A powerful Bon god obviously invoked to frighten off his pursuers.

203. I.e. 'Why should I solve other people's problems?'

204. A cave, which according to tradition was used by Pelgyi Dorje, may still be seen at Yerpa. His hat was kept there until 1959 (Dowman, *Power-places*, p. 75).

205. This name appears twice, spelled *snubs* and *gnubs*, respectively.

206. In another version, when the Seven Men from U and Tsang returned to Samye from Kham, they inquired if anyone had seen monks before that time. An old woman of seventy-six said that she had seen monks when she was a girl of six (Shakabpa, *Political History*, p. 55). The motif of an old woman with knowledge of a forgotten religion is also found in the *Blue Annals*. In that instance, the old woman identified a ruined temple and a hidden pillar, relics of an earlier and now-forgotten attempt to introduce Buddhism to China (Roerich, *Blue Annals*, p. 18).

207. In this case, the heretics were probably Muslims.

208. I.e. Atisha.

209. I.e. Kubilai Khan.

210. I.e. the *Mani kabum*.

211. Including the *Testament of the Pillar*.

212. Tselpa Kunga Dorje, author of the *Red Annals*.

213. The text reads 'Earth-male-dragon Year', which equates with the year 1328, at which time the author was only 16 years of age. Kuznetsov (*Rgyal rabs*, p. ix) argues that this is when he began to compile this work, an undertaking that continued for the next forty years. Sørensen (*Fourteenth Century*, p. 64) holds that '*brug*, 'dragon', is a scribal error for *spre'u*, 'monkey', and that the actual date of the composition is therefore 1368. We have accepted the latter argument.

Glossary

Arhat One who has attained liberation, which is the cessation of afflictive emotions that bind one to the cycle of compulsive rebirth.

Bodhicitta 'Enlightenment thought'. The aspiration to attain enlightenment in order to benefit all beings.

Bodhisattva A being dedicated to the welfare of others. Bodhisattvas vow to remain within cyclic existence in order to work for the benefit of others, rather than seeking liberation for themselves alone.

Bon The religion of Tibet before the advent of Buddhism.

Dakini A 'sky-walker'. A female celestial who embodies divine wisdom.

Dharma The teachings of the Buddha.

Dharmakaya 'Truth Body'. The ultimate form of the Buddha, enlightenment itself.

Karma 'Action'. According to the law of cause and effect taught by Buddha Shakyamuni, one's present experience is directly produced by one's past thoughts and actions, and one's future experience is produced by one's present thoughts and actions.

Mandala A circular design representing the mind and environment of an enlightened being.

Manifestation The physical emanation, often in human form, of the mind of an accomplished being or deity.

Mantra Sanskrit words or syllables that represent the pure speech of enlightened beings.

Naga A being with a human head and a snake's body. Nagas live in water or underground, where they guard great treasures. They may influence weather, crops and the health of humans and livestock.

Nirmanakaya 'Emanation Body'. The form in which an enlightened being appears in the physical world.

Nirvana The state of permanent cessation of ignorance and suffering.

Sambhogakaya 'Complete Enjoyment Body'. The spontaneously appearing light body of the buddhas which manifests to highly realized beings.

Samsara Cyclic existence, characterized by the ceaseless round of birth, suffering, old age and death.

Shravaka 'Hearer'. One who seeks individual liberation and relies primarily on the spoken words of the Buddha for attaining liberation and for instructing others.

Stupa A Buddhist sacred monument often housing relics. Stupas are constructed in specific designs, usually with a dome shape resting on a square base of several layers, surmounted by a multilayered column.

Tathagata 'Thus Gone One'. A synonym for 'buddha'.

Three Jewels The three perfect objects in which one can seek refuge from cyclic existence: the buddha, or the expression of ultimate reality; the dharma, or the true path and the states of realization to which it leads; and the sangha, or ideal spiritual community.

References

Aoki, B. 1955. *Study on Early Tibetan Chronicles: Regarding Discrepancies of Dates and their Adjustments.* Tokyo: Nippon Gakujutsu Shinkokai.

Demiéville, P. 1952. *Le Concile de Lhasa.* Paris: Impr. nationale de France. Bibliothèque de l'Institut des Hautes Études Chinoises no. 7.

Dowman, K. 1973. *The Legend of the Great Stupa and the Life Story of the Lotus Born Guru.* Berkeley: Dharma Publishing.

——. 1988. *The Power-places of Central Tibet: The Pilgrim's Guide.* London and New York: Routledge and Kegan Paul.

Gyatso, J. 1989. 'Down with the Demoness: Reflections on a Feminine Ground in Tibet.' In: Willis, J. D. (ed.) *Feminine Ground: Essays on Women and Tibet.* Ithaca, NY: Snow Lion Publications.

Haarh, E. 1969. *The Yar-luṅ Dynasty: A Study with Particular Regard to the Contribution by Myths and Legends to the History of Ancient Tibet and the Origin and Nature of Its Kings.* Copenhagen: G. E. C. Gad's Forlag.

Hoffmann, H. 1961. *The Religions of Tibet.* London: George Allen and Unwin Ltd.

Hoog, C. (trans.) 1983. *Prince Jin-Gim's Textbook of Tibetan Buddhism.* Leiden: E. J. Brill.

Kuznetsov, B. I. (ed.) 1966. *Rgyal rabs gsal ba'i me long (The Clear Mirror of Royal Genealogies).* Leiden: E. J. Brill. (Scripta Tibetana I).

Obermiller, E. 1931. *History of Buddhism (Chos-hbyung) by Bu-ston.* Heidelberg: Harrassowitz.

Richardson, H. E. 1952. *Ancient Historical Edicts at Lhasa and the Mu Tsung/Khri Gtsug Lde Brtsan Treaty of A.D. 821-822 from the Inscription at Lhasa.* London: Royal Asiatic Society of Great Britain and Ireland.

———. 1962. *Tibet and Its History.* London: Oxford University Press.

———. 1985. *A Corpus of Early Tibetan Inscriptions.* n.p.: Royal Asiatic Society.

Rockhill, W. W. 1907. *The Life of the Buddha.* London: Kegan Paul.

Bsod nams rgya mtsho. 1968. *Sa skya pahi bkah hbum. The Complete Works of the Great Masters of the Sa skya Sect of Tibetan Buddhism.* Tokyo: Toyo Bunko.

Shakabpa, W. D. 1967. *Tibet: A Political History.* New Haven and London: Yale University Press.

Snellgrove, D. L. 1957. *Buddhist Himalaya: Travels and Studies in Quest of the Origins and Nature of Tibetan Religion.* Oxford: Bruno Cassirer.

———. 1967. *Nine Ways of Bon.* London: Oxford University Press.

Snellgrove, D., and Richardson, H. 1968. *A Cultural History of Tibet.* London: Weidenfeld and Nicolson.

Sørensen, P. K. 1986. *A Fourteenth Century Tibetan Historical Work: Rgyal-rabs gsal-ba'i me-loṅ.* Copenhagen: Akademisk Forlag.

———. 1994. *Tibetan Buddhist Historiography: The Mirror Illuminating the Royal Genealogies. An Annotated Translation of the XIVth Century Chronicle* rGyal-rabs gsal-ba'i me-long. Wiesbaden: Harrassowitz Verlag.

Tucci, G. 1950. *The Tombs of the Tibetan Kings.* Rome: Istituto Italiano per il Medio ed Estremo Oriente.

Vogel, C. 1981. *Thon-mi Sambho-ta's Mission to India and Sroṅ-btsan sgampo's Legislation.* Göttingen: Vandenhoeck and Ruprecht.

Wylie, T. V. 1962. *The Geography of Tibet according to the 'Dzam-gling-rgyas-bshad.* Rome: Istituto Italiano per il Medio ed Estremo Oriente.

Index

Anantanemi (Mu 'khyud mtha yas) Indian king 36

Anantapala (Anantapāla, mTha yas skyongs) Indian king 34

Aniruddha (Ma 'gag pa) Buddha's cousin 34

Aranemi (rTsibs kyi mu khyud) Indian king 34

Ariq-Boke (Ba ri bo kha che) Mongol emperor 50

Arjiba (Ra khyi phag) Mongol emperor 50

Arog De (A rog lde) King of Yatse 278

Aryapalo Ling (Aryapalo gling) Shrine 235, 238

Ashoka (Aśoka, Mya ngan med) Indian emperor 36, 80

Asholeg (A sho legs) One of the Six Leg, early kings of Tibet 86

Ashvakarna (Aśvakarṇa, rTa rna) Mythical mountain 31

Asog De (A sog lde) King of Yatse 278

Astrology, introduced from China 90

Atisha (Atiśa, Jo bo rje) Indian pandit 36, 174, 209, 277, 282

Atsara (Atsara) Descendant of Yumten 269

Avalokiteshvara (Avalokiteśvara, sPyan ras gzigs) Bodhisattva of Compassion 11, 27, 28, 29, 53, 55, 56, 64, 65, 66, 67, 68, 74, 75, 78, 95, 96, 98, 103, 105, 112, 114, 115, 116, 127, 161, 169, 171, 172, 180, 182, 183, 184, 185, 186, 187, 189, 190, 207, 209, 215, 216, 235, 236, 284

Ayur-Paribhadra Buyantu (Bu yan) Mongol emperor 50

Ba Sangshi (sBa sang shi) Father of Ratna 233

Bai-shingqor-dogshin (Ba'i shing thor dog shing) Mongol king 49

Bar Rinchen (sBar rin chen) Disciple of Yo Gejung, etc. 272

Barchukha (Bar chu kha) Place-name 164

Barnang-gang (Bar snang sgang) Place where Mangsong Mangtsen died 221

Bartan-ba'atur (Bar than pa dur) Mongol king 50

Barti Mel (Bar rti smal) King of Yatse 278

Baso Lhakhang (Ba so lha khang) Shrine 240

Batachiqan (Ba chi) Mongol king 49

Batselkhar (sBa tshal mkhar) Site of Me Agtsom's death 229

Batsun Lodro Wangchug (sBa btsun blo gros dbang phyug) Sent for ordination to Kham by Tsana Yeshe Gyaltsen 273

Be Chang Pelgyi Legzang (sBas lcang dpal gyi legs bzang) Minister of Songtsen Gampo 106

Be Chang Pelgyi Pagzang (sBas lcang dpal gyi pags bzang) Minister of Songtsen Gampo 208, 214

Be Selnang (sBa gsal snang) Emissary of Trisong Detsen 231

Be Tagnachen (sBas stag rna can) Anti-Buddhist minister at court of Relpachen 260, 262

Be Tenzang Pelleg (sBas kyi bsTan bzang dpal legs) Minister of Trisong Detsen 247

Bel Dorje Wangchug (Bal rdo rje dbang phyug) Disciple of Yo Gejung, etc. 272

Belpatsel (sBal pa tshal) Place in Central Tibet 155

Belza Tritsun (Bal bza' Khri btsun) *see* Tritsun

Bende Yeshe De (Ban de ye shes sde), Translator at the time of Trisong